Hard-Luck Harvey Haddix
and the Greatest Game
Ever Lost

Hard-Luck Harvey Haddix and the Greatest Game Ever Lost

LEW FREEDMAN

McFarland & Company, Inc., Publishers
Jefferson, North Carolina, and London

All photographs provided through the courtesy of the
National Baseball Hall of Fame Library, Cooperstown, New York.

LIBRARY OF CONGRESS CATALOGUING-IN-PUBLICATION DATA

Freedman, Lew.
　　Hard-luck Harvey Haddix and the greatest game ever lost /
Lew Freedman.
　　　p.　　cm.
　　Includes bibliographical references and index.

　　ISBN 978-0-7864-4124-2
　　softcover : 50# alkaline paper ∞

　　1. Haddix, Harvey, 1925–1994.　2. Pitchers (Baseball)—
United States.　3. Milwaukee Braves (Baseball team)—History.
4. Pittsburgh Pirates (Baseball team)—History.　5. Baseball—
United States—History.　I. Title.
　GV865.H23F74　2009
　796.357092—dc22　　　　　　　　　　　　　　　　2009017878
　[B]

British Library cataloguing data are available

©2009 Lew Freedman. All rights reserved

*No part of this book may be reproduced or transmitted in any form
or by any means, electronic or mechanical, including photocopying
or recording, or by any information storage and retrieval system,
without permission in writing from the publisher.*

On the cover: Pittsburgh Pirates pitcher Harvey Haddix (National
Baseball Hall of Fame Library, Cooperstown, NY)

Manufactured in the United States of America

McFarland & Company, Inc., Publishers
　Box 611, Jefferson, North Carolina 28640
　　www.mcfarlandpub.com

For Harvey Haddix and
the 1959 Pittsburgh Pirates

Table of Contents

Introduction   1

1. All Pitchers Should Be So Sick   5
2. Bad Baseball   12
3. First Inning   19
4. Harvey   27
5. Second Inning   33
6. The Worthy Opposition   38
7. Third Inning   44
8. Pittsburgh   49
9. Fourth Inning   54
10. Branch Rickey   59
11. Fifth Inning   65
12. A Prince of a Guy   70
13. Sixth Inning   76
14. Speaking Spanish   82
15. Seventh Inning   90
16. The Boss   96
17. Eighth Inning   102
18. Ninth Inning   107
19. Tenth Inning   114
20. Eleventh Inning   120
21. Twelfth Inning   127
22. Thirteenth Inning   135
23. Aftermath   146
24. The 1959 Season   155

Table of Contents

25. The Year All Pittsburgh Went Crazy — 162
26. Waxing Eloquent Over Haddix — 171
27. Life After Imperfection — 179
28. Upon Further Review — 184

Box Score: Milwaukee 1, Pittsburgh 0 — 189
Chapter Notes — 193
Bibliography — 203
Index — 205

Introduction

It was early in the 1959 season, before school was out for the summer, when Pittsburgh Pirates southpaw Harvey Haddix took the mound for what shaped up as a nothing-special, routine night in the major leagues at Milwaukee's County Stadium.

Instead, the theatrical performance in the evening mists in Milwaukee turned into an unforgettable game, a spectacular accomplishment that defined the career of the pitcher and remains one of the most glorious achievements in baseball history.

For many baseball fans this unpredictability is what makes the sport great. No matter how many games are witnessed, each trip to the ballpark holds the promise of uniqueness. No matter how many times the spectator has watched baseball drama unfold, it is possible on any given day that he will see something he has never seen before. There are no scripts followed on the stage, only improvisation.

That was most assuredly true on May 26, 1959, when Haddix was called upon by Pirates manager Danny Murtaugh to pitch against the Milwaukee Braves. It was just another road trip for the Pirates, and the 1959 season had not played out long enough to establish its personality. It was too soon to know who the stars of the season would be or what team would prevail at the end of the 154-game schedule.

The Braves of Hank Aaron, Eddie Mathews and Joe Adcock were one of the best hitting teams of their time, with power aplenty. The club had been the National League representative in the World Series two straight seasons, winning it all in 1957. Haddix was new to the Pirates, coming over in a multi-player trade with the Reds. After some awful years in the early 1950s, the Pittsburgh franchise was on the rise. The Pirates were determined to become a factor in the pennant race and they soon did so. But on this night there was no way to predict something special was in the offing, either at "Play ball!" or in the months down the calendar.

Perfect games are rarities. They seem to appear on the baseball landscape about as rarely as Halley's Comet. If that is not literally true, then

Introduction

it is mentally accurate. No one goes to the ballpark expecting to see a perfect game. Perfect games appear out of the atmospheric conditions roughly once a decade. A few things set Harvey Haddix's pitching performance apart, though. A perfect game normally consists of 27 men up and 27 men down. No flaws for nine innings. The law of averages dictates that while your arm for this night is the best on the planet, your cohorts will at least nick the other pitcher for a run somehow, some way. That did not occur on May 26, 1959.

The fellow assigned mound duty for the Braves that game was Lew Burdette. In some ways, Burdette's showing was the opposite of Haddix's. Inning after inning, the Pirates examined Burdette's stuff and sprayed it all over the yard. They compiled 12 hits and threatened on the base-paths. But neither Haddix nor the Pirates had much good luck that game. Pittsburgh could not push across a single run of support.

So inning after inning Haddix toiled, throwing the heat, baffling the batters, nodding to his fielders if they made a good play. After nine innings the score was 0–0. Haddix was still perfect and Burdette was still lucky.

In the 10th inning, it was more of the same. Haddix put three more men out. Now he was at 30 batters straight retired and counting. In the 11th, three more Braves were sent back to the dugout without visiting the bases. The same thing transpired in the 12th inning. Thirty-six Braves had carried lumber to the plate and all 36 had trudged back to the dugout, unsuccessful. On and on the game went. Haddix mowed down his 36 consecutive batters. The Pirates swung away at Burdette, but except for the occasional paper cut, never harmed him. The game remained a double shutout entering the 13th inning.

It was in the 13th that Haddix proved fallible. Apparently, the gods who had favored him grew bored with the Pirates' lack of support and decided to teach them a lesson. The Braves began to touch Haddix for a walk here, a hit there, and despite one of the most bizarre endings to a game in baseball history (as a bonus to 12 innings of perfection), they walked off the diamond as the victors—even if no one was quite sure about the final score.

The men who played in the game, the fans who saw the game from the stands, and the sports writers who covered the game for their newspapers immediately realized they had witnessed something unique. In the 50 years that have followed, Haddix's feat has never been approached. He pitched a perfect game—and lost it. Dazed by the outing, Haddix didn't know whether to laugh or cry. Newspaper headlines the next morning were printed in massive banner type, and they proclaimed the game an instant classic, calling it the greatest game ever pitched.

It was an impossible scenario, really, with the man who pitched so well going into the books as a loser that night. Haddix knew that he would never pitch better, certainly not as effectively, for so long, and eventually predicted that when he died the game would be mentioned prominently in the first paragraph of his obituary.

What neither Haddix nor anyone else present that night imagined, was that many years in the future, Major League Baseball officials would re-examine the definition of a no-hitter and wipe the record books clean of Haddix's accomplishment, as if he had never pitched the game. The game didn't count as a no-hitter, they said, because even if it lasted much longer than the generally accepted norm of a regulation 9-inning game, Haddix ultimately did surrender a hit.

For those who participated in the game and for those who saw it or read about it, the ruling misses the mark. They know that for one game in his major league career, Harvey Haddix was better than any other pitcher who ever lived. And that's not philosophy or make-believe. That's baseball fact.

1

All Pitchers Should Be So Sick

On the morning of the greatest pitching day of his life, Harvey Haddix wondered if he was too ill to take his turn in the Pirates' rotation against the Milwaukee Braves. He was sneezing and felt weak. A virus of some sort was creeping into his body.

For the Pirates, that Tuesday began in Pittsburgh, where they gathered for a 6 A.M. flight. The Pirates had swept the Cincinnati Reds in a doubleheader Sunday and had Monday off to spend with families or go fishing. They were beginning a three-game series against the Braves. By the time he met up with his teammates, Haddix was pretty sure he had identified the culprit weakening his body. "I had the flu," Haddix said.[1]

Although it was a late spring day, May 26, 1959, the weather was cool in Milwaukee. Rain was in the forecast and mist sprayed periodically from the clouds. It was not a day conducive to keeping a pitcher's arm warm without the aid of an electric blanket. The team checked into the Hotel Schroeder, a stately hotel built in 1928 that was the largest in Wisconsin, an 811-room monster large enough to get lost in, which was exactly what Haddix chose to do. He went into hibernation. Haddix spent much of the day lying around his room. Haddix's roommate, Bob Skinner, said he thought his friend's lethargy indicated he was going to opt out of the mound assignment that night claiming illness.

Looking out the window, Skinner felt there was a chance the game might even be postponed. But the clouds just hung there, thick in their grayness, without unleashing a downpour. On this day, more because of his own bodily weather report than the National Weather Service's, Haddix had no desire to walk around the city the way they often did together. "You know how you feel when you have the flu?" Skinner said. "He was just resting."[2]

It's possible, Skinner believes, that if the Pirates and Braves were scheduled for an afternoon game at County Stadium, Haddix might have scratched. But the pitcher took advantage of the long empty day and husbanded his strength. Later in the afternoon, before heading to the ballpark, Haddix ate a hamburger and a milkshake, but described his condition as "not feeling good."[3]

On the day they are in the lineup for a start, pitchers usually come into the clubhouse focused and, depending on their personal preferences, either making jokes with teammates or with a silent approach, shooing away all conversationalists. The first thing Haddix did was lie down in the trainer's room away from the locker room hubbub. The major league clubhouse of 1959 did not have the amenities of the major league clubhouse of 2009. Couches and soft landing spots were at a premium. It was testimony to the power of Haddix's illness that he sought out a hard, flat spot to lie down. The likelihood of Haddix taking the ball from manager Danny Murtaugh and actually starting the game seemed to diminish in Skinner's mind.

"He really felt punk," said Skinner, the Pirates' left-fielder that day. "He was wondering if he could pitch or not. He lay around the clubhouse and I guess he got to feeling a little bit better."[4] Haddix never told Murtaugh that he was sick. He waged an internal war, talking to himself, telling himself he could do it. It was a point of pride not to miss a pitching turn. "I intended to pitch no matter what," Haddix said.[5]

The starting time was scheduled for 8 P.M. Roughly an hour before the game Murtaugh, Haddix, and some of the other players met in the clubhouse to discuss strategy and how best to approach a powerful Braves lineup that was loaded with fierce hitters. Haddix did most of the talking.

"I got on the old thing of pitching high and tight and low and away," Haddix said, "and at the end of the meeting, when it broke up, Don Hoak spoke up. He said, 'Harv, if you pitch those guys that way, you're gonna pitch a no-hitter.'"[6]

Shortstop Dick Groat, who was not in the lineup that night because he hadn't been hitting, had his locker next to Hoak's, and he chuckled when Hoak made the comment.[7] There actually was a lot of laughter among the players when Hoak made his casual observation. If there had been pre-game tension, the tease cut through it. Haddix said, "The heck with it. Let's go."[8]

The season was less than two months old and Haddix brought a 4–2 record to the mound. The Pirates were 21–19. Not many years earlier, the Pirates were the most woeful team in the National League, but in

1. All Pitchers Should Be So Sick

the mid–1950s they started to make the move into the first division and show the general improvement that by 1960 paid off in a NL pennant and the World Series championship in one of the most stirring Series of all time.

The 1959 Pirates understood they were on their way up, but were still feeling their way. A key step on the road from ignominy to respectability to triumph was the multi-player trade that brought Haddix to Pittsburgh from the Cincinnati Reds. Haddix, third baseman Hoak, and catcher and pinch-hitter supreme Smokey Burgess were acquired for Frank Thomas, Whammy Douglas, Jim Pendleton, and John Powers. The trade essentially made the Pirates into contenders.

"We had been such a bad baseball team for so many, many years, and then, all of a sudden, in 1958 we learned how to win," Groat said.[9] "Then they made the trade that filled in all the gaps. We got Haddix and Hoak and Burgess. We thought we would be all right. We didn't have a great year in 1959, but then we turned it around and won it in 1960. Harvey and Burgess and Hoak were tremendous assets to that team."

Haddix had a fastball that was not as fast as the best, but he possessed exceptional control. He was a southpaw who broke into the majors with the St. Louis Cardinals during the 1952 season. One of the other pitchers on that club was Harry Brecheen, who was nearing the end of a 13-year Major League career that produced 133 wins. Another

Harvey Haddix was the unlucky 1–0 loser as the pitcher who threw a perfect game for 12 innings, only to falter in the 13th inning and lose to the Braves on May 26, 1959.

crafty left-handed pitcher, Brecheen had acquired the nickname "The Cat." Teammates took one look at Haddix's similar style and nicknamed him "The Kitten." The appellation stuck.

Haddix had a limited rookie season, going straight from his U.S. Army discharge to the Cardinals' roster. He finished with a 2–2 record. In Haddix's Major League debut against the Braves the opposing hurler was Lew Burdette—the same Lew Burdette scheduled to throw for the Braves, on the drizzly night in May of 1959. At that time the Braves were completing their half-century run in Boston, with one foot out the door to Milwaukee and moving vans half-packed.

The game was not one of Burdette's finer outings. The Cardinals thumped the Braves 9–2 and 26-year-old newcomer Haddix got the win. He also stroked the ball well at the plate. "My first time at-bat off Lew Burdette and I had a base-hit with two RBIs," Haddix said.[10] Making for a notable all-around box score, Haddix also stole a base. It was a memorable debut from all angles. "Of course I knew it wasn't going to be that easy all the time," Haddix said.[11]

Haddix was born September 18, 1925, in Medway, Ohio. He grew up in small Ohio farm towns and lived most of his life in them between Major League seasons. His family moved to South Vienna when Haddix was in high school and he remained in the community after that.

Haddix's fastball was not the type that crackled and smacked into catcher's mitts so hard that fans turned their heads at the sound. He was also slightly built at 5-foot-9. Although the *Baseball Encyclopedia* lists Haddix's playing weight at 170 pounds, some of his closest friends on the Pirates laugh at the notation as the greatest form of exaggeration. "He probably didn't weigh over 140 pounds," Pirates pitcher Bob Friend said. "He had the same build as Harry Brecheen."[12]

Haddix could not make the ball whistle, but he could make it do tricks. Haddix had all the fastball he needed when mixed with a curveball, a change-up and a slider. Those were the main tools he employed to fool batters. But those weapons are more subtle than raw speed and scouts missed Haddix at Catawba High School and did not latch onto him until he was playing in a neighborhood summer semi-pro league in 1943.

A bird-dog scout named Pat Donahue who appraised local talent approached Haddix after he saw him pitch and announced, "I'm going to write to Connie Mack about you." Years later, Haddix chuckled that the

1. All Pitchers Should Be So Sick

emphasis was on the slower means of communication, a letter, rather than contact made by phone call. While flattered, Haddix did not hear back from either Donahue or Mack, then the Philadelphia Athletics manager who was in the middle of his own season.

However, one day Haddix was perusing the local newspaper and saw an item that grabbed his attention. The St. Louis Cardinals were scheduled to hold open tryouts in Columbus, the state capital, just 30 miles east of South Vienna. Haddix told his father about the opportunity and pushed for a ride. "I'd like to go over there and see what those scouts think of me," Haddix said.[13]

Although Haddix had only pitched his senior year, he had thrown a few no-hitters and that gave him the confidence to think he could play baseball for money. In the years before major league western expansion, the Cardinals were the westernmost team in the game and their fan base far exceeded Missouri boundaries and close-by locales. When Haddix arrived on the scene, some 350 hopefuls from surrounding states were clamoring to be noticed by two St. Louis representatives in the course of a three-day tryout camp.

The team officials asked players to fill out cards with their names, backgrounds and position specialties. Haddix had been playing first base and outfield when he wasn't pitching, so he wrote down all three positions.

"With two fellows running the camps, you can imagine how busy they were," he said. "They didn't have time for all that foolishness, so they wiped out the last two (positions) and said, 'You're a pitcher.' The first day we went from nine in the morning till four in the afternoon. When they finally called me I threw fastballs, about seven or eight, and he said, 'That's enough. You can come back tomorrow.'"

On the second tryout day, once again Haddix's name did not come up until the end of the session; this time the Cardinals' representative told him to throw what the catcher signaled. That time Haddix threw about five fastballs and the scout said, 'That's enough. Do you want to sign?'"[14]

Haddix became property of the St. Louis Cardinals and its huge farm system developed by Branch Rickey. Haddix made a two-week road trip with the Columbus Redbirds, but his assignment from 1944 to 1946 involved service to the U.S. Army. After his time away from the game, the Cardinals tried Haddix at Class C Winston-Salem, where he won 19 games with a 1.90 earned run average. That impressed the administration and he made a fast leap to AAA Columbus. Perhaps too fast. "It was a struggle," Haddix said. "It was a learning process is what it was."[15]

Haddix possessed a reliable off-speed pitch that was effective in Columbus, but this pitch was something he had just developed rather than gained through instruction. One day, he said, a player on the other team came up to him after a game and asked when he had begun throwing a slider. "Which was almost unheard of in those days," Haddix said. "Well, I didn't know I threw a slider, so I didn't say anything. I found out that when I was pitching, when I got a little tired, instead of staying on top of the ball, I was a little bit off to the side of it and made the ball slide. That wound up being a pretty good pitch for me because then I knew what I was doing with it."[16]

Haddix spent the 1948, 1949, and 1950 seasons with Columbus, at the top of the minor league rung, but so many frustrating miles from St. Louis. Haddix also played winter ball in Puerto Rico, where because of his small stature he was nicknamed "Rabbit."[17] In 1950 Haddix went 18–6 in AAA and felt he was close enough to the majors to sense his breakthrough, but instead he was scooped up by the Army again for the Korean War. The second time around in fatigues Haddix stayed in the service from 1950 to 1952, but went directly to the Cardinals after his release.

All of the time spent in the Army could have ruined Haddix's chance to pitch in the big leagues, but he overcame that disruption with a philosophical attitude. "It's one of those things that happens," he said. "Some people are more fortunate than others" in time missed.[18]

Dismantling rifles, doing pushups, and running over hills with a full pack instead of tweaking his delivery and gaining experience against hitters did not dissipate Haddix's talent. He was an old rookie, but a mature one, and after his four-decision rookie year, Haddix made an unexpected but welcome splash in 1953. Moving into the starting rotation, Haddix produced an exceptional 20–9 season, with a 3.06 earned run average, 19 complete games and six shutouts. That caliber of play earned him the first of three selections for the National League All-Star team.

To the sportswriters who covered the team Haddix was a revelation. He had appeared in seven games after being discharged by the Army and all of a sudden he seemed to be the second coming of Warren Spahn. "A pint-sized southpaw who played shortstop, of all things, in his high school days, looks like one of the budding pitching greats of the National League," a Milwaukee writer commented. "So rapid has been Haddix's progress in only four full years in organized baseball that it is difficult to believe that he never was a pitcher until his senior year in high school."[19]

"It was all new to me," Haddix said of his first full year in the majors and the best overall season he had in his career. "It was very exciting. I didn't worry about who I was pitching against. It didn't matter to me. You just went out there and pitched and evidently I had good enough stuff. You just learned as you went along what guys' weaknesses were."[20]

The next season Haddix finished 18–13, but a fast start promised much more. He had 13 wins in hand by July 1 and teammate Al Brazle told Haddix he was doing so well he was going to win 30 games that year. "And I felt like I could, but of course you don't count your eggs before they're hatched."[21]

As a whole baseball players are superstitious, but neither Brazle nor Haddix foresaw what kind of disaster lay ahead. Soon after, Haddix was pitching against the Braves in Milwaukee. He took a 4–1 lead into the fourth inning, cruising along confidently the way he had been much of the season. Muscular Joe Adcock walked into the batter's box and waved his big stick at Haddix. Haddix delivered, Adcock stepped into the ball, and blasted a rocket straight back to the mound, where the ball ricocheted hard off Haddix's left knee.

Haddix went down, had to leave the game, and suffered permanent damage that affected the stability in his leg when he tried to complete his pitching motion. The swat had long-term repercussions for Haddix's career. "I had no spring to push off and I never, ever threw the same after," Haddix said.[22]

In 1955, Haddix slipped to 12–16 and the Cardinals shipped him to the Philadelphia Phillies, which after a season-plus traded Haddix to Cincinnati for one year. When Haddix was traded again, this time to Pittsburgh, he was looking for some redemption, and he felt he found it when the Pirates installed him in the starting rotation at the beginning of the 1959 season.

And at 8 P.M. Central Daylight Time, May 26, as Braves pitcher Lew Burdette stepped onto a soggy mound with Haddix watching from the visitors' dugout, history began to unfurl.

2

Bad Baseball

The Pirates of the early 1950s were as bad as the New York Mets of the early 1960s without the publicity or Casey Stengel to rub salve on the wounds.

In 1952, Pittsburgh finished 42–112, a .273 winning percentage, a record that ensconced the Pirates in last place in the eight-team National League, 55½ games behind the first-place Dodgers. In 1953, the Pirates finished 50–104, a .325 winning percentage, a record that once again planted them in last place.

"The '52 Pirates suffered through the worst season that any major-league team had the misfortune to endure," said slugger Ralph Kiner, who was in the midst of leading the National League in home runs a record seven consecutive years. "That [the horrible record] left us 22½ games behind the seventh-place Boston Braves, who were so embarrassed by their year they moved to Milwaukee."[1]

Funny man catcher Joe Garagiola, who earned a more favorable reputation in the sport for his one-liners than his batting average, was a member of the 1952 Pirates. "The 1952 Pirates were so bad, when we had a rainout, we had a victory dance," Garagiola said. "We gave the fans their money's worth. They always saw the bottom of the ninth. We finished in last place ... on merit."[2]

Growing up in St. Louis with fellow catching pal Yogi Berra, Garagiola thought he achieved his dream by reaching the majors. He ultimately enjoyed a longer, more profitable career as a broadcaster, author, and after-dinner speaker. His stay with the Pirates regularly provided fodder for self-deprecating humor. He talked about 1952 club manager Fred Haney "before he got his parole to Milwaukee." And Gargiola said the players were so unaware they couldn't decipher their own signs. "Nobody ever got our signs," he said. "Many of the clubs thought they had them, but we would miss our own signs so much they could never prove it."[3]

One player on the hapless 1952 team who went on to a more successful career in another field was John Berardino, who batted .143 in 19 games as an infielder. Eventually, Berardino found a better role. He played a prominent doctor on the daytime TV soap opera *General Hospital* for 25 years.

After his arrival in the majors in 1946 until 1953, Kiner was the cornerstone of the franchise. Kiner was born October 27, 1922, in New Mexico, where his father operated a bakery. He was four when his dad died and his mother moved to California. Kiner was handsome, a muscular 6-foot-2, and 195 pounds, and was the darling of many young female admirers. He ran with the Hollywood set in the off-season. Kiner casually dated actress Elizabeth Taylor (a photograph of them in evening attire backs this up) and more seriously dated Janet Leigh. He later married tennis star Nancy Chaffee.

Between 1947 and 1950, the Pirates drew more than 1 million fans each season. At the time that was a notable achievement. The 1,517,021 fans that passed through the turnstiles of Forbes Field in 1948 set an attendance record that stood until 1960, the year the resurrected Pirates won the World Series.

As a slugging outfielder, Kiner provided many of the fan thrills during the lean times. He led the National League with 23 home runs as a rookie in 1946 and he blasted 54 in 1949, just two behind the then-league record of ex–Cub Hack Wilson, a mark set in 1930.

Like all other power hitters of the era (and perhaps all eras), Kiner admired Babe Ruth. But he also had a special place in his heart for Hank Greenberg, the Tigers' bomber who once smashed 58 home runs and drove in as many as 183 runs in a season. Kiner called Greenberg "one of the heroes of my youth, which was spent in Southern California."[4] In 1948, the Pirates flirted with respectability, finishing 83–71, and in fourth place, but except for that season, Kiner was a Don Quixote of sorts, a lonely figure tilting at windmills as the remainder of his teammates floundered.

It had not always been so for the Pirates. Pittsburgh was a proud franchise with a long track record of honor and success, and the city fawned over its Pirate heroes when they came along. From Honus Wagner to Paul and Lloyd Waner to Pie Traynor, Pittsburgh had embraced its baseball stars with enthusiasm. For the first half of the 20th century and beyond, the Pirates were the premier sporting attraction in town. The football Steelers did not begin to challenge for supremacy until their Super Bowl–winning stretch began in the 1970s.

Officially, the Pirates claim their roots in Pittsburgh stem from the creation of the Pittsburgh Alleghenies on April 15, 1876. However, that team went out of business in 1878. In 1882, the Alleghenies were rejuvenated and played in the American Association. The club joined the National League in 1887 and remains one of the circuit's oldest members. In 1900, new Pittsburgh owner Barney Dreyfuss merged his Louisville team into the Pirates, bringing along 14 players, including a clever batsman and all-around star named Honus Wagner.[5]

Wagner was born John Peter (and was variously referred to as Johannes, Honus, or Hans) in the town that became Carnegie, Pennsylvania, on February 24, 1874. Nicknamed "The Flying Dutchman," Wagner was already established as a star player after three seasons in Louisville and his adjustment time to the National League was nil. Wagner batted .381 in 1900 to win his first of eight league batting crowns.

Wagner's extraordinary skills at bat and as a shortstop quickly stamped him as one of the best the game had ever seen. He played for 21 seasons, hit .328, and was enshrined in the first Hall of Fame class in Cooperstown, New York, in 1939.

"Honus Wagner was a man who could win with his glove, his arm, his bat, or his head," one of his biographies states. "He set new benchmarks for hitting, base-running, and fielding. As a major leaguer, he played every position except catcher, and many who watched him said he would have been a Hall of Famer at any of them."[6]

Wagner grew up in the coal mining community then called Chartiers, just a few miles outside of Pittsburgh near the Monongahela River. Wagner's family called him "Hans." Although bow-legged, Wagner was very athletic and he was a strong 5-foot-11 and 200 pounds, yet still capable of stealing 723 bases.

After watching Wagner perform in the field and at bat during one series against his New York Giants in 1907, legendary manager John McGraw could not stop spewing compliments about the Pirates star. "Wagner is just in a class by himself and that's all there is to it," McGraw said. "The fans in other cities throw spasms when he makes a play. His equal has never been known. Wagner is a whole team in himself."[7] Over time Wagner grew so popular in Pittsburgh because of his diamond exploits, a song was written about him named "Husky Hans."[8]

Despite his early stardom, less is remembered about Wagner's play a

2. Bad Baseball

century after his prime than is commonly known about Cy Young, Ty Cobb and Babe Ruth—with one major exception. Just about anyone who collects baseball cards recognizes that the most valuable card of all is a tobacco portrait card of Wagner called the T-206, one among many the American Tobacco Company issued between 1909 and 1911.

Even then the cards were very popular and players (524 of whom were approached) liked to see their images on the 1½ inch by 2½ inch cardboard inserts in various cigarette packs. The manufacturers, who had already started the presses, did not reckon on Wagner's puritanical streak. They wrote him and said they planned to pay $10 for his permission to use his image on a card. Wagner wrote back saying he didn't want to encourage smoking by youngsters or ballplayers. The print run of Wagner cards was halted.[9]

No one knows precisely how few Honus Wagner baseball cards made it into circulation before the cease-and-desist command stopped the presses. No one knows how many survive, either, but the card remains the most coveted and sought-after in the hobby. One particular Wagner card has fascinated buyers and observers alike. At one point it was owned by hockey superstar Wayne Gretzky. It has since passed through several hands, with a 2007 purchase calculating the value at a record $2.8 million for any single card. Wagner, who died in 1955, never could have anticipated such a frenzy.

What Wagner did live long enough to see was how the World Series—which he first played in when the classic end-of-season tournament made its debut in 1903—grew and established a hold on fans.

The older National League made peace with the fledgling American League long enough to get the first World Series out of the talking stages and onto the playing field. The American League pennant winner was Boston, at the time called the Pilgrims, on their way to making a bigger name for themselves as the Red Sox. The Pirates won the National League pennant with a 91–49 record that season. Boston's mark was 91–47.

The first World Series game was played on October 1, 1903, at Boston's Huntington Avenue Grounds. Pitching for Boston was Cy Young. The Red Sox won that game and captured the first Series, though at least the Pirates could always claim they had been part of the first one, a feature in the event that became an American institution.

By 1909, with eight years to go in Wagner's career, the Pirates had moved into their first true ballpark, the steel and concrete structure known as Forbes Field. Located adjacent to the University of Pittsburgh campus, the stadium opened for use on June 30 with a capacity of 25,000, although the $1 million structure was expanded to hold 35,000 people in 1938. When Harvey Haddix, Bob Skinner, and Dick Groat competed in the 1950s, Forbes Field was still the Pirates' home field. It remained so through the 1970 season.

Wagner lived in Pittsburgh for the rest of his life and was a great booster of city programs. At one time, during a Made in Pittsburgh traveling exhibition that Wagner joined, he was touted as "The Greatest Man in Our Town."[10] The city proved what it thought of Wagner when a statue was erected in his honor and dedicated on April 30, 1955, less than a year before his death.

By winning pennants in 1901, 1902, and 1903, and the World Series in 1909, Wagner and his teammates established Major League baseball in Pittsburgh with their early success, but pennants became scarcer as the century aged. Pittsburgh won another Series in 1925 and another pennant in 1927, but did not finish in first place again until 1960.

The key Pirate figure in the 1920s run was third baseman Harold "Pie" Traynor, who earned his nickname because of the fondness he demonstrated in scarfing down anything wedged-shape with the appropriate crust. Traynor played the hot corner for Pittsburgh from 1920 to 1937 and authored a lifetime batting average of .320. Traynor had a reputation as a superior fielder, as well, and in 1948 was the first third baseman elected to the Hall of Fame. The team retired his number 20 jersey.

Traynor was another star ballplayer who endeared himself to fans on and off the field. He was, as one historian said, "a local legend, renowned for field leadership and his personable nature. Everyone, from the low-level grunt to the business executive, found him easy to talk to and get along with."[11] Those traits, when Traynor neared the end of his playing career at age 36 because of an arm injury, convinced the Pirates to make him their manager in 1934, a position he held until 1939.

Of course, right from the start Traynor knew he was signing on for a job that provided less security than that promised by the steel plants operating down the street. "I wasn't looking for a job," Traynor said. "Managers are a dime a dozen, and I knew it wouldn't be steady."[12]

The brother duo of Paul and Lloyd Waner, two of the Pirates' greatest

2. Bad Baseball

stars, and both Hall of Famers, overlapped with Traynor. Paul broke into the Pittsburgh lineup in 1926 with a sensational .336 hitting season which few could believe because he was so skinny that his flannels flapped in the breeze. Paul Waner, who played the saxophone as a youth (though no one suggested he could have a musical career instead of playing ball), stood 5-foot-8 and his listed weight was 153 pounds. But he definitely carried a big stick.

There is an old joke about talented older siblings saying to agents or owners that if they liked what they saw they should see the other brother back on the farm. In this case it was true. The Waners were from Harrah, Oklahoma. Lloyd was three years younger, but when Paul used his own performance as evidence the Pirates should give his brother a tryout, he was persuasive. Lloyd broke in with Pittsburgh in 1927 and hit .355. Although he put on some weight as he aged, he weighed 132 pounds at the time.

The Waners were farm boys whose youth was defined by the Great Depression, but who worked hard at the one activity they loved and felt could uplift them from poverty. Baseball was their game, their tool, their path to a future with paved streets instead of cow manure underfoot. The Waners were so poor as youngsters that even to play baseball they had to manufacture their own equipment out of tree limbs, corn cobs, and rocks.[13]

It was widely known that Paul Waner liked to trip the light fantastic on the evenings after day games and that his drink of choice was measured in proof volumes rather than fat content. He was no milk drinker. A sports writer of the time said that Paul Waner "hit doubles and triples during the games and drank them after."[14] He was a party boy who liked to have a good time, but who never let his extra-curricular activities interfere with a baseball career that produced 3,152 hits and a .333 batting average in 20 seasons. He once clouted six hits in a game. Lloyd was the more reserved of the duo, less inclined to drink anything stronger than soda pop. He batted .316 with 2,459 hits in 18 big-league seasons.

Most memorably, in the inevitable pairing of brother nicknames, Paul the elder was known as "Big Poison" and Lloyd was called "Little Poison." Those were brilliant appellations, stingingly accurate in the way pitchers must have looked at the siblings: if Big Poison didn't get them with a hit, then Little Poison would. However, the story Lloyd tells about the origin of the nicknames has nothing to do with that otherwise felicitous application.

Hard-Luck Harvey Haddix and the Greatest Game Ever Lost

Lloyd Waner said that a particularly vociferous New York Giants fan in the Polo Grounds was of Italian descent and yelled with an accent. He actually hailed the Waners in a friendly manner and the brothers once gave him an autographed baseball. The man was actually calling them "Big Person" and "Little Person," according to Lloyd Waner.

"We would wave at him and he became our biggest rooter in the Polo Grounds," Lloyd Waner said. "But whenever we came in there he would yell that and the newspaper people finally picked it up. Only they thought he was saying 'Poison' instead of 'Person.' It became a newspaper nickname because no ballplayers ever called us that."[15]

The brothers were separated in 1941 when Paul Waner was sent to Brooklyn. Lloyd Waner rounded out his Pirates tenure in 1945. They were indisputably two of the greatest stickmen in Pittsburgh history, but their power hitting was almost incidental.

It was left to Ralph Kiner's vastly different style of swinging at the fences to excite the Pittsburgh fans anew and provide individual glory when there was no team glory to be had. The cast of players surrounding Kiner in the early 1950s was less well known than supporting actors in a Hollywood movie extravaganza. Kiner's name appeared above the title, but his teammates' names came and went on an ever-changing roster.

A part-owner of the Pirates was crooner Bing Crosby, who dreamed more of a pennant than a white Christmas. He donated a record player for use in the Pirate clubhouse. Kiner said the most popular song played (the title of which he didn't remember) repeated themes of "cigarettes and whiskey," and "wild women." He called it the team's "fight song."[16]

Once, the players attended the wedding and reception of a coach, then, still wearing tuxedos, adjourned to the ballpark to play the Cincinnati Reds. "We didn't win many games in Pittsburgh, but we did manage to have some fun," Kiner said.[17]

Kiner was reminded of just how few games the Pirates won when, after hitting 37 round-trippers in 1952 to share the league lead, he tried to browbeat general manager Branch Rickey into a pay increase at the same time Rickey wanted to cut his salary by 25 percent. As a result, Kiner was holding out. In one of the most famous lines in baseball negotiation history, Rickey said, "We finished last with you and we can finish last without you."[18]

Some 41 games into the 1953 season Kiner was traded to the Cubs, and that season the Pirates did finish last without him.

3

First Inning

As the visitors, the Pirates batted first against Braves starter Lew Burdette. Manager Danny Murtaugh did not have as many weapons at his disposal in writing out the lineup card as did his counterpart Fred Haney, the Pirates' ex-manager.

The Braves were World Series champions in 1957, interrupting the New York Yankee dynasty with a seven-game victory. They returned to the Series in 1958, this time losing to the Yankees. But the core of the Braves remained the same, and they were favored to win a third straight National League pennant.

On this night the Pirates were without right fielder Roberto Clemente, who was nursing a sore arm, and Murtaugh rested shortstop Dick Groat, who spent the night in the dugout. Dick Schofield was penciled in to play shortstop in Groat's stead and Roman Mejias began the game in right field. Decades later Groat said it was simply a case of the manager's decision to give him a night off.[1]

Schofield was the leadoff batter, followed by centerfielder Bill Virdon and then catcher Smokey Burgess, who was far more respected for his hitting prowess than his lumbering on the basepaths, where he resembled a truck moving without tires. Rocky Nelson was at first, Bob Skinner in left, future Hall of Famer Bill Mazeroski at second base, and the pugnacious ex–Marine Don Hoak was at third. Mejias held the eighth spot in the order and pitcher Harvey Haddix rounded out the nine.

Burdette won 203 games in an 18-year career, but in contrast to Haddix in this game, he was far from untouchable. Even with a slightly weaker lineup the Pirates rapped out 12 hits. However, all of them were singles and Pittsburgh could never put enough of them together to move a single runner around the bases.

The game started inauspiciously. Schofield popped up to third baseman Eddie Mathews. Virdon topped the ball in front of the plate and was thrown out at first by Del Crandall firing the ball to Joe Adcock. Then Smokey Burgess flied out to left field. No problems for Burdette.

"We had 12 hits and we couldn't score," said Schofield, who slapped three singles in six at-bats. "We had some chances. Burdette wasn't a bad pitcher either."[2]

The night was humid and damp as Haddix warmed up. Fans still trickled into County Stadium, but the park was far from full.

The stadium, with a capacity of 53,192, was built for $5 million between 1951 and 1953 as a home for the Milwaukee Brewers of the American Association. But there was also an eye to luring Major League baseball to Milwaukee and the plan of ambitious city fathers worked. The moneymen of Wisconsin built it, and Braves owner Lou Perini came from Boston.

County Stadium's dimensions were not extraordinary, measuring 315 feet down both the left-field and the right-field lines and 402 feet to the deepest point in center field. Six years after the Braves became the primary tenants, there was still a bit of a shine on the ballpark that sometimes hosted Green Bay Packers football games as well.

The Braves' leadoff hitter was second baseman Johnny O'Brien. O'Brien, 28, and his twin brother Eddie, were born in South Amboy, New Jersey, and both had played for the Pirates in the mid-1950s. They were the first twins to play second base and shortstop in the same game in the majors. Pirates general manager Branch Rickey had signed the O'Briens together with $40,000 bonuses with the belief they could become Pittsburgh's permanent double-play combination.

The brothers had already proven to be excellent all-around athletes. Johnny O'Brien was a multi-sport high school star and is in their hometown's Saint Mary's High School Hall of Fame. The O'Briens, who attended Seattle University as business majors, played in a shocking, 84–81 upset of the Harlem Globetrotters, a game in which Johnny scored 43 points. Johnny scored more than 3,000 points in his three varsity seasons for the Chieftains.

The identical twins were not above impersonating one another. When they played for the same team they sometimes acted out roles to fool the manager, and when posing for their Topps baseball cards purposely deceived the photographer. One year Topps solved the problem by putting both on the same card.[3] Later, Eddie returned to his alma mater as athletic director.

In 1959, Johnny O'Brien filled in at second for 44 games for the

3. First Inning

Braves, mostly because they were missing Hall of Fame second-sacker Red Schoendienst, who battled tuberculosis and played in just five games while undergoing surgery that removed part of a lung. O'Brien hit just .198; that season marked the end of his six-year Major League career.

Barely more than two weeks before Haddix's start, Cincinnati Reds manager Mayo Smith was worried about O'Brien's bunting ability and walked him intentionally to face sluggers Mathews and Hank Aaron. Not even O'Brien could believe that maneuver. Opening this game, that idea did not occur to Pirates manager Danny Murtaugh as a strategy. O'Brien's lead-off appearance was not a bothersome at-bat for Haddix. Swinging at the first pitch, O'Brien topped it to the left side of the infield, where shortstop Dick Schofield scooped up the ball and threw to Rocky Nelson at first base for the first out.

A much more feared hitter was holding down the second spot in the Braves lineup. Third baseman Eddie Mathews, one of the greatest hitters to ever play his position, strode to the plate. The fact that Mathews was batting second demonstrated the strength of the Milwaukee lineup, heavily packed with home-run hitters. But it also showed that manager Fred Haney was short on table-setters. Mathews was not the type of player expected to bunt for a single or be disruptive on the basepaths. He was a swing-away slugger who smacked 512 home runs in his 17-year Hall of Fame career. In 1959, Mathews led the National League in homers with 46, the second time he did so.

The left-handed swinging Mathews was a little less hasty in the box than O'Brien, but not much. He swung at a 1–1 pitch and lined out to Nelson. That brought up Aaron. Aaron was deep into a career that at retirement after 23 seasons made him the leading home-run hitter of all time. Aaron's 755 homers shattered Babe Ruth's seemingly unreachable mark of 714. Aaron drove in 2,297 runs and batted .305, and he was the first player in Major League history to stroke more than 500 home runs and 3,000 hits.

With the exception of the recognition provided by regular elections to the National League All-Star team, many of Aaron's kudos came later, after retirement, when fans and baseball scribes took the time to reflect on what he accomplished. Soft-spoken and a player who performed efficiently, with economy of motion rather than flamboyance, Aaron often was slighted in the public spotlight when compared to Willie Mays and

Mickey Mantle. But every pitcher knew that the littlest mistake could result in the ball disappearing over the ballpark fence with a mere flick of Aaron's exceptionally powerful wrists.

"He's simply the smoothest player in the history of the game," one magazine writer observed about Aaron's style. "His wrists are legend. His running gait, resembling a speeded up motion picture of a participant in the 20-kilometer walk, is effective, if not picturesque. He never seems to be going very fast, but he almost always gets where he is going, and on time."[4]

Aaron was born in Mobile, Alabama. Growing up in the Deep South in the 1930s was not an easy experience for any black man. Despite leading the league in average and RBIs with Jacksonville in 1953 in the South Atlantic League, where Aaron was one of the first African-American players in the Sally League's half-century existence, he experienced scarring discrimination in the way of name-calling and being forced to use facilities separate from white teammates.

During his prime, Aaron was often misjudged or underestimated as a person because he was not loquacious and spoke with a Southern accent. What Aaron excelled at was playing at a high level, day after day, year after year, not only being reliable while staying healthy, but coming through in the clutch game after game. He played the game in his head, he said, not taking days off and not taking at-bats off.

"Pride is what helps anybody," Aaron said. "I take pride in what I'm doing every day I go out there. I know there will be bad days and bad games, but I want to be consistent. That's pride. This is a grueling game, the toughest. It is a mental strain to go out there daily and concentrate the way you should."[5]

If a pitcher lost his concentration against Aaron he could be in trouble quicker than it took for a 90 mph fastball to soar into the right-field stands. Vern Law, a right-hander in the Pirates rotation who won 18 games in 1959 and 20 in 1960 when he captured the Cy Young Award, and later was a Pirates coach and assistant baseball coach at Brigham Young University, can deliver a graduate-school lecture on how he tried to prevent Aaron from ruining his night.

"You just didn't throw the ball belt high to him," Law said. "You kept the ball down, and if you could, you also kept the ball away from him on the outside part of the plate. But still you had to let him know

3. First Inning

Hank Aaron, who became major league baseball's all-time leading home-run hitter, made a base-running gaffe in the decisive 13th inning, but it did not prevent the Milwaukee Braves from scoring the winning run off Harvey Haddix.

you were going to come inside occasionally. You had to keep him honest because a pitcher has got to have both the inside and outside corners. He can't just pitch one way.

> I remember a game in Atlanta when I'd gotten Aaron out three times in a row, all on balls away from him. I kept everything away from him that time. So his last time up I see him going right out to the corner of the plate, stepping in that direction to pick up the ball. Well, I came inside. I wasn't more than five or six inches off the plate and he wanted to get out of the way. But because he was diving into the pitch and it was just above the belt, he stepped right into it and the ball glanced off the top of his helmet. After the game the reporters asked him if he thought Law was throwing at him. He said, "No, I don't think so. I think it's probably just as much my fault as his because I was looking for the ball away." So that's the way you had to pitch Hank. He was one of those first-ball, fastball hitters. I'd throw him a straight fastball, but I would take enough off from it that he would be out in front on his swing and I could get a nice little ground ball out of him. On the first pitch he would be looking for something straight and be cutting away."[6]

Haddix sneaked his first pitch over the plate without Aaron reacting for strike one called. The count quickly moved to 0–2 when Aaron fouled the next offering behind the plate. He took a ball low, then hit another foul ball to the left side. On the 1–2 count, Aaron hit a fly ball to center field, where it was hauled in by Bill Virdon. Haddix was out of the inning without a hit or base runner.

As Haddix looked around County Stadium that night he saw one surprising sight. Attendance was just 19,194. Visiting players had become used to the sight of packed houses in Milwaukee. When the Braves shifted from Boston to Milwaukee, they arrived to considerable fanfare. They were treated like long-lost sons returned from a distant war. The love affair reached its apex in 1957 when the Braves knocked off the Yankees for a world championship and in 1958 when the club returned to the Series. For any Braves fan of the 1950s it would have been difficult to imagine that by 1966 their team would be located in Atlanta and a diminishing amount of spectator interest would be cited as one of the reasons.

If in later years fans said they had been in County Stadium the night Harvey Haddix threw his perfect game, photographs of banks of empty seats could refute them.

When Haddix walked to the Pirates' dugout at the end of the first

3. First Inning

Bill Virdon did not get to cross home plate in Harvey Haddix's gem, to his and his team's eternal lament.

inning, he was aware that he had had a three-up, three-down inning, and that no one had reached base. "I was conscious of it all the way," he said.[7] But 1–2–3 innings are common for pitchers to start ballgames. They are not necessarily omens. The jump from three men out to 27 is a huge one, and that was not a subject in the forefront of anyone's mind at the moment.

Virdon, who made one of the putouts in the first inning, was regarded as one of the top fielders at his position during his 12-year career, finishing with a .982 fielding percentage. Working behind Haddix that day was a breeze, he said. "That was the easiest game I ever took part in," Virdon said. "They were all easy fly balls. There were fly balls that didn't have a chance of going out of the ball park and were easy to get to, just routine pitches. I don't know if I ever played in an easier ball game, watching the whole ballgame."[8]

When the first inning ended, Haddix took a seat in the Pirates dugout, pulled on his warm-up jacket and rooted for his team to score some runs. He never mentioned having a cold or the flu to his teammates again that night.

4

Harvey

Harvey Haddix was a good guy who was soft-spoken, but who had a good sense of humor. He was a man who liked the outdoors and spent a chunk of the off-season hunting and a chunk of the baseball season reading about it. Those are some of the ways long-ago Pirates teammates remember the small left-hander away from the mound. He was from the middle of the country, from Ohio, and to them he seemed like a middle-of-the-road fellow.

In most photographs of Haddix in a baseball uniform, he appears very serious. He has a thin, somewhat elongated face, wide lips, large ears, and seemingly sad eyes. But in the pictures where he is smiling, his face is transformed. A wide grin becomes him, widens his eyes, and is more appropriate as an indicator of his personality, former Pirates say. He was not the gloomy man that those who studied the pictures might conclude, they note.

Dick Schofield met Haddix for the first time when they both played for the St. Louis Cardinals. Schofield, who was born in 1935, was a scrappy shortstop just 18 years old when he made his Major League debut. Haddix, who had been in the service and was an elderly rookie, seemed like an old wise man to him. "He was just a super guy," Schofield recalled. "He was one of my best friends in baseball. I guess the best way to put it is he was just one of the good guys. He was 10 years older than me, so he took care of me a little bit when I first started. He was nice to me. We were close for a long time."[1]

When he was on the mound, Haddix displayed solid concentration and was very businesslike. Whether the situation was going his way or it was tense, his fielders didn't see any difference in the consistency of his approach. He did not get flustered and he did not express joy. He just took care of his assignment with authority and appeared unflappable. "Harvey was pretty much the same when he pitched," Schofield said. "He didn't change from one time to the next. On the day of the perfect game, he didn't do anything different, except he just didn't give up any hits."[2]

Haddix met his wife Marcia in Ohio and their marriage produced two daughters, Teri and Ann, and a son, also named Harvey.

Baseball teams take longer road trips than other professional sports teams, sometimes staying in a single city for four days or so, depending on the length of the series. There is a considerable amount of down time before and after games in hotels and plenty of empty time to fill. Players drift into routines, groups develop habits, and individuals establish their own patterns. If it's Boston I will visit my cousin Joey. If it's Chicago I will visit my brother Alan.

Haddix was an avid reader on subjects that entertained him. Outfielder Bob Skinner, who spent many nights sharing a hotel room with the pitcher, and other pals said Haddix was rarely without magazines that told hunting stories or advertised the latest in hunting rifles. Haddix might lie around the room for hours, relaxing and poring over the magazines. "He was a real outdoorsman," Skinner said. "He always had a gun magazine with him. He always had his books and magazines. He read *The Sporting News*, too."[3]

Although many baseball players through the years have expressed an affinity for fishing—none more than Ted Williams, who was regarded as being as able with a rod as he was with a bat—most of the fishing lifestyle was out of reach because the prime fishing season coincided with the baseball season. However, the hunting season began in earnest at the end of the baseball season.

That's when Haddix returned to Ohio and engaged in bird hunting. In autumn, doves, pheasants, ducks and geese are all in season. Haddix also hunted rabbits on his 408-acre farm. In November of 1964, after his first season with the Baltimore Orioles, Haddix was on a low-key hunting trip carrying a low-power .22 rifle when he became enmeshed in a surprising big-game hunt.

A neighbor who was a member of the Champaign County Livestock Association had done business for some time with Arthur Godfrey, the widely popular radio and television performer. Godfrey once gave him a gift of two bison, one male and one female. The animals were not comfortable in the barn, so Haddix's neighbor allowed them to roam in his pasture.

The 900-pound bull that had been transferred from Virginia apparently did not like its new home and at mid-day on the last day of November,

4. Harvey

it went berserk on the local farm, at one point heaving a cow over its horns with a shake of its head. The owner, knowing that Haddix was a hunter and believing he had a large caliber rifle, called for assistance. According to Haddix, the phone call came in this way from his friend: "You have to shoot this thing for me. It's mad and dangerous. There are children around and who knows what other damage it might do. You've got to help."[4]

The only thing was, the distraught man kept repeating "bull" on his side of the conversation. The word buffalo, or bison, was never mentioned, or else Haddix might not have shown up. Because he only hunted small game or birds, Haddix had traded in his old deer gun for the .22. Still, envisioning more of a Texas ranch bull, he grabbed the rifle and jumped in a Jeep. When he arrived at his neighbor's farm and realized the crazed animal was a bison, he balked. "I told him I couldn't do it because my gun was too small," Haddix said. "But he said I had to."[5]

Haddix began hunting the beast. It had been 80 years since buffalo hunting had virtually disappeared on the Plains, so it was a rare opportunity for an avid hunter, even given the emergency nature of the stalk. Haddix began thinking like a hunter on a special trip.

After some time, Haddix spotted the bison on the edge of the woods, took careful aim, and hit it. Only the big animal didn't go down. Haddix continued his pursuit, finally catching up and then slowing the big beast with additional shots. It took five hits to kill the big animal and the chase was probably the most demanding of Haddix's hunting career. He compared the experience favorably with his 12-inning perfect game against the Braves. "It would have been a big thrill killing a buffalo with a deer rifle, but getting one with such a small-caliber gun was an even greater thrill," Haddix said.[6]

All of those hours spent reading hunting magazines in his hotel rooms on road trips had prepared Haddix more than adequately for his unexpected local safari. He posed for a photograph with the furry buffalo head and it appeared bigger than the tires on his Jeep.

The Pirates of the late 1950s and early 1960s were close-knit. It was not a case of seven cabs for seven players on nights back at the hotel. Many of the guys went out to dinner together on the road. Haddix hung out with Skinner, Dick Groat, Bill Mazeroski, Hank Foiles and others. Sometimes they frequented 24-hour coffee shops after night games when they were too restless to sleep. After day games they enjoyed fine quality dining in a variety of cities. One of their favorite places for seafood was the renowned Bookbinder's in Philadelphia, according to Skinner. They were good customers. "If we had a Saturday day game, Harvey would always take me and we'd eat like kings," Skinner said.[7]

The reason Haddix had that wherewithal to dine like royalty had nothing to do with his making a vastly superior salary in an era when Skinner was making in the $20,000-plus range, the norm for good but not star ballplayers. Haddix and other Pirates were regular diners at the establishment as much as possible given their schedule, but when Haddix pitched his near-perfect game, restaurant owner John Taxin endowed him with a lifetime gold pass. "Harvey goes into my Hall of Fame even if he didn't win in Milwaukee," Taxin said, "and he can eat free at Bookbinder's as long as he lives."[8]

Not every meal out was a dining extravaganza. Haddix and his teammates visited greasy spoons for coffee and to just hang out and kill time. Part of the exercise was the camaraderie built from being with buddies who were involved in a shared experience. Teams bond more away from the field of play than on them. Often the foursome consisted of Haddix and Skinner, Bill Virdon and Groat.

"We were dear friends," Groat said of Haddix. "Harvey and Skinner roomed together and Virdon and I roomed together. The four of us spent an awful lot of time together. Mostly going to dinner. We went out together almost after every game. We were big buddies."[9]

One thing that Groat noticed about Haddix was how much he smoked. This was an era before the surgeon general of the United States took note of cigarette smoking as a bad habit that carried health risks, and professional team sport athletes were no different from members of the general American population. They smoked up a storm. Groat, who had been an All-American basketball player at Duke University and played briefly in the NBA before devoting himself full-time to baseball, didn't hesitate when invited to do a cigarette commercial.[10] In the 1950s, endorsing tobacco products was no different from endorsing a brand of automobile. Players, who were making salaries more in line with what Americans working at other jobs made, were darned happy to have the extra income from product endorsements.

Groat, who operates Champion Lakes Golf Club in Ligioner, Pennsylvania, won a National League Most Valuable Player Award in 1960 and

4. Harvey

was the shortstop on a World Series champion, but might have been become a bigger basketball star. Yet he was ahead of his time in basketball. The professional game was not as evolved as baseball and the National Basketball Association still fielded teams in smaller cities like Sheboygan, Wisconsin, and Anderson, Indiana. It was hard to make a living.

Born in 1930, Groat grew up in Pennsylvania in the era where high school athletes who excelled were routine multiple-sport players. At Duke University, a school where the men's basketball team has become one of the most spectacular successes in the nation, Groat was the first true Blue Devil. In the autumn of 2007 he was inducted into the College Basketball Hall of Fame. As a long-time radio broadcaster for the University of Pittsburgh, he remains involved in basketball. "I love college basketball," Groat said. "It's always been my first love. I was a much better basketball player."[11]

Although Haddix certainly never served as an official at any basketball game Groat played in for Duke, Schofield, who answered to the nickname "Ducky," remembers the pitcher carrying around a whistle in his pocket and using it on selected occasions as an ongoing joke. "Harvey had this whistle and if he saw you someplace doing something that he thought you shouldn't be doing, he'd take out this whistle and blow it, like he was calling a technical foul on you!" Schofield said. "He'd get on an elevator and if there was some big, tall girl on the elevator, he'd blow the whistle and holler, 'Jump ball!' He just enjoyed life. I think he was liked by everybody. You could say he never changed from the farm boy from Ohio. I don't think he ever really changed about anything."[12]

Schofield, who had been a Ted Williams and Boston Red Sox fan while growing up, broke into the majors in 1953 as a $40,000 bonus baby with the Cardinals. He played 19 seasons, retiring in 1971. That made him one of a limited number of big leaguers to compete in three different decades. He is also one of a small number of big leaguers who had future generations of the same family follow them into the game. His son Dick, Jr., played 14 seasons from 1983 to 1996. Grandson Jayson Werth was a member of the Baltimore Orioles' organization and then the Phillies'.

Never lacking for confidence after being pursued by 13 major league clubs and being offered a basketball scholarship to Northwestern, Schofield bristled when it was suggested he was going to be consigned to mop-up duty behind Groat and Mazeroski. He recognized they were stars, but refused to admit he couldn't win a job. "I'm not conceding anything to anybody," Schofield announced. "All I want is a chance to play and I'll show them."[13]

He did, in spurts, but it took a broken wrist to Groat to earn Schofield major playing time in 1960. Otherwise manager Danny Murtaugh just worked Schofield into the lineup for spot duty periodically. One of those odd days happened to be the Haddix game and Schofield played a significant role in the field and at bat.

When Schofield retired he went to work for the state government of Illinois in his hometown, and as an example of how baseball salaries were for backup infielders, he was as happy as a lottery winner when he got paid about $1,300 a month. "I thought, 'Gee whiz,'" Schofield said, "that's more money than I made playing baseball most of my life so this ought to be pretty good."[14]

The job lasted one year before the legislature cut back on the budget. However, besides watching the younger generation play ball, Schofield managed to stay close to sports while working 23 years for the Josten's company that manufactures championship rings.

Schofield won a World Series ring with the Pirates, played in the 1968 World Series for the Cardinals, and led the National League with a .981 fielding percentage in 1965, but no thrill exceeded his participation in Haddix's masterpiece. "I think the most memorable game I ever played in was 1959 when I was with Pittsburgh," he said. "We couldn't score a run and they couldn't get a hit."[15]

5

Second Inning

Dick Groat thinks it was after the second inning when he first lighted a cigarette for Haddix. Things were going so smoothly on the mound that when Haddix returned to the dugout after the third, he asked Groat to fire him up again. Then it became ritual, or superstition, as Braves batter after batter made outs and trudged back to the home dugout. On a night when Groat was perched in his own dugout sitting out the game, he acquired another job. "Harvey was a heavy smoker and he refused to light a cigarette after I lit a cigarette for him," Groat said. "And I lit a cigarette for him for every inning he smoked after that."[1]

Such a thing would never happen during a game in a Major League dugout now. In the 1950s, cigarette smoking was still a manly pursuit that only enhanced the image of a professional athlete. In the 2000s, the behavior is considered unhealthy and socially inappropriate and besides, intrusive TV cameras would be able to pick up the first flick of a match and broadcast such action nationwide. If a player still smokes heavily and must partake during a game, he surely does so now by retreating to the clubhouse.

Superstition or not, Haddix was setting Braves hitters down with the grace of his curveball and the location of his other pitches. Cigarettes, it can safely be said, played no practical role in the zeros going up on the County Stadium scoreboard.

The Pirates got their second chance to assess Lew Burdette's stuff when first baseman Rocky Nelson led off the second inning. Nelson was a veteran journeyman ballplayer who broke into the majors with the St. Louis Cardinals in 1949. He never played 100 games in a season and generally was the Pirates' backup. The club had begun the season with Ted Kluszewski holding down first.

Kluszewski, a former National League home run champ, famously used scissors to snip the ends of his short-sleeved baseball jerseys to the shoulder, thereby highlighting his bulging biceps. It was never 100 percent clear if it was a fashion statement, a showoff move, or a ploy to psych out enemy pitchers. Before the end of the season Kluszewski was shipped to the Chicago White Sox and helped the Sox win their first American League pennant in 40 years.

Kluszewski became expendable because the flamboyant Dick Stuart had moved into the job more or less full time. Stuart was a legendary minor-league home-run hitter, with matinee-idol looks, a party-boy outlook, and a limited fielding capability that was ridiculed far and wide. Stuart earned his designation as "Dr. Strangeglove" because of his shakiness defending the bag. On this night, manager Murtaugh sat Stuart, so it was Nelson's opportunity to swing in the clean-up spot.

Nelson came through with the first hit of the game, singling to center field. Skinner wanted to make something happen, but instead grounded to Braves shortstop Johnny Logan, who threw Nelson out and doubled up Skinner at first base.

Skinner, who had a 12-year Major-League career as a corner outfielder and batted .277, was a reliable hitter who typically stroked more than 10 homers and drove in 60-plus runs. After he retired, Skinner stayed in the sport for decades coaching, and in his later years scouting for the Houston Astros. His son Joel also enjoyed a nine-year big-league career.

Skinner classified Haddix as a close friend and said if he could have had one more hit on his resume than the 1,198 he retired with, he wishes it would have been a run-producer in that game against the Braves and Burdette. "Burdette was very tough in the crunch," Skinner said. "He pitched a heck of a game."[2]

Nelson and Skinner were erased and when second baseman Bill Mazeroski stepped in, the bases were clear. Burdette struck out the future Hall of Famer, ending the Pirates' half of the second.

It was Haddix's throwing turn again. Haddix had not magically gotten fully healthy since the game began. His adrenaline was carrying him and he was busy with the assignment of getting hitters out, but once in a while he took note of his bothersome upper respiratory system. Early in the game he began popping throat lozenges to ward off illness.

"I felt lousy," Haddix said. "I sucked on throat lozenges the whole ball game so I wouldn't cough while I was out there on the mound." Once in a while, he added, he was conscious of the damp weather and how that might affect his health. Then he forgot about it and went back to throwing.[3]

5. Second Inning

An illustration of how much power the Braves featured top to bottom in the batting order was that neither Eddie Mathews nor Hank Aaron was batting cleanup. The fourth hitter was first baseman Joe Adcock. Adcock stood 6-foot-4 and weighed 210 pounds. He was born in a flyspeck of a community named Coushatta, Louisiana, that had 500 people. He attended Louisiana State on a basketball scholarship. In the spring, when he joined the Tigers' baseball team, Major League scouts took notice of Adcock's power, if not his smoothness. He was considered a not-fully-formed but potentially great slugger in need of coaching. There was a reason why he looked that way — Adcock had never played baseball until he went to college.[4] Cincinnati signed him, but while Adcock looked like a baseball player, he couldn't swing like one at first. In spring training of 1948 Adcock counted it a victory if he could even swat a foul ball. It was as if every hurler was Bob Feller. An embarrassed Adcock caught only air on the majority of his cuts. "Guess I was overanxious," he said a few years later.[5]

After two nondescript years playing for Columbia, South Carolina, in the Sally League, Adcock began lighting up the Texas League. He broke into the majors with the Reds in 1950. Following some seasoning, and a trade to the Braves in 1952, Adcock emerged as a fully developed power hitter. On April 29, 1953, the lanky blaster hit a fastball so hard that he became the first batter to hit a ball into the centerfield bleachers at the Polo Grounds. The ball landed 10 rows up, 475 feet from home plate. Adcock also became the first batter to hit a ball over the left field stands in Ebbets Field.

Those blows awed onlookers, but Adcock's crowning moment at the plate — one of the greatest days ever recorded by a batsman — occurred on July 31, 1954, when the Braves crushed the Dodgers, 15–7, in Brooklyn. Adcock cracked a Major-League-tying four home runs in a game (a record that he still shares) and added a double in a fifth at-bat. Adcock always hit well against the Dodgers in Brooklyn, and New York sports writers said Ebbets Field might as well be "Adcock's Alley."[6] And that was before his finest display.

Ironically, Adcock did his slugging with a borrowed bat. The night before, in his final at-bat of the evening, Adcock broke his own favorite bat. The next day he picked up a heavier bat belonging to teammate Charlie White, a seldom-deployed backup catcher. Adcock's first impression was that he made a mistake because White's bat felt a lot heavier—weighing perhaps five ounces more than Adcock's usual stick. But after he hit a Johnny Podres fastball for a homer in his first at-bat, he decided to stay with it throughout the game. White later told Adcock the bat was only two ounces heavier, but in Adcock's hands that day it was a war club put to positive use. "I never hit more than two in one game before, even in the minors," Adcock said.[7]

Adcock was still finding his groove in the majors, coming to understand just how menacing a hitter he could be. In a 1956 triumph over the Giants, Adcock went four-for-four with eight RBIs that included a grand slam and a two-run homer—in six innings before going to the bench. At the time he had hit nine home runs in his previous 11 games.

Haddix knew he had to pitch Adcock carefully. Haddix's first pitch to the first baseman was high and inside for a ball, a fairly safe place to put a pitch. A moment later Adcock went down on strikes.

Braves left-fielder Wes Covington hit a grounder to Mazeroski at second for the second out and catcher Del Crandall grounded to Don Hoak at third to get Haddix out of the inning.

Bob Friend, who was not only Haddix's friend, but another of the Pirate pitchers in the regular rotation, had a seat in the dugout that night, bundled in his warm-up jacket against the cool evening, watching intently. He felt from the first pitch Haddix had command and that his pitches were crisp and working.

"Harvey had terrific stuff that night," said Friend, who won 197 games in his career and was coming off his finest season, a 22-win effort, entering the 1959 campaign. "Everything was sharp. It looked like he had life on his fastball. He had a real good slider coming in there. Slider, curveball, he used all the pitches and the location was terrific. He was just mowing them down. There wasn't any fluke about it."[8]

Two innings does not a ballgame make, given that pitchers are perfect for the six straight hitters many times each season. But sometimes baseball men can tell when a good player has taken his game to a higher level that day. Braves manager Fred Haney observed right from the start that Haddix was on and that Haddix was going to be difficult to work for bases on balls. "He had terrific control," Haney said. "Haddix held us in the palm of his hand."[9]

Some fans go to baseball games rooting for a no-hitter every time.

Pitchers who focus only on home plate and the next batter can be oblivious to the fact that they are pitching a no-hitter, but all it takes is a 180-degree spin of their bodies to gaze at the outfield scoreboard and the line score to answer that question. Batters hit by a pitch are rare enough that pitchers don't forget it when they have bonked someone. But walks don't go up on the board. No posted number signifies that method of putting opposing hitters on base. As the game wore on and the score remained a double shutout, Haddix didn't remember whether he had walked a Braves hitter or not in the early innings.[10]

Sometimes it's the guys who are on the bench, the backups in uniform, who may or may not get in, who have more awareness of the entire game situation. Mel Roach, the Braves' second-base backup, was in the dugout that night and he said the team could tell in the early going that Haddix was going to be hard to hit. "We knew all along," Roach said of no men reaching base.

Roach also said being in the field during a no-hitter could sometimes change a man's attitude. "I played in three no-hitters. When the game is far along you actually pray nobody hits the ball to you. It's tough."[11] Roach meant he never would want to be the fielder who made an error that cost a pitcher a perfect game.

6

The Worthy Opposition

Lew Burdette liked to confuse people. On the baseball diamond, it was with the pitches he threw. Off the field, it was with his first name.

Burdette's given name, when he was born in 1926 in the creatively named town of Nitro, West Virginia, was Selva Lewis Burdette, Jr. The closest he ever came to answering to Selva was when he was accused of putting saliva on a spitter before his windup. Most often he used the name "Lew," but frequently, when others spelled it, he was referred to as Lou. Burdette signed "Lewis" to contracts and alternated between "Lew" and "Lou" for autograph seekers and said he wasn't picky how his first name was spelled.[1]

While Burdette was paid to get batters out, no one on his teams seemed overly curious as to how he managed the feat. For two decades he was accused of employing the illegal spitball, moistening those stitches before he palmed the ball and heaved it to the plate. He never admitted to doing so. He called his out pitch a sinker. "My best pitches were a sinker and a slider," Burdette said. "I'd move the ball in and out. I always tried to keep it down."[2]

Growing up in Nitro, where the primary manufacturing product was explosives, Burdette honed his throwing accuracy by throwing rocks at church windows. That may not have been a popular pursuit with the religious folks in town, but the atheistic arm got Burdette signed by the New York Yankees in 1947.

It was the luck of the rotation on May 26, 1959, that the Milwaukee Braves sent Burdette to the mound to face Harvey Haddix. Haddix always recalled beating Burdette for the first win of the slight southpaw's career. But Burdette got the best of most teams. During an 18-year career, Burdette compiled a record of 203–144, a winning percentage of .585.

At the time of this showdown with Haddix, the right-handed throwing Burdette was in his prime. He won 17 games in 1957, the year the Braves captured their only World Series in Milwaukee, won 20 in 1958, and was on his way to a career high 21 victories in the season of Haddix's 12-inning perfect game.

6. The Worthy Opposition

Right-handed pitcher Lew Burdette was Harvey Haddix's mound opponent in the 13-inning masterpiece between the Braves and Pirates and managed to shut out Pittsburgh while scattering 12 hits.

Throughout the long, misty night, Pirate bats regularly got in the way of Burdette-thrown pitches, but he issued no walks. Superb control was a Burdette trademark. He surrendered just 1.84 walks per nine innings during his career, a mark that placed him fourth-best on a list of pitchers who threw 3,000 or more innings after 1920. Those ahead of him are Robin Roberts (1.73), Carl Hubbell and Juan Marichal.[3]

Although it had nothing to do with his pitching (so it didn't stick),

Burdette's nickname as a youth was "Froggy." He was enamored of the outdoors, took long walks in the woods, and collected bugs, lizards, frogs and the like. Often he brought them to school and, while ignoring the lesson on the blackboard, took his collectibles out and occupied himself with them on his desk. One day a frog leaped from his desk and disrupted the class, blowing his cover.

The teacher threatened to whack Burdette on his butt. He pleaded with her not to and explained why. "I got three of my pet caterpillars in my back pocket," he said. "I wouldn't want them to get hurt." The teacher laughed and relented, and from then on Burdette was allowed to bring his finds from the natural world to school as long as he shared them for show-and-tell.[4]

Burdette became friendly with Mickey Mantle in the Yankees' organization and received some advice from a paternalistic Joe DiMaggio when he joined the big club. But he was not a Yankee for long. In 1950, Burdette made two appearances for New York, but his destiny was rearranged when he was included in a trade with the Braves that brought Johnny Sain to the Yanks.

This was a significant trade for the Braves. When the pitching-thin team had battled through long campaigns in the late 1940s, it relied on Warren Spahn, the winningest left-handed pitcher of all time, and Sain, to anchor the rotation. The phrase "Spahn and Sain and pray for rain" indicated just how important Sain was for Braves' hopes of winning games.

Burdette gradually grew into his role as a star pitcher for the Braves, the number two starter behind Spahn. The pair became buddies and running mates on the road. Burdette had become a Brave not long before the team was vacating its half-century home in Boston for the prime baseball real estate of Milwaukee.

When the official team welcome was held in 1953, featuring a parade, Burdette sat with Spahn gulping down the adulation of Wisconsin's hungry baseball fans. "Hey, Warren," he said, "Isn't this the greatest thrill you've ever had? We're sitting on top of the world. It's the biggest parade I've ever seen." Spahn was equally impressed. "It's like V-E Day and V-J Day rolled into one," he said.[5]

Burdette never lacked for confidence, and in the 1950s the savviest pitchers were given more leeway in protecting their share of the plate from hitters who crowded it. If a hitter inched his toes too close to the dish, pitchers didn't hesitate to fire a fastball in tight. Burdette got on hitters' nerves more than most because he talked to them from the mound 60 feet, 6 inches away, and he fiddled around with the ball in his glove for what seemed like an inordinate amount of time. This behavior seemed to bother the Dodgers more than other teams. "He's simply got the edge on us because he outtalks us and we get all riled up for nothing," said Brooklyn's Hall of Fame shortstop Pee Wee Reese. Centerfielder Duke Snider chimed in, "It's not only the chatter. He does all kinds of things out there and he drives you crazy waiting for every pitch."[6]

For a brief period of time in the late 1970s, Detroit Tigers pitcher Mark Fidrych endeared himself to chuckling fans with antics on the mound, including talking to the baseball. In retrospect, some called Burdette the Mark Fidrych of his era.[7] Burdette's was the type of behavior that could distract hitters from their main task—and that was the point. The Dodgers also began questioning the true origins of that "slider" Burdette threw so effectively. "And about that spitball," Jackie Robinson said. "This guy's been throwing a spitball ever since he came into the big leagues and nobody ever did anything about it."[8]

After the Braves compiled a 5–0 lead, the Dodgers were furious. Burdette taunted Brooklyn catcher Roy Campanella, one of his most vociferous foes. "You've been talking so much about how you can hit me, let's see what you can do with the next pitch ... it's going to be a fast one down the middle."[9]

Not quite. The next pitch sailed in towards Campanella's head. The war of words escalated, pausing with a promise from Campanella to knock any similar pitch over the fence. Once again the ball came in high and tight. Campanella once again threatened to bash the ball out of the park. However, the next pitch fooled him completely and he struck out with a wild swing. Campanella actually started walking towards the mound, with the suggestion of violence in his face. Burdette yelled, "Get back there in the dugout with the rest of those Brooklyn bums!"[10] That lit the fuse and a brawl ensued.

Unperturbed, in his next outing, Burdette shut out the Pirates, 1–0.

In an eight-team National League, the Pirates got used to seeing Burdette, so he wasn't throwing anything unusual or special during the Haddix game. Of course, the Pirates didn't know what to call Burdette's best pitch. Despite their anger and best efforts, the Dodgers had not proven that Burdette threw the illegal spitter and neither had anyone else.

"It was either a great sinker or he had the spitter working," said Pirates pitcher Bob Friend, observing Burdette that night from the dugout. "Probably one, or both. He had pretty good stuff. To throw a spitter you must have a good fastball because if you can't throw hard, the spitter isn't any good."[11]

Years later, Don Hoak, who was the Pirates' third baseman in Haddix's game, and who made a thorough tour of the National League, gave an interview on the subject of the spitball. "Only once did I see water fly off a spitball and the man who threw that pitch was Lew Burdette," Hoak said.[12] It was not raining that day. Just as he did when confronted by such alleged evidence of his doctoring of the ball as a player, at the time of that 1967 discussion, Burdette replied, "Who, me?"[13]

Burdette pretty much thrived on implausible denial. In 1969, Burdette was hired by a chewing tobacco company to endorse the product that carried the slogan, "Bring back the spitter." Coincidence? Burdette had no comment on that. However, he did campaign for baseball to make the spitball legal again, saying (it was not clear if this was a facetious or serious statement) that if the spitball was employed, hitters would reduce the ferocity of their swings and their batting averages would rise.[14]

The spitball was banned by Major League baseball in 1920. However, players who had been using it legally were grandfathered in under the new law and allowed to finish their careers with the pitch. The last legal spitball was thrown by Burleigh Grimes in 1934. Grimes served as Burdette's pitching coach in the minors in Norfolk, Virginia.

The way Burdette told the story, he asked Grimes for spitball throwing lessons, but the old-timer refused to provide them. Burdette recounted Grimes' response this way: "Nothing doing. If you throw the spitter, you'll get caught and you'll be in trouble. But if you can make hitters think you're throwing a spitter you won't even need one. You'll have them guessing." Burdette said he adopted that psychology.

"If I could get one of the first three hitters to go back to the dugout and say, 'That so-and-so is throwing a spitter,' I'd be liable to have a good game." Even better, Burdette said, is when the constant complaints of opposing players or a manager got on the umpire's nerves. "He'd come out to the mound with a disgusted look and say, 'Let's see the ball.' I'd toss it to him and he'd glance at it and toss it back. Umpires don't like long games more than anyone else."[15]

6. The Worthy Opposition

Burdette said that the first time he was accused of throwing a spitter (at least in the public realm, no telling what type of curses were being leveled at him in the confines of clubhouses) was by Phillies manager Steve O'Neill in 1957. A little later, Reds manager Birdie Tebbetts took measures beyond visiting with umpires during games, lodging a formal protest with the National League office. President Warren Giles, however, declared Burdette not guilty. Burdette asked Tebbetts for an apology, but it was not forthcoming. "It got a million dollars worth of publicity," Burdette said of the newspaper reports, thinking once again of how his "spitball" played with hitters' minds. Not all of that publicity was good. Burdette said his young son got into scrapes at school because kids taunted him with the phrase "Your father's a cheater."[16]

In a small-world development, Tebbetts eventually became manager of the Braves while Burdette was still on the team. Enterprising newsmen, recalling the earlier flap, asked Tebbetts about his pitching ace's spitball. "What spitball?" Tebbetts said. "Lew Burdette throws the best sinker in the National League."[17] If Grimes actually taught Burdette the spitter when they were chatting between games—despite Burdette's protestations—is unknown. Neither man is alive to pursue the topic.

No baseball games are the same. The same team can face the same opposing pitcher two days in a row and the results can be totally different. The Pirates were familiar with Burdette, respected him for the All-Star he was, but remained confident that they could reach him for hits, and eventually, runs.

"We had hits," said outfielder Bob Skinner. "They were throwing runners out at third and all over the place."[18] The Pirates wanted those runs to make Harvey Haddix's night a little bit easier, but they just couldn't get a runner beyond third base.

7

Third Inning

Third baseman Don Hoak began the Pirates' half of the third inning with an infield single off Lew Burdette. The next batter up was back-up right-fielder Roman Mejias. Mejias, who hailed from Abreus, Cuba, was in the lineup because the team star, Roberto Clemente, was nursing a sore throwing arm.

At a time when few major league teams employed Latin American players on their rosters, the Pirates were in the forefront of signing Hispanics. Mejias, 29 at the time, had a nine-year major league career, but only twice participated in as many as 100 games in a season. The 1959 campaign was his busiest of six with Pittsburgh; he appeared in 96 games.

Mejias hit a grounder to Eddie Mathews covering third, who fired the ball to second to get Hoak out on the force play.

Harvey Haddix was the next Pittsburgh hitter. Designated hitter in the American League or not, National League pitchers have always taken their own turn at the plate. This added responsibility was just part of the game and didn't seem to affect Haddix's pitching one way or the other on this night. Haddix beat out an infield hit back to the mound, but Mejias was thrown out trying to advance to third. Given how few times the Pirates had opportunities, the Mejias gaffe was later seen as significant. If Mejias had held on second, he likely would have scored on the next play after shortstop Dick Schofield singled, sending Haddix to third base. Center fielder Bill Virdon got a piece of one of Burdette's offerings, but flew out to left. Pittsburgh, as would become a common sight, stranded two runners on base.

Watching from the dugout, Dick Groat spent his night off chatting with Haddix about everything except how he was pitching, and when he wasn't talking, he was observing how his teammates seemed to have Burdette's number until it really mattered.

"It was one of those nights where we just couldn't get a big base hit when we needed it," Groat said. "We had our opportunities and we didn't produce."[1]

7. Third Inning

Sometimes it becomes apparent early in a game when a pitcher is on, but it also seems like little things are working against a team trying to score runs. This was one of those occasions when fellow Pirates hurler Vernon Law sensed that every run Pittsburgh scored would be important for Haddix. Even early in the game he had a bit of uneasiness over the way the ball was bouncing and wanted to see the Pirates put up some runs quickly.

"I was rooting like heck for somebody to get a base hit and for us to get a run in for him," Law said. "I just had a feeling that the way things were going, you know, we were struggling to score. I was just hoping somebody could break out for him."[2]

By the bottom of the third inning, Haddix had set down the Braves' most dangerous hitters once apiece. But the Braves had power distributed throughout the lineup. The lead-off man in the third was veteran Andy Pafko, the centerfielder. Compared to the prowess of Hank Aaron, Eddie Mathews and Joe Adcock, Pafko was not considered a home-run hitter. But given that he was batting seventh in the order, his presence was evidence of the Braves' great depth at the time.

Pafko, of Czechoslovakian extraction, whose name was Anglicized from Pruschka, grew up in Wisconsin and was happy to be playing in Milwaukee, where he once had a fan club called the "Pruschkettes." But he had also been happy for the chance to play Major League ball in Chicago, for the Cubs, when they won the 1945 pennant, and for the Dodgers, in Brooklyn, where he won another pennant after being traded there in 1951. The .285 lifetime hitter was part of the Braves when the club won two pennants and a World Series, too.

"It felt like everybody went 0-for-4 that day," Pafko recalled of Haddix's day, an observation that was pretty much accurate. "You feel helpless when a pitcher seems unstoppable. You feel good when the game is over and that there'll be another day coming. Some days you hit the ball so hard and it's right at somebody. You have to give the credit to the pitcher."[3]

At the time Pafko spoke, the Cubs had not played in a World Series in 63 years, and he was one of three living members of that club. Pafko's stay in Brooklyn lasted just a year and a half; wherever he went pennants followed. There was a great hullabaloo in the baseball world when the Cubs parted with Pafko during the middle of the 1951 pennant race. Giants manager Leo Durocher had wanted him and been told that Pafko was unavailable. Then, as a key figure in an eight-player deal, Pafko was traded to Durocher's chief rival. "Leo thundered that Pafko alone was worth more than the four new Cubs," a sportswriter noted.[4]

Of course, the Giants overtook the Dodgers for the pennant, anyway, on Bobby Thomson's famous home run. But Brooklyn bested New York the next season, with Pafko contributing a solid, 19-home run, .287-hitting season. Although Pafko played on pennant-winners for three organizations, he had no doubt that the Braves team that Haddix faced was the powerhouse among the three good clubs.

"That was the best group I ever played with," Pafko said. "It had to be. Playing in Milwaukee was also exciting for me because I grew up in Wisconsin. It was great to come back to play in my home state to finish out my career. The people treated us right. Oh, my gosh, we had free meals and cars and everything else. We practically owned the town. It was just terrific. I'll never forget that."[5]

Pafko was always grateful for his Major League opportunities. He grew up on a farm in Boyceville and as a youth was diagnosed with severe high blood pressure. On his seventh birthday, Pafko also survived an explosion of a stove that nearly blinded him when he and buddies tossed gasoline in a stove instead of kerosene. One friend was killed; Pafko was hospitalized in the resulting blast, and he was left with some small scars on his forehead.

In a first-person story written for *Sport* magazine during his playing days, Pafko extolled the wonders of being a ballplayer in Milwaukee, which made major leaguers feel so at home. After a home game once, he reported, he approached his car, only to find an elderly woman, leaning part of her weight on a cane and the rest of it on a friend, patiently waiting for him for an autograph.

"Her long wait told me how strongly she felt about the Braves," Pafko wrote. "People like that old lady contribute to Milwaukee's great baseball spirit. I'll take Milwaukee. Coming to Milwaukee was the greatest thing that has happened to me in more than 10 years in the majors."[6] When he was active, Pafko said, he got fan mail from as far away as Korea and Alaska.[7]

Many times during his major league career Pafko looked at the battle between the pitcher and the batter as the irresistible object meeting the immovable force, especially on the occasions when the batter was hot and

7. Third Inning

the pitcher had his best stuff working. Batters are deemed successful when they hit safely on a pace approaching just 30 percent of the time. When a pitcher is on fire, Pafko said, the odds might tilt. "On some of those days you're hot and you can just do no wrong," he said. "When the pitcher is hot I would say the pitcher wins nine out of 10 times."[8] As hot as Haddix was that night, he was in the 90 percent realm by Pafko's calculations.

Pafko hit a fly ball to right field and Mejias squeezed it for the first out. Johnny Logan stepped in. As a young man, Logan had always aspired to play shortstop, but felt he was in need of coaching. From a distance he admired Yankee shortstop Frankie Crosetti and wrote him a letter seeking advice. Crosetti responded with some pointers. The key element in Crosetti's tips was this: "Play every ball hit to you as though it is going to take the last bad hop."[9]

With the same zeal, Logan, who is of Ukrainian heritage and grew up in upstate New York, had focused on making himself a better hitter, as well. He took extra batting practice and learned situational hitting, the best approaches to hitting behind the runner. Logan evolved into a holler guy with the Braves, the player who would yell to stoke up the more reserved players. He was a chatterbox on the bench and in the field. When he spoke to newspapermen he was jolly and frequently had malapropisms attributed to him. Popular at sports banquets, once while making an acceptance speech Logan said, "I'm very, very speechless." He also said of the Cardinals' Hall of Famer, "It's a pleasure to share the rostrum with Stan Musial, one of baseball's great immorals." Such skewed phrases became known as "Loganisms." Logan, who also penned baseball poetry, later in life shared a Milwaukee broadcast booth with Bob Uecker.[10]

During his first time at bat against Haddix, Logan caught a pitch over the plate with the fat part of his bat and hit a stinging shot towards shortstop. For a second, it appeared the ball was through the infield for the Braves' first hit. Later, in retrospect, several players felt this was the closest Milwaukee came to recording a hit. In subsequent years, when Haddix pondered his own performance that night, he too remembered the Logan swat as an almost. "Johnny Logan hit a real hot scooter at Dick Schofield," Haddix said.[11] The ball rocketed off the bat, but Schofield was positioned well and didn't really feel it was that difficult of a chance. "Johnny Logan hit a line drive kind of in the hole, but I caught it," Schofield said. "There just weren't many balls hit very good at all."[12]

That fact stuck with players who were on the field that night. After a few innings of watching Haddix throw they could tell he was on, that the spin of his curve was baffling the hitters and even when bat struck ball it didn't really travel anywhere.

"As the innings went by and the game grew longer and longer, it just became apparent that Harvey could do whatever he wanted to do with the ball that night," said Pirates reserve catcher Hank Foiles, who watched the game from the visiting team bullpen and who also regularly caught Haddix.

"Harvey was a very clever pitcher. He was very agile and he didn't overpower you, but he made you hit his pitch. He very seldom shook off a catcher. He would talk over the hitters with you before you were out on the field."[13]

Foiles, who spent 11 seasons in the majors and turned 30 that year, early on was less conscious of watching history unfold than of the game being just like one of the many he participated in or watched. At least in the third inning it was too soon for him to think of it as an event that was truly special. "Each game was a game you played," Foiles said, "whether you were on the field or on the bench, or in the bullpen. You were part of the game. You played it. Eventually, it was going to end somehow."[14]

Not yet, though. After Logan's liner died in Schofield's glove, Haddix was at the end of the order. Burdette, the opposing pitcher, came to bat for the first time and he struck out looking.

About that time, Pirate pitchers who had the day off were starting to look at one another. They said nothing, not even to each other, but they felt Haddix was looking as sharp as they had ever seen him. Elroy Face, who was in the middle of the best season of his career, made a habit of watching games in the dugout at their start and then moseying over to the bullpen in the later innings when he might be needed. Face was needed often in 1959 and his 18–1 record was the best ever compiled by a reliever, but he was not needed on that night. "You're not supposed to talk about it," Face said of the way major league ballplayers skirt around the topic of a no-hit game. "It spoils the chance. It's superstition."[15]

The smooth way the ball emerged from Haddix's hand and approached the plate that game seemed more like magic than superstition.

8

Pittsburgh

The city that worshipped the Pirates was built on the backs of steel workers, later symbolized by a football team named for them.

Pittsburgh of the 1950s was a blue-collar community. Men as tough as the product they produced were the foundation of a steel industry that was a cornerstone of American growth in the post–World War II era. It was a friendly town, without pretensions, with a shot-and-beer clientele at the neighborhood tavern after the shift ended at the plant. There was nothing frou-frou about Pittsburgh. Imbibers drank Iron City beer, or Rolling Rock, made in nearby Latrobe, Pennsylvania.

Pittsburgh was also a city whose air quality suffered from the smoke stacks belching black particulate substances into the sky. For decades, before there was either a U.S. Environmental Protection Agency, or an American populace conscious of the opinion that children should be able to differentiate between sunny days and cloudy ones, Pittsburgh's nickname was "The Smoky City." It was neither insult nor compliment, but statement of fact.

In the 1950s, the Pirates were the number one game in town, and the awful records kicking off the decade notwithstanding, it was good to be a Pirate in Pittsburgh. It was a different age of celebrity than what a star might face today, but if you were a regular on the Pirates you were known. You might be recognized when you went shopping with the family, but you were not mobbed. You might be asked for an autograph when dining in a restaurant, but you were not interrupted so frequently you couldn't get the fork to your mouth with a bite of baked potato.

This was a pleasant type of celebrity. It was good to be noticed, but you could still function in day-to-day life, something that was truer in the 1950s, except among the biggest stars, than it is in the 2000s. For the most part, the players were regular guys who were year-round members of the community. The ballplayer of the 2000s routinely makes $1 million or more in a season. The ballplayer of the 1950s, even a starter like outfielder Bob Skinner, might make $20,000 or so. That meant the players were looking for off-season work to supplement their incomes.

"None of us made any money," Skinner said many years later. "We all worked, or most of us worked, in the wintertime. I had a 40-hour-a-week job in an aircraft plant as a spot weld inspector." A machine welded airplane wings with markings no bigger than a dime and Skinner made his rounds double-checking to see if the welds held. And he played ball on Sundays in an industrial league until it was time to re-join the Pirates for spring training.[1] "I love the Pittsburgh fans," Skinner said decades later while living in San Diego and working as a scout. "Even to this date [1992] the fans recognize me and treat me great."[2]

The Pittsburgh area was inhabited by Native Americans for an estimated 10,000 years before what is considered the modern era began. Located where the Allegheny and Monongahela Rivers intersect the Ohio River (hence the future name of a baseball field called Three Rivers Stadium) Pittsburgh was viewed as being of strategic importance when the Indians, the French and the British sought territorial privilege.

When the French built Fort Duquesne in 1754, the British resented it and the construction project, coupled with the countries' hostile attitudes, led to the French and Indian War. After the American Revolution, Pittsburgh became a growing metropolis whose navigable waterways turned it into a hotbed of commerce. Steel production began in 1875 and by 1911 the city met half of the nation's needs. The Heinz family opened their food manufacturing company, eventually giving the world "57 varieties," and the coal mining industry in the region surrounding Pittsburgh prospered.[3]

A natural offshoot to being the United States' leading steel producer was that the Pittsburgh Pirates, under the ownership of future Hall of Famer Barney Dreyfuss, acquired one of the first steel framed ballparks in 1909. Forbes Field, named after John Forbes, a British general in the French and Indian War, was built for $1 million next to the University of Pittsburgh.

Forbes Field was not the fan-friendliest ballpark in the majors. Sight lines for some of the 25,000 fans (at first, then 35,000) were poor—if seated in the upper left corner of the left-field bleachers, ticket holders could not see the batter. Although Wrigley Field's ivy is much more famous because the park continues to serve the Chicago Cubs, Forbes Field's left and center fields also featured ivy covering a brick wall. Other characteristics were a very hard infield and a vast swath of empty space behind the catcher, good for running down foul pop-ups. In 1934, following the death of team founder Dreyfuss, a statue of the magnate was installed near the right–center field exit gate. There was also a 457-foot mark on the left-center brick wall, a spot that would have taken a gargantuan blast to clear with a home run.[4]

No one was prouder about the erection of the stadium than Dreyfuss, who always believed—and was proven correct—that the Pirates would only grow in popularity as the years passed. When Forbes Field was being built, Dreyfuss heard from many naysayers who thought that any stadium capable of holding 25,000 spectators was too grand in ambition. The first Pirates game was played at Forbes Field June 30, 1909. Mayor William A. Magee threw out the ceremonial first pitch. "A friend of mine bet me a $150 suit of clothes that the park would never be filled," Dreyfuss said. "We filled it five times the first two weeks."[5]

Forbes Field remained the Pirates' home park for 68 seasons. Lights to play night baseball were installed in 1940, but by then sometimes the plumes of smoke radically altering the air were so widespread that street lights were turned on during the day in order to conduct average business activity.[6]

Although Honus Wagner was the most popular Pirate of his generation and endured in popularity in Pittsburgh for the rest of his life, arguably the community's foremost citizen was Andrew Carnegie, who not only maintained a mansion on Millionaire's Row on the East Side of town, but was the ruler supreme of U.S. Steel. Steel making was a sooty, dirty profession. Men walked out of the factories covered in grime. But Carnegie romanticized his emotions about the steel world with words from the heart, penning a poem called "Ode to Steelmaking." He wrote,

> The eighth wonder of the world is this:
> two pounds of iron-stone purchased on
> the shores of lake superior and
> transported to Pittsburgh;
> two pounds of coal mined in Connellsville
> and manufactured into coke and
> brought to Pittsburgh;
> one half pound of limestone mined
> east of the Alleghenies and
> brought to Pittsburgh;
> a little manganese ore,

> mined in Virginia and brought to Pittsburgh.
> And these four and one half pounds of material
> manufactured into one pound of solid steel
> and sold for one cent.
> That's all that need to be said
> about the steel business.[7]

Carnegie was born in Dunfermline, Scotland, in 1835 and grew up in poverty. The Carnegies moved to Pittsburgh in 1848 and young Andrew was introduced to labor as a teenager. When he rose in stature to the job of secretary and telegrapher to the operator of the Pennsylvania Railroad, Carnegie was paid $35 a month and said, "I couldn't imagine what I could ever do with so much money."[8]

Over the years, as he made millions, Carnegie figured out what do with his money, especially after 1901, when he sold his company to J.P. Morgan for $480 million. When the deal was struck, Morgan said to Carnegie, "Congratulations, Mr. Carnegie, you are now the richest man in the world." Not only did Carnegie supervise the leading company in one of the most powerful industries in the United States, he was generous with his riches, endowing more than 2,800 public libraries and educational institutions. It was estimated at the time of his death in 1919 that he had given away $350 million. His largess helped shaped Pittsburgh for generations.[9]

People shrugged off the smog that hung in the air. "There were legends about the workers who didn't get out of breath," said William Kennedy, Sr., an engineer for Bell Telephone systems in the 1950s. "It [the steel industry] was loved by most Pittsburghers because it gave them a big source of employment and income."[10]

Author John Wideman, who had a hardscrabble upbringing in Pittsburgh during the 1940s and 1950s before he found success, described the city as a place that admires hard work, puts up with hard weather, and is very much a mix of attitudes. He wrote that Pittsburgh's destiny was "to be a polyglot, patchwork town, never a smooth, swaggering, big city. Lots of churches and plenty of Iron City beer at home in the fridge. We tiptoed around each other in Pittsburgh, more aware of our differences and similarities than we were willing to admit; proud, maybe, not to make a public fuss about such stuff."[11]

The first efforts to eradicate Pittsburgh's image as "The Smoky City"

8. Pittsburgh

and to improve air quality took root after World War II, but the atmosphere was not going to be cleared in a day. In the 1950s, the ballplayers didn't worry too much about environmental causes, just about getting themselves into the first division of the National League and making a living for their families.

Pirates backup catcher Hank Foiles said when he broke into the majors with Cincinnati in 1953 and his mind drifted to a paycheck, he talked over the big money that awaited him with his wife. "We felt if we ever made $10,000 a year we'd be on top of the world," Foiles said.[12]

All the regular working stiffs thought that way, unless you were Ted Williams or Stan Musial, Willie Mays or Mickey Mantle, seeking those $100,000-a-year contracts. During 1950s summers, the Pirates were the ones who provided Pittsburgh with its main source of entertainment, even more so after the decades-long ban on selling beer inside Forbes Field was lifted. Now a guy could sit back in the sunshine and not only cheer for Haddix, Friend, Clemente and Hoak, but he could sip a cold one, too.

Part of the Pittsburgh ritual when going to the ballpark was stopping at Gustine's for a good meal, too. Frankie Gustine was a former Pirates third baseman who played 12 years in the majors. He came up with Pittsburgh in 1939 and spent all but his final two seasons with the team until his retirement in 1950. When he left baseball, Gustine opened a restaurant. It soared in popularity and it became a must-see place for fans and players.

Bill Kennedy was a huge Pirates fan. He was going to night school to improve his career prospects and listened to many games on the radio, but when he could get away, he watched the Pirates in person. "You would go out to the ball game and stop and have dinner," Kennedy said. "Having dinner there and going to the game was the thing to do. It was sort of medium priced to high class. You could get a steak there."[13]

It was a special time for the players themselves as the 1950s was coming to an end and the 1960s was dawning. The record on the field was improving and the chemistry in the clubhouse was first-rate. Sometimes players recognize those moments when they are happening, when prospects seem to be on the rise, when a group of guys is going out to dinner and everyone is welcome to come.

"That was a bunch of nice guys," shortstop Dick Schofield said. "I guess it happens in different places at different times, but that was kind of special."[14]

9

Fourth Inning

Pittsburgh had a wealth of catching during the 1959 season. Hank Foiles and Danny Kravitz shared the role, but when manager Danny Murtaugh was looking to beef up the hitting from the receiver's spot, he tended to turn to Smokey Burgess.

Burly Burgess stood just 5-foot-8 and weighed around 190 pounds. He was not the guy a skipper asked to bunt. But he was one of the best pinch-hitters in history. A clutch hitter who packed some wallop in his bat, he had broken into the majors in 1949 and came to the Pirates in the same swap with Cincinnati that brought the man on the mound, Harvey Haddix.

Burgess, who lasted 18 years in the big leagues, possibly without ever beating out an infield hit except by accident, compiled a .295 lifetime average. Pitchers worked him carefully. Braves pitcher Lew Burdette knew all of this about Burgess, and sure enough, when Burgess led off the visitors' half of the fourth inning, he caught hold of a Burdette throw and smacked it on a line to center field. Only it traveled directly into Pafko's mitt for the first out.

First baseman Rocky Nelson hit a grounder to Braves second baseman Johnny O'Brien and was thrown out at first. However, the next batter, Bob Skinner, looked as if he might start a Pirate rally with his clean single to center. Pittsburgh second baseman Bill Mazeroski got good wood on a Burdette pitch, but it also settled into Pafko's glove, ending the Pirates' chance to score the first run.

"We had opportunities," said Pirates pitcher Bob Friend, thinking of all the innings Pittsburgh put men on base. "Lew Burdette, the crafty, old right-hander, would always get out of it. Sometimes we'd load 'em up and he'd throw a double-play ball. Lew pitched a great game. To give up 12 hits and have a shutout, I don't know how he did it. That's pretty good pitching."[1]

Haddix had been through the Braves' order once without incident. Nine up, nine down, nobody on base. He had no trouble in the fourth inning, either. O'Brien led off and took a called third strike. Then followed the meat of the order. Eddie Mathews stepped in for his second try. He did get the ball out of the infield, this time flying out to Bill Virdon in center field.

Haddix's third challenge of the inning was Hank Aaron, one of the greatest hitters of all-time. Aaron could break up the perfect game, the no-hitter, and the game with one stroke quite easily. Not this time, however. Haddix induced Aaron to replicate Mathews' swat and he also flied out to Virdon.

After four innings and the Braves not even sniffing a hit, players were beginning to take notice that Haddix had nasty stuff in his repertoire that night. Some of them watched the scoreboard and studied the "0" under Braves hits. Some of them knew that Haddix hadn't allowed a base runner.

One of the keenest observers in the Pirates' dugout was pitcher Vernon Law. Law was scheduled to pitch the next day in the series finale against Warren Spahn. Law, who after retiring as an active player coached baseball, possessed a natural instinct for closely following the game as it played out, rather than chatting with other players or pacing up and down in the dugout. Because he followed Haddix in the rotation, he wanted to see how the Braves reacted to certain types of pitches and their location. He also charted the game pitch by pitch as an additional reference.

The two men were nothing alike on the mound. Law was right-handed, Haddix left-handed. Law stood 6-foot-2 and Haddix was five or six inches shorter, depending on who was measuring. Law relied more on his fastball. But the hitters were still the same hitters, likely to be in the lineup again the next game. And there was this: Law recognized early on Haddix was pitching a masterpiece.

"You're aware of what's going on if you're paying any attention to the game at all," Law said. "In all the years I coached afterwards I told guys I never missed a pitch during a ball game. I watched every pitch, watched every hitter, what they've swung on. You're aware of everything because it's important. Things like that can help you when you need to get a hitter out. You know that so-and-so got him out this way or that way."[2]

Haddix was one of the boys, a guy who liked to hang out with his Pirate teammates during evenings on the road, but he was never a rowdy character. Perhaps precisely because he was not, Pirate friends teased him about being loud and cocky, particularly after his near-perfect game. "We kidded and agitated one another from that day on," Haddix said of how his game helped bring the club together. "They always had the thing about me that I was cocky, which was not true. I think this carried over into the next year and we were the loosest bunch of ballplayers you ever saw."[3]

They were jokesters after the game, not during it. No one said a word to Haddix in the dugout when he sat down between innings and none of his fielders said a word to him when he was on the mound throwing. If you were the shortstop or catcher that day, there was really no reason to visit. Haddix just kept befuddling the Braves.

When he came to County Stadium that night, Braves backup infielder Mel Roach was half expecting to play. He never knew for sure if manager Fred Haney would have him in the lineup or not on a given night, but he frequently got the call when Milwaukee faced left-handers. He pored over the posted lineup card, but saw his name was absent from the list of those called to duty. So Roach took a seat on the bench and watched teammates flail away at Haddix's best offerings.

As the game progressed and Haddix's sharpness came into increasingly clear focus, Roach had mixed feelings. He wanted to be part of the action, to be in the Braves lineup to get his licks in, and at the same time he could stand back somewhat detached and admire what Haddix was accomplishing.

"It was a mixture of both," Roach said. "You're just in awe to see this guy. He wasn't the biggest guy and he was just standing out there mowing them down, one after the other. Just amazing."[4]

Roach, who broke into the majors in 1953 as a 20-year-old, spent most of his eight-year career with the Braves and much of it backing up his hero, Hall of Famer Red Schoendienst. He experienced the best of Milwaukee baseball, being part of two World Series clubs when fans adored the players and set attendance records.

"The Yankees called Milwaukee 'Bush Town,'" Roach recalled of the homey nature of Milwaukee, Wisconsin's largest city back then. "The ballpark was not very big, by design. Somebody said they wanted to have people wait in line to get tickets. That way they'd always be full. But it was always a good crowd. They had cookouts in the parking lot and all that stuff."[5]

9. Fourth Inning

Tailgating was big in Wisconsin, home of the grilled brat and at the time many popular local beers. The fans had developed the habit of pregame partying at Green Bay Packers football games and discovered that it translated well.

By Milwaukee standards, it was not a big crowd that night, with fewer than 20,000 in the stands who were not frightened off by the damp weather. One observer seated under the clouds was Roland Hemond. Hemond, who has spent more than a half-century in baseball and is most identified with his tenure as general manager of the Chicago White Sox, was at the beginning of his baseball administration career.

In the late 1950s Hemond worked as assistant farm and assistant scouting director for the Braves, and his duties had him in attendance at almost all of the team's home games. In Hemond's decades of watching baseball, Haddix's performance is the closest he has come to witnessing a full perfect game in person. Coincidentally, Hemond was doing an old friend a favor that night by providing game tickets. Hemond had served in the Coast Guard for four years, and a pal, Rudy Blenig, was in the area and stopped by to see him. Hemond invited Blenig to sit with him that evening. Decades later Hemond marveled at his friend's timing, picking the day of Haddix's effort. "He was so elated, but he was rooting for the Braves," Hemond said.[6]

Hemond's own slight build has more in common with Haddix's than it ever did with a behemoth slugger like Ted Kluszewski. Each inning when Haddix took the mound, Hemond ruminated about the pitcher's size. On size alone Haddix looked like a boy throwing against men. Haddix was 5-foot-9 tops. Aaron was 6 feet tall and a husky 190-ish. Joe Adcock was 6-foot-4 and weighed around 220. Mathews was 6–1 and played at 200 or so. He was the lone Lilliputian against a squadron of Gullivers and each Gulliver in turn took his unproductive club and returned it to the bat rack.

"He was pitching against such a great ball club and I don't know if he weighed 170 pounds," Hemond said. "He was a relatively small guy. It was amazing the way it just went on and on, and he continued to pitch so gallantly and so well."[7]

Haddix baffled the hitters rather than overpowered them. "The Kitten" accumulated a fair number of strikeouts by confusing hitters, but he was never among National League leaders. In 1959, Haddix pitched 224⅓ innings and struck out 149 men. That meant he was going to get you some of the time, but couldn't count on blowing batter after batter away.

Pirate backup catcher Danny Kravitz caught Haddix many times and they never had a problem with signs or pitch choice, Kravitz said. Once they reviewed the hitters before the game, Haddix knew what he wanted to do, and he executed.

"We got along well," Kravitz said. "We had those meetings in the clubhouse all of the time. He pitched to the hitters the way he wanted to and that's the way we went. Once in a while his view would shift, but mostly that's the way he pitched the game, the way we went over it."

Haddix, like all pitchers who don't live and die with the knuckleball, had a pitch he called a fastball. Pitch speed was not really catalogued in the 1950s, but sports cars, not Haddix's pitches, traveled 100 mph. Kravitz said Haddix had other strengths that compensated for a routine fastball. "He had a good curveball," the catcher said. "His slider wasn't exceptionally good, but he was sneaky with it."[8]

Reliever Roy Face often began watching games in the dugout and then moved to the bullpen as innings passed. He was in the midst of putting together the best relief pitcher won-loss record of all time in 1959 with his 18–1 mark, and he knew that in a close game Murtaugh would signal for him. Watching Haddix work in the early going against the Braves, Face had a sense that he would be keeping his team jacket on all night, not limbering up his arm.

Some Pirates who played that night recall Face warming up in the bullpen, a just-in-case scenario if Haddix suddenly weakened along the way in the double shutout. Face said that is not so. He never budged from his seat, and if anyone else warmed up that night it wasn't because Murtaugh was worried about Haddix, it was probably because they wanted to loosen their arms a bit for the exercise. It's possible, Face said, despite the superstition of not mentioning an ongoing no-hitter in front of a pitcher, that somebody on the bench took note when Haddix was on the field. "I just sat back and enjoyed the game," Face said.[9]

For a guy who appeared in 57 games that season, it was a rare night of complete freedom.

10

Branch Rickey

The man who invented the farm system brought glory to the St. Louis Cardinals and success and notoriety to the previously hapless Brooklyn Dodgers with his vision and commitment to equality on the baseball diamond.

Branch Rickey lost a power struggle with strong-willed Dodger power broker Walter O'Malley and was looking for a new job in baseball when he joined the Pittsburgh Pirates as executive vice-president and general manager in 1951. Branch Rickey believed he could bring the same positive on-field results to a third organization, though he discovered that rebuilding the Pirates into contenders was a monumental task.

Rickey, whose massive cigars could be as intimidating as a baseball bat when waved in front of a young player's face, was born in Portsmouth, Ohio, in 1881 into a very religious household that held the Sabbath to be holy. Despite his devotion to baseball, he promised his mother he would not indulge in the pastime on Sundays, and he maintained that vow throughout his career. Rickey was a good enough player to reach the big leagues as a catcher, but not good enough to become a regular or last very long. In parts of three years between 1905 and 1907, plus a brief comeback try in 1914, he batted .239.

Earning an undergraduate degree at Ohio Wesleyan, where he also coached the baseball team, Rickey, whose bushy eyebrows were a distinctive facial characteristic that seemed to announce his arrival in a room, continued his education by working his way through law school at the University of Michigan. Degree or not, rather than follow a career path as a trial lawyer, Rickey moved into baseball administration. He actually joined the St. Louis Browns' front office in 1913 and managed the team for two seasons—hence the power to insert himself into two games in 1914. Rickey's main claim to fame with the Browns was signing future Hall of Fame first baseman George Sisler. It was the first indication that Rickey had a gift for recognizing young talent.

Rickey became field manager of the Cardinals in 1919, a job he kept until 1925. More influentially, he served as Cardinals general manager between 1925 and 1942. The Cardinals evolved into a National League powerhouse under Rickey's tutelage, and the famous "Gashouse Gang" won the 1931 World Series and again in 1934 with such pitching luminaries as Dizzy and Daffy Dean holding down key mound slots.

Rickey made the people of St. Louis happy, but his most enduring contribution to the sport during his tenure in Missouri was the creation of baseball's farm system in the 1920s. Rickey hired scouts and had them fan out across the country seeking talented prospects. The idea was to grow his own ballplayers, to obtain the boys young and nurture them into men, much like harvesting mature farm crops. The youthful players progressed from the comparatively easy competition in the low minors to AAA advanced competition. Then Rickey plucked the crème de la crème for the Cardinals, while sometimes using the second-tier talent as trade bait.

The Rickey system, copied by all other major league teams, replaced independently owned minor-league teams. In his zeal to snap up every talented ballplayer in the country, Rickey was chastised by Commissioner Kenesaw Mountain Landis. Twice, with an eye to the future of other minor-league clubs and Rickey's seeming monopoly on young players, Landis ordered the release of about 70 Cardinal prospects.[1]

After the 1942 season Rickey was hired as president and general manager of the "Bums," the scuffling Brooklyn Dodgers of little baseball accomplishment. Within a few seasons the fortunes of the Dodgers improved, and in the front office move he is most famously remembered for, Rickey signed Jackie Robinson as the first modern African-American player to break the national pastime's color barrier. Robinson's ascension to the Dodgers for the start of the 1947 revolutionized baseball and was a landmark in the movement toward racial equality in American society.

Well aware that Robinson, who became a Hall of Fame player, would face abuse from fans and opposing ballplayers, Rickey issued an order for Robinson to hold his temper in check and sacrifice his emotions for the larger cause.

Rickey-operated Dodger teams emerged as the best in the National League. Dodger ownership, however, underwent a shakeup and Rickey sold his 25 percent stake in the club. New Pirates owner John Galbreath was trying to turn the team into a winner and eagerly sought new leadership.

10. Branch Rickey

With his decorated history, Rickey shifted to Pittsburgh at age 69 with the aim and confidence he could resurrect the franchise, announcing a five-year plan to put the Pirates on a victorious path by building with youngsters. Instead, the Pirates of 1951, 1952, 1953, and 1954 as a group proved to be the losingest in team annals. Their sole bright, shining knight in armor was the perennial NL home-run champ Ralph Kiner. The team was so bad that it became referred to sarcastically as "the Rickey Dinks."[2]

Rickey, because of his wisdom as an administrator, coupled with his religious focus, and the fact that India's Mahatma Gandhi was in the news, was called "the Mahatma" by many in the game. He called upon his skill as a talent evaluator to sign Pittsburgh area athletes by the bushel. Some panned out with the Pirates or other major league clubs, including pitcher Ron Kline and outfielder Bobby Del Greco, but they did not lift the Pirates into the first division.

In 1951, the Pirates leapt into the talent hunt in a headline-making way, paying out a $100,000 signing bonus to a California schoolboy southpaw named Paul Petit. Petit was baseball's first six-figure bonus baby. The day of the lone scout driving through the backwoods of the nation in search of the dream prospect was drawing to an end. As the sport moved towards an organized draft, a rule was passed requiring that any so-called "bonus baby" signed for more than several thousand dollars would have to remain on the big club's roster for two years or risk being lost to another team in a special draft.

When Ralph Kiner, whose track record glittered in neon lights compared to his teammates', saw how much Petit was making, he was astounded. In his capacity as reigning National League home-run champ, and as a proven commodity, he went looking for a raise even though he said he was well enough off to be driving a Cadillac. Kiner was additionally stunned to note that the Pirates in their contract were even obligated to pay for Petit's honeymoon; the slugger later sarcastically wrote, "The fine print specified Petit had to provide his own bride."[3] Petit barely got off the bench in his two seasons in the majors, finishing with a career 1–2 record.

As Rickey settled into his position, his keen eye did pay dividends. He signed Dick Groat, the Duke All-American basketball player, who gave up that sport after one year as a pro to become the Pittsburgh shortstop, pitchers Bob Friend, Roy Face and Vern Law, all of whom would contribute to a pennant-winner, though long after Rickey was gone, and

Vic Janowicz, the Heisman Trophy–winning football player from Ohio State. Backup catcher and humorist Joe Garagiola took note of Groat's and Janowicz's all-around athletic credentials as the Pirates teams he served on slumped to the bottom of the standings. "We could beat any other team in basketball or football," Garagiola said. "Unfortunately, we couldn't win baseball games."[4] "In an eight-team league, we should have finished ninth."[5] Fans were furious when Rickey traded Kiner to the Chicago Cubs in 1953 and the team still did not improve.

Rickey conducted a fall tryout camp for 65 of his best hopefuls—Bob Skinner, Law and Friend were among them—and Garagiola said it was the first time he ever heard the phrase "purpose pitch" uttered. Rickey may have been a man of God, but he also seemed to realize that a pitcher had to have the high, inside fastball in his arsenal to make good. "When you throw it, let it serve a purpose!" Garagiola said Rickey shouted.[6]

In 1952, the Pirates became the first team in the majors to try out the plastic hard-shell batting helmets now required to be worn on top of caps when hitters come to the plate. Garagiola said the fans thought the helmets looked ridiculous, and on the night the protective gear made its debut they screamed insults at the ballplayers, calling them "everything from coal miners to space cadets." Much of the conversation revolved around the unlikely prospect of Pirates getting hurt, he said, because "Who's going to throw at a .210 hitter?"[7]

Given Rickey's voracious appetite for uncovering unknown ballplayers and converting them into major leaguers, and his pivotal role in shattering baseball's color barrier, it is of no surprise that one of the players he signed for the Pirates was the team's first black player.

Curt Roberts was a 5-foot-8, 165-pound infielder who was from Pineland, Texas, but by 1947 had broken into pro ball with the Kansas City Monarchs of the Negro Leagues. He had put in three seasons with the team when Rickey signed him for the Pittsburgh organization. Roberts was just 21 in 1950, but he never matured into another Jackie Robinson. He spent three seasons with Denver in the minors before making his Major League debut as the first black Pittsburgh Pirate in 1954.

Rickey gave Roberts and his wife, Christine, the same instructions and pep talk that he had given to Jackie Robinson and his wife Rachel—turn the other cheek and ignore all nasty verbiage, whether on the field or in the stands.

10. Branch Rickey

Seven years had passed since Robinson's inaugural Major League campaign, but integrating a new team still stirred up emotions, Roberts found. In a Pittsburgh newspaper interview, Christine Roberts said sitting in the stands at Forbes Field was disturbing. Listening to insults spewed towards her husband and calls to "Knock the nigger down!" provoked her into changing her usual seat close to the field to the upper deck, which she considered more peaceful and less threatening.[8]

As a rookie in 1954, his first of three big-league seasons, Roberts was the team's primary second baseman, appearing in 134 games and batting .239. Roberts' strength was his fielding, but he was beaten out for the job the next year in new manager Fred Haney's judgment, and Roberts was out of the majors after the 1956 season. Essentially, so too was Rickey, who gave up his quest to remake the Pirates into winners when he resigned as general manager after the 1955 season, though he stayed on behind the scenes in the front office.

Rickey deserves some credit for the Pirates' greatest personnel coup of the era—spotting a young Roberto Clemente playing in Puerto Rico and stealing him from the Dodgers. The Dodgers wooed 18-year-old Clemente first. He signed in February 1954 for a $10,000 bonus and a $5,000-a-year rookie salary and was assigned to their AAA Montreal Royals farm club. This was a dangerous move. By signing Clemente to a significant bonus and then not keeping him on the Major League roster, the Dodgers risked losing him. The Royals moved Clemente in and out of the lineup, trying to prevent buzz spreading about his skills. The strategy did not work. Clemente was noticed and the Pirates swooped in and plucked him from Brooklyn.[9]

It has been widely reported in Puerto Rico that while on a scouting mission to Puerto Rico in 1953, Rickey noticed the raw Clemente playing for Santurce and, impressed by his all-around prowess, made contact with him. Supposedly, Rickey told Clemente at that time that he was going to be a star. Clemente biographer David Maraniss questions the validity of the story because Rickey kept copious notes of his travels and there are no known notes about this encounter. Notes from a 1955 Latin American scouting mission by Rickey do record the general manager's impressions of Clemente. Rather than praise Clemente as an up-and-coming sensation, there is considerable criticism of how much the player had to improve and indicated it was too bad that under the bonus signing rules he couldn't be sent to the minors that season for seasoning.[10]

If the Pirates believed Clemente needed seasoning it was too bad. They were stuck with the same deal the Dodgers wrought—he had to stay in the majors or be drafted away, a procedure that worked out well for Pittsburgh. Clemente appeared in 124 games for the 1955 Pirates and batted .255, but a year later he was a star, hitting .311.

Some of the players Rickey ferreted out in his tryout camps, by deploying scouts wherever the Greyhound Bus system traveled and by picking others' brains, made it big with the franchise during the 1950s. Clemente, Dick Groat, Bob Skinner, Vernon Law, Bob Friend, and Roy Face grew up together in baseball and with the Pirates. Several of them were together on the field the night Haddix pitched his 12-inning perfect game and were still playing together a year later when the Pirates won the World Series. They were Branch Rickey's legacy.

11

Fifth Inning

Third baseman Don Hoak led off the fifth inning for the Pirates. At this point in the game Burdette was throwing nearly as crisply as Haddix. He was not perfect, but he was stingy, giving up a single here and a single there, mostly keeping the basepaths unclogged.

Hoak was an ex–Marine and wore the designation proudly. He came to the Pirates earlier in 1959 in the same trade that transferred Haddix and Smokey Burgess.

Hoak did not have to burnish his image or play the role of tough guy. His resume spoke loudly enough. With a listed date of birth of February 5, 1928, in the coal mining community of Roulette, Pennsylvania, Hoak was pretty much an underage Marine when he fought the Japanese during World War II on Iwo Jima and Okinawa. He came by his nickname of "Tiger" honestly after the war when he became a professional boxer in Florida. At 6 feet, Hoak both fought and played ball at around 165 pounds (at first), making him a middleweight in all endeavors. Before he signed with the Brooklyn Dodgers, Hoak compiled a 28–11 record as a fighter.[1]

An older rookie when he broke into the majors in 1954, Hoak planted himself at third base and survived many experiences that proved to him that the description of his location on the diamond truly was the hot corner. In 1960, Hoak admitted that between the war, boxing, and getting hit by grounders and airborne bats, he had had his nose broken nine times. When a sportswriter suggested that Hoak might be better off—or at least his insurance company would—if he took a step back from his innate aggressiveness, Hoak scoffed. "That's the only way I know how to play," he said.[2]

After the country was no longer at war, it became a popular thing to say of a partner you could count on that you would want him in a foxhole with you in hard times. Hoak was the real deal. He had been in the genuine foxholes and carried his feisty attitude with him into his sporting competitions. By Hoak's fourth season in the majors he was toiling for the Cincinnati Reds. In 1957 he led National League third basemen with a .971 fielding percentage and batted .293.

Baseball in the 1950s was a little bit rougher game than it is in the 2000s. If a pitcher knocked down a batter, retaliation was expected. If a fight broke out in one game, it was expected that there at the least would be talk of revenge. A brawl in a 1957 series between Cincinnati and the Dodgers prompted Hoak to utter inflammatory phrases that were seen as part of the game 50 years ago, but surely would have gotten him fined and suspended in the modern game.

Hoak promised to beat up Brooklyn second baseman Charlie Neal before the series ended, and his intentions were made known in graphic terms. "His wife won't know him when I get through with him," Hoak said. "If I don't catch him in the ballpark, I'll catch him outside. I'll be looking for him and I'll whip his hide, I guarantee you that."[3]

Hoak didn't even call Neal by name, simply referring to him as "number 43," and he interspersed profanity with the words that were quoted in print. Hoak's beef was the belief that the night before, during the teams' fight, as Hoak tried to pull Brooklyn catcher Roy Campanella off Cincinnati reliever Raul Sanchez, Neal blindsided him with a punch to the eye that knocked him flat. "Who does he think he is?" Hoak continued. "He's a big man when he's got eight or 10 guys around him to help him. He'll need some help when I get through with him."[4]

Neal, Raul Sanchez, who the Dodgers claimed aimed at hitters, and Brooklyn second baseman Junior Gilliam were tossed out of the game. Despite Hoak's bravado, there was no repeat of violence in that night's game, possibly because Commissioner Ford Frick and National League President Warren Giles sent telegrams warning that there had better not be. "I was just mad for a few hours," Hoak said.[5]

During the same season, Hoak was involved in a peculiar on-field incident that provoked Major League powers to write a new rule. In an April game between his Reds and the Milwaukee Braves, Hoak was on second base while teammate Gus Bell occupied first. Wally Post was at bat and he stroked a ground ball to short, where the Braves shortstop Johnny Logan prepared to field it and turn an easy double-play.

Much to the shock of the players, the fans, and especially the umpires, Hoak, seemingly about to be forced out on the play, reached out and speared the bouncing ball bare-handed as he was running past Logan. Hoak was ruled out automatically for interfering with a batted ball, but the other Cincinnati players were given their bases. After the game, feverish

11. Fifth Inning

consultation took place between umpire Cal Hubbard, Giles, and Frick. No one could remember such a blatant attempt to actually field a ball in play by a runner during the history of the game and there was no rule that flat out prevented it. A rule was immediately crafted that called for the interfering runner to be called out and also the runner trailing him, thus creating an automatic double play.

"A certain amount of grudging admiration must be directed at Don Hoak for having the ingenuity and the daring to thumb his nose at precedent and tradition in the way he did," a *New York Times* columnist opined. "He found a loophole in the rules."[6]

The incident helped establish Hoak's image as a ballplayer that would do anything to try to win. That reputation was enhanced as time passed. During August of 1960, in the heat of the pennant race that would propel the Pirates into the World Series against the Yankees, the Pirates were slumping. They had dropped two straight games to the St. Louis Cardinals. For a night of relaxation, to take their minds off the tension of the game, a handful of players gathered at a private party convened at a pool belonging to a friend of outfielder Gino Cimoli.

Cimoli and the other Pirates in attendance, Bob Friend and Bill Virdon, were aghast when climbing out of the pool, Hoak sliced open his right foot on the ladder. The cut between his second and third toes gushed blood. It was not a cut that could be simply sealed up with a Band-Aid. The players thought Hoak should go to a hospital, but there was a doctor in the house at the party. Hoak requested that the cut be stitched on the premises.

The doctor had his little black bag with him and it held a needle and stitching equipment, but no anesthesia. The wound took eight stitches and Hoak took no pain killers as he watched the needle pulled through his skin time after time. Hoak swore the other Pirates to secrecy and the next day suited up for a doubleheader against St. Louis. It took 20 innings to complete the two games and Hoak played all of them, turning in his usual reliable fielding performance and knocking in the game-winner with a single in the 11th inning of the second game.

Friend was so impressed he insisted that he had the right to tell the story later after the pennant was won. "You should have seen him," Friend said. "You should have seen the rest of us watching him getting sewn up like that without novocaine or anything."[7]

Hoak was sensitive about word of his injury getting out when it happened for a couple of reasons. He was sure the players would be portrayed as guys fooling around when in reality the foot-gashing was just a fluke accident. He didn't want to have to do any explaining to manager Danny Murtaugh and he didn't want to sit out any games.

"It hurt," Hoak said of the night the injury occurred and the follow-up doctor care. "But the next day was much worse. I sneaked into my spikes and I couldn't walk. I took off the newer spikes and put on the oldest ones I own and I still couldn't walk. The foot had stiffened up on me a little and knowing the stitches had just been put in scared me a little, but I knew I just had to try and play."[8]

Hoak said he forced himself not to limp or show pain in the clubhouse or going to and from the field. He stayed in his uniform until well after the game ended and others, including sports writers, departed. When he peeled off his shoes he knew what he would find. His sock was soaked with blood.[9]

Friend, who felt his friend's on-field heroism of sorts should be credited, convinced Hoak to allow him to inform a newspaper reporter about what he had endured. Hoak was reluctant, but cooperated. Friend said Hoak had put up with a great deal of pain, but the Pirates needed him down the stretch and they might not have won the National League pennant if he had sat out any length of time because of the cut. Hoak would have preferred to keep his discomfort a secret for all time. When a reporter asked him, "Would you have told it if Bob hadn't?" Hoak replied, "Hell, no."[10]

Besides Hoak's solid fielding and clutch hitting, the Pirates looked to their third baseman for other assistance. "There's no question about it," Friend said, "Hoak's the leader of our club. He gives 200 percent effort. He keeps everyone else on his toes. Everyone listens to him."[11] It was long-time Pittsburgh sports writer Les Biederman who suggested that Hoak was "the best third baseman Pittsburgh has had since Pie Traynor. He started the rallies. He kept them going."[12]

During the fifth inning of Haddix's gem, Hoak could not start anything. He made the first out with a grounder to short. Right-fielder Roman Mejias deposited a single into right field. It was Haddix's turn at bat with a chance to aid himself and put the Pirates on the scoreboard, but he made it easy for Burdette. Haddix hit a grounder to Eddie Mathews at third and he started an inning-ending double play. It was back to the mound for Haddix.

11. Fifth Inning

The Braves game was still early in Haddix's tenure with the Pirates after the trade that delivered him from the Cardinals. He had been around the league for a few years, though, and Pirates players knew what they were getting. There was a sense of optimism in 1959, especially among the older players who had been through the dreadful times in the early days of the Rickey regime, that the corner had been turned, that the arrival of Haddix, Hoak and Burgess would pay off.

"When we got hold of them from Cincinnati," Roy Face said, "that boosted the morale of the whole team. That was probably the best trade that Joe [L. Brown] ever made."[13]

Joe L. Brown, Rickey's successor as general manager, was the son of comedian and Hollywood personality Joe E. Brown, who was best known for bellowing out of a very wide-open mouth. The younger Brown became the Pirates' general manager in 1956 and held the position for 21 seasons, then stayed with the team as a scout until 1992. He applied a stern philosophy to the Pirates that sounded harsh. "If you let your business be run by the fans and don't do what's right, then you're a coward," Brown said, though he also knew he had to appease and please the fans.[14]

Brown was the beneficiary of the good things Rickey had started and the quality players he had acquired. But Brown knew that the Pirates still weren't ready to be serious pennant contenders, that they could not yet hang with the Braves and Dodgers over the long season. His answer was the four-for-three trade with the Reds. The only outgoing Pirate missed in any way was departing outfielder Frank Thomas, the power hitter who played two generations before the White Sox's Frank Thomas.

The Pirates were just starting to realize the dividends from the deal. At the moment, as the game wore on, Haddix was looking like the best component in it.

Big Joe Adcock grounded out, third to first, Hoak to Rocky Nelson, for the Braves' first out. Wes Covington hit a fly to left field that was grabbed by Bob Skinner. And catcher Del Crandall ended the fifth with another fly out to left.

By the fifth inning, Crandall said, the Braves in the dugout watching Haddix move his sly stuff around the plate with impeccable control were starting to talk about the zeroes piling up on the scoreboard. "We were sitting around watching and wondering how he was doing it," Crandall said. "He didn't have overpowering stuff."[15]

12

A Prince of a Guy

Bob Prince's plaid sport coats spoke louder than his words. And that was pretty hard to do. Prince was not official royalty by title, but he was the Prince of the Pirates by station—radio station. He earned his status by long-time affiliation with the Pittsburgh ballclub as the man who was the voice of the team, visiting living rooms and front porches with his play-by-play reports and his colorful stories.

If a fan followed the Pirates in the 1950s his ears were filled with Prince's favorite phrases and his personalized description of the action at Forbes Field. And not just in the 1950s, since Prince joined the Pittsburgh broadcast team in 1948 and was a featured performer until 1975. In all, he produced 28 years worth of gab. "Bob Prince had a passion for life and for baseball that made him the fan's announcer," wrote Pittsburgh author Jim O'Brien.[1]

If the phrase "shrinking violet" connotes the image of a wallflower at a dance, Bob Prince was the opposite, the cut-up who took over a room upon entrance. He was the big man on campus with the campus being the entire city of Pittsburgh, indoors and out. He greeted everyone by name and remembered them the next time, shook hands until his own was bruised, slapped backs until he needed to wear a cast, and shared drinks and stories in taverns until the clocks froze on closing time.

Prince, who was as noticeable by his horn-rimmed glasses as his personal brand of sport coat, was born in Los Angeles in 1916, made a stop at the University of Pittsburgh on his way to earning a degree at Oklahoma University, was a star swimmer in both places, and joined the Pirates broadcast team as Rosey Rowswell's junior partner in 1948. When Rowswell passed away, Prince became the main man in the broadcast booth in 1955.

When it came to style, Prince could best be summarized as a showman, but he also had substance. He knew his stuff, but sprinkled his baseball information with bon mots, stories, and flashy favorites. He was a nickname guy, bestowing pet names on Pirate players for years.

12. A Prince of a Guy

Rowswell had his quirks and personal phrases, too. His signature comment was uttered when a long home run was bashed. As the ball left the bat and was clearly going to sail over the fence, he shouted, "Open the window, Aunt Minnie, here she comes!" As Rowswell's assistant, Prince sometimes contributed by making the sound of breaking glass.[2]

When Prince became king of the booth and teamed with Nellie King, he moved out from under Rowswell's shadow. Prince used established nicknames like Dick "Ducky" Schofield and Vernon "Deacon" Law, but he also created his own. As a compliment, Prince attached the name "Arriba" to Roberto Clemente, the Spanish usage in honor of the player's Puerto Rican heritage. The word means "the great one" and the description stuck so that even when he returned to the island, Clemente fans began using it.

Prince used "Kitten" when talking about Harvey Haddix, the nickname he brought with him from Cincinnati. But when chatting about Jesse Gonder, Prince said, "Way up yonder with Jesse Gonder."

With all of Pittsburgh tuned in to the Pirates' fortunes, Prince worked to entertain, as well, with phrases he employed again and again for years when certain developments in the action arose. If a pitcher was throwing the ball very fast and it slammed into the catcher's mitt with a thump, Prince might call the pitch "a radio ball," one that was heard but not seen. When there was a close play with a runner on first or any other close call, Prince might say, "By a gnat's eyelash." One of his true signature descriptions was deployed when the Pirates overcame a deficit to win a game. "We had 'em all the way," Prince never tired of saying.[3]

Rowswell was not an easy act to follow. He was popular for many of the same reasons that baseball fans gravitate to their hometown announcers. Rowswell was around for a long time—19 years. So fans got used to him. Rowswell rooted for the home team; he was not critical. Fans identified with that. And he was funny in a down-home way and fans laughed along with that.

No matter how good a baseball team is, even if it becomes the World Series champion, in a long season mistakes are going to be made. Strange, unflattering things are going to occur. When the Pirates made those unforgivable errors, Rowswell was consistent in his commentary. "Oh, my achin' back."[4] That might have been a more polite reaction to the doings on the field than even managers had at the time. Rowswell's charm was evident in his repeat trademark comments. When a Pirate pitcher whiffed an opponent and Rowswell was pleased with the pitch, he declared, it was "the old dipsey doodle." And when a Pirate player clocked a pitch for a double or another long hit, he said it was a "doozey marooney."[5]

From the vocabularies, delivery and enthusiasm of the Rowswell-Prince tandem, it was apparent that the Pirates players and their fans of the 1950s listening to a broadcast were regaled with as much funny business as baseball business. Rowswell didn't mind having his imagination challenged when the Pirates went on the road and he had to re-create away games on the radio with sound effects. Prince was often required to dip into an arsenal of utensils to simulate the crack of a bat or the roar of the crowd. Nothing topped Aunt Minnie's window being in jeopardy, however, when Rowswell sadly lamented, "She never made it." The fact that "she never made it" was part of the charm.[6]

Rowswell, and then Prince, became much sought after-dinner speakers at sports dinners, banquets and for occasions of all types. In his heyday, Prince dashed from event to event, attending more than one in the same day or evening. Prince was renowned for helping out charities and he frequently went out of his way to help aspiring broadcasters and journalists from Pittsburgh get started in their careers. "Pittsburgh was lucky to have a booster like Bob Prince," wrote Jim O'Brien, who was one of the young men whose careers were given a boost by Prince.[7]

Although Rowswell and Prince commanded the airwaves throughout the 1950s, their styles had evolved considerably from the early days of broadcasting. And Pittsburgh was the city that probably knew this best because the first Major League game to be broadcast emanated from the Steel City. The first baseball radio broadcast in history dates to August 5, 1921, when Pittsburgh's KDKA told the story of the Pirates-Phillies game at Forbes Field. The announcer was Howard Arlin. As might be expected, the equipment and the setup were rudimentary. To reach the listeners Arlin deposited himself in a box seat behind the first-base dugout and used a hand-held microphone and a "converted" telephone to reach his public.[8]

At the time of this modest start symbolizing a coming revolution that would lift baseball coverage from telegraph reports posted in windows or at street corners to a direct connection to the fans, Arlin was a 25-year-old engineer at Westinghouse. The Pirates won the game, 8–5, but few

12. A Prince of a Guy

recognized the larger victory of technology for the moment. "I did this as a one-shot project," Arlin said. "Our broadcast, at least back then, wasn't that big a deal. To tell the truth, our guys at KDKA didn't think that baseball would last on radio."[9]

Wrong. Radio connected baseball to fans in a way no other medium had to date, as it spread and increased the visibility and accessibility of the sport. Radio broadcasting, it turned out, was pretty much a two-and-a-half-hour long advertisement for the sport. This awareness was slower to evolve in some cities than others, and the Pirates didn't hire a full-time announcer, Rowswell, for 25 years after Arlin's broadcast.

William Kennedy, Sr., the Bell engineer and Pirates fan, said baseball on the radio was the background soundtrack of his life in the 1950s. He was a big Rowswell fan, though he liked Prince, too. "Rosey was a little more homespun," he said. "They were both energetic. They were both able to present the game and describe it well. But Rosey always invented a bunch of euphemisms that he would throw in like, 'Clemente was diseased with speed.' Whatever it was that we were doing, we had the radio on listening to the Pirates while we were doing it."[10]

Thundersticks—plastic sticks that fans bang against one another as noisemakers—are the rage in the 2000s, but decades earlier, Prince invented "the Green Weenie." In a similar concept, the green plastic hot-dog-shaped thingies that Prince exhorted fans to wave in the air were intended to jinx opposing teams. If things were looking bad for the Pirates, sometimes fans turned and yelled to Prince in the broadcast booth, urging him to wave the green weenie out the window. Prince also created "Babushka Power," anointing female Pirate fans with magical prowess to dim the luck of the opposition.[11]

Prince was so adept at appraising players and dropping nicknames on them there was no surprise that he too was adorned with one. Prince was called "Gunner." Some people said the nickname stemmed from his rapid-fire radio delivery. Others said an angry husband once pulled a gun on the party animal for cavorting with his wife.[12] Either way it stuck.

Prince was considered color blind by the players. He was friendly with Roberto Clemente when many others in the sports media either didn't understand him or failed to recognize his talents. "From the beginning, the Gunner seemed to appreciate Clemente, at first as a circus barker might appreciate the virtuosity of his most dazzling trapeze artist, and later as a friend would admire a friend," one of Clemente's biographers wrote. "There was rarely tension between the two as there was between Clemente and many members of the press."[13]

Prince was one of the guys. On the road he drank with the players. He offered advice. He wanted them to do well. "He was part of us," shortstop Dick Groat said. "He wanted it as badly as we did." At one point Groat surprised sports reporters by writing them thank-you notes for their compliments. He later admitted Prince was "an influence" on Groat's actions.[14]

Pitcher Bob Friend said that Prince's comments about the regulars and the team over the years accumulated in the public mind and helped shape a good image for those players and the Pirates, as well. "Bob Prince built up a very positive image of us over a long time," Friend said.[15]

That was one way of saying that Pirate players owed Prince. Win or lose, pennant-winning play or basement-level play, Prince made it clear he was in the Pirates' corner. He was around all of the time, not a fair-weather friend. Groat believes the Pirates' big 1959 trade that involved the acquisition of Haddix set up the team for success and Prince recognized it. "Bob was thrilled to have a winning ballclub to talk about," Groat said.[16]

On the night when Harvey Haddix chose to pitch the greatest game in baseball history, Bob Prince was in the radio booth in County Stadium beaming the story back to Pittsburgh. In an unusual development that was only coincidental, Prince's wife, Betty, made a very rare road trip. Prince was known for schmoozing with celebrities in all walks of life and Mrs. Prince, who was married to the broadcaster for 44 years, was the recipient of prime tickets and seated with some famous athletes. "I had tickets by the dugout," she said many years later. "I was sitting with Sam Snead, the great golfer, and his young nephew, J.C. Snead, who later became a pretty good golfer on the pro tour. I have no idea what I was doing with them. Bob must've given them tickets."[17]

Prince was as happy for Pirate success as any player was, and as gloomy about disappointment as the rest of the locker room. As the Haddix game wore on and he realized he was viewing something remarkable, Prince made no secret of his allegiance. He worked the drama to let the fans back home know this was some kind of game.

"Bob Prince was definitely partisan. He couldn't be a disinterested observer if he tried," said Sam Hazo, president of the International Poetry Forum, in 1998. "During the Haddix game Prince was literally cheering for him all the way even though it was supposed to be an unwritten law that you never breathed the words 'no-hitter' while a no-hitter was in progress. Prince was never fettered by such superstitions and that was part of his appeal."[18]

Pirate fans back home let the broadcaster's voice take over their living rooms, kitchens or bedrooms, radio turned up loud to hang on every word, as Bob Prince told them what an extraordinary thing was going on during this regular-season baseball game in Milwaukee.

13

Sixth Inning

The teams were more than halfway through a normal game with a double shutout going and Harvey Haddix knocking batters down like tenpins. "I think people were aware of the perfect game," Dick Schofield said. "I don't remember anybody saying anything to him."[1]

Schofield was the Pirates' leadoff man in the top of the sixth. He hit a grounder to Johnny O'Brien at second and was thrown out at first, one of the 17 putouts Braves first baseman Joe Adcock registered that night. Centerfielder Bill Virdon stepped up to the plate and grounded out, too. Adcock fielded the ball and tossed it to pitcher Lew Burdette covering. Next up was Smokey Burgess. The Pirates had a mix of seasoned catchers on the roster, with Hank Foiles and Danny Kravitz, plus Burgess. But there was no debate who was the best hitter among them. Burgess, who in the later stages of his career was regarded as the best pinch-hitter in the National League, wielded a sturdy stick.

Burgess, who retired in 1967, was ahead of his time. He was the prototype designated hitter. His value as a batter exceeded his value as a receiver, though he was a six-time National League All-Star. He was also one of the slowest runners around. Burgess was neither going to leg out infield hits nor steal bases. He definitely was a feared hitter and part of the reason was his own lack of self-consciousness. He didn't worry about who the pitcher was. Burgess had the confidence to hit against the best.

"That Smokey Burgess will hit left- or right-handed pitchers," said Dick Groat. "He'll hit late in a game or early. He'll hit with men on base or with the bases empty."[2] Occasionally, the phrase "a hitter's hitter" was applied to certain players. Burgess filled the bill.

Burgess' playing weight is listed as 187 pounds in the *Baseball Encyclopedia*, but some teammates, like Haddix, felt a more accurate reading was 200 pounds, which translated to some bulk on a man standing 5-foot-8. "Smokey didn't like to catch," Haddix said of the man he was throwing to during his 12-inning perfect outing. "It became more and more a tough job for him because of his build. He said he gained weight even when he wasn't eating. I told him, 'Smokey, you're the only one I know who gains weight just breathing air.' I don't think he felt good much. I don't think his health was up to par. [But] my, how Smokey could hit that ball."[3]

The subject of Burgess' less-than-Olympic-type body structure was periodically noted in the press. "There's teetotaling Smokey Burgess, who looks less like an athlete than like a traveling salesman for a farm-implement company," wrote well-known Pittsburgh sports media figure Myron Cope. "He has a figure shaped like a head of cabbage, a slick of sparse, black hair atop his head, and the small, fat hands that one sees folded across laps at luncheons of the Daughters of the American Revolution."[4]

Descriptions of that sort would not get Burgess recruited for modeling campaigns, but his forte was hitting under all circumstances. Long-time Major League manager Birdie Tebbetts was another who admired Burgess' ability to crunch the ball in the clutch. "You can wake Smokey up on Christmas morning and he'll get you hits," Tebbetts said.[5]

Burgess had the tools to be a good catcher, he just didn't have great maneuverability behind the plate. But he was also one of those catchers who tries to distract hitters with conversation when they step into the batter's box. It may have been a strategy, but it also came naturally to Burgess, who chitchatted with teammates at a non-stop rate, too. Phillies Hall of Fame outfielder Richie Ashburn was one of Burgess' favorite gossip targets and he blabbered every moment Ashburn was trying to set up his stance to hit. Ashburn even pleaded with umpires to make Burgess stop talking, but there was no rule against it, so they didn't interfere.

Willie Mays did not like Burgess' chatter and Burgess realized it did more harm than good to rile up certain players. Same with Stan Musial, whom Burgess did talk to, but whom he never seemed to seriously discomfit. Two of his choice targets were Hank Aaron and Joe Adcock, the Braves' home-run sluggers. He admitted when he started to ask them about how were the wife and kids and such innocuous topics they snarled back at him saying, "Don't talk to me, I'm trying to concentrate." Burgess said he recognized how good Aaron was and that nothing he said was going to disrupt his focus at the plate, but he once said rather plaintively, "Aw now, Henry, you're hitting the ball too hard and I'd like to get you out just one time today."[6]

There was a certain irony in Burgess offering greetings and the time of day to most batters on opposing teams. That's because Haddix was a purist, a player who followed the letter of baseball's fraternization law during his playing days. He did not hang out and shake hands and talk to foes when they came to town, or when he was preparing to pitch. "He was a real professional," said outfielder Bob Skinner. "When I was rooming with him, I remember he never spoke to opposing players in the field. They were the enemy. He'd talk to them in the hotel or in a restaurant, but not on the field."[7]

Burgess talked enough for the entire battery. Once, proving he could hit just about any offering from a pitcher, whether it was in the strike zone or not, Burgess startled Lew Burdette. Burdette unleashed a bad pitch. It was destined to be called a ball because it was so slow the catcher might have to employ a steam shovel to haul it out of the dirt. But much to Burdette's astonishment and chagrin, Burgess swung at the pitch. If Burgess had his eye on a pitch nothing would dissuade him from taking a crack at it. In this instance, he connected, the bat struck the ball and the ball swung out of play—home run. Burgess' swing on the play would have been more likely highlighted on the cover of *Golf Digest* than *Baseball Digest*. "If you didn't hit that pitch, it would have hit you on the ankle!" a disgusted Burdette shouted from the mound.[8]

If he said it, the statement is not easy to uncover, but Burgess could have retorted to Burdette, his opponents and even his teammates who blinked at his off-the-wall swings, that it was not a beauty contest in there, but a hitting contest. "He looks like a butcher in a supermarket," said Skinner. "But oh, boy, how he could hit."[9]

Only not during this at-bat. Burdette didn't give Burgess anything good to hit (down at the ankles or over the plate), but induced him to swing and Burgess lofted a fly ball out to Covington in left. It was still 0–0 with the Braves marching to the plate in the bottom half of the sixth inning. Pafko was first up.

Many fans have referred to the 1950s as a golden era of baseball because of the overlapping generations of older stars like Joe DiMaggio, Stan Musial, Ted Williams, Bob Feller and Warren Spahn, the arrival of young stars like Mickey Mantle and Eddie Mathews, and the first major influx of black stars like Willie Mays, Hank Aaron, Ernie Banks, and Roberto Clemente. And there was one other important element that helped the 1950s overshadow the weak 1940s. World War II had ended, and veterans returned to their teams.

13. Sixth Inning

"I didn't think of that as a golden era at the time," Pafko said, "but nobody was in the service and there were so many stars around. Against Haddix, there were some hits that were hard, but right at people. When he's pitching a no-hitter, you have to give credit to the pitcher. If a pitcher doesn't have it that day he has to wait four days for another turn. But there's a little bit of luck, too, and your luck isn't good sometimes."[10]

Pafko was the type of player who could hurt a pitcher if the thrower sighed with relief after successfully working his way through the murderers' row of Mathews, Aaron, Adcock, Covington, and Del Crandall. Pafko, who had a lifetime .285 average and drove in nearly 1,000 runs, was hitting seventh in the order. He was just the type of reliable hitter who could break up a no-hitter if a pitcher didn't bear down. Handy Andy was well-liked in Wisconsin.

Pafko said he was inundated with fan mail in Milwaukee. He was pleased to get it, but laughed at some of it. He liked the idea that youngsters became baseball fans at an early age, but some of the spelling in the letters demonstrated just how youthful they were. One letter read in part, "You are my favorit player and the Braves my favorit teem. Please send me some baseballs, bats and a picture. Also a glove." That kid may have mistaken the centerfielder for Santa Claus. Pafko did answer the letter, at least. He said he also got several marriage proposals in the mail and he turned those letters over to his wife, Ellen, to answer.[11] Milwaukee fan devotion was so legendary that when County Stadium was about 2,000 short of capacity, Pafko said a teammate looked at him and said, "Gee, what's the matter, Andy, don't the Wisconsin folks like us anymore?"[12]

As a native of Wisconsin, perhaps Pafko was idolized even more than the other Braves, for in his first couple of seasons playing for Milwaukee local businessmen presented him with a new set of luggage, a set of clothes, a wheelbarrow full of roses, vast amounts of locally produced sausage and cheese, a clothes dryer, an outboard motor, a TV set, and Mr. and Mrs. automobiles. Pafko said even without the gifts, "I still would have been strongly convinced that Milwaukee is America's greatest baseball town."[13]

The way things were going, if Pafko had broken up Haddix's no-hit bid in the sixth inning, his next present might have been a free trip for two to Paris. Instead he hit a popup to first base for the first out of the inning.

Johnny Logan succeeded Pafko in the batter's box and produced no result resembling the spectacular. He grounded out to shortstop. The final batter of the Braves' half-inning was the pitcher. It was Burdette against Haddix, but Burdette did not help his own cause. He struck out.

Some remember that there was a point in the middle to late innings when some members of the Pirates bullpen got up and began throwing. Such a thing was a rarity when a pitcher was cruising along the way Haddix was and in that era, with his man pitching a shutout, regardless of how many pitches he ran up, manager Danny Murtaugh would have left Haddix in. There was no hint of Haddix injury, either.

Memories are dim on the topic. Some players say George Witt might have warmed up. Roy Face, who in any case would have been the player Murtaugh turned to in a close game, said it was possible that Fred Green, or Witt, might have just stood up to fling a few pitches as part of their routine to loosen up. He certainly never warmed up with any intent that day, Face said. "They might have been throwing just to get some work," Face said. "It sure didn't look like Harvey was fading."[14]

According to one much later account of the doings of that night, there was more activity occurring on the Braves' bench. Nothing the Braves did helped them solve the puzzle of Haddix's pitching repertoire that day. If they hit the ball it ended up being an easy out. Yet the Braves had one quiet trick up their sleeves. In 1993, the late Bob Buhl, one of the regulars in the Milwaukee rotation, told a baseball historian named Danny Peary that the Braves had stolen Pittsburgh's pitching signs. Buhl, who spent 15 years in the majors and won 166 games, said that the Braves picked up the signals from Burgess. Whenever the Pirate catcher flicked his fingers for a fastball, curve or slider, members of the Braves on the bench adjusted a towel to inform the hitter what pitch was coming.

"His catcher, Smokey Burgess, was tipping them off," Buhl said. "Burgess was chubby and couldn't squat all of the way down." So the Braves had a better view of his fingers.[15] The way Buhl described the scene, the bullpen group employed binoculars to study Burgess' hands. Sign stealing was nothing special at the time.

"Back in those days, you stole signs all the time," Buhl said. "We'd get them from the bullpen and a lot of times the third-base coach could steal them because catchers ... didn't hide them very well. We used a towel system in the bullpen to signal the hitters. Most of our guys took the signs. Others thought it would foul them up if they knew what was coming."[16]

13. Sixth Inning

On this particular night it didn't matter what Braves pitchers in the pen told their hitters. Regardless of how many times Braves hitters were tipped off that a fastball was next, a curveball was coming, or a slider was headed their way, they couldn't hit safely off Haddix. "Harvey was doing such a good job of putting on and taking off speed that the hitters couldn't time him," Buhl said.[17]

After Buhl spoke up some 34 years after the game was played, Haddix was asked for his reaction to the likelihood that some of the Braves were actually aware of what pitch he was about to hurl, and yet he still got them out. "About them stealing the signs," Haddix said, "we all knew that a lot of teams stole signs. It was something teams did to win because they wanted it so bad. But I never really had any idea the Braves were stealing signs that night. But doesn't that just go to show how the game is so strange and so great at the same time?"[18]

14

Speaking Spanish

The Branch Rickey philosophy of searching the wide, wide world of sports for top talent regardless of location and ethnic background was transferred to Puerto Rico, Cuba, and other Latin American baseball strongholds by the Pirates in the 1950s and accounted for the acquisition of several members of the team's roster by 1959.

Above all, there was The Great One, Roberto Clemente. But Roman Mejias was on the team and in the lineup for the Harvey Haddix game. Mejias was born in Abreus, Cuba, in 1930. Outfielder Joe Christopher was born in Frederiksted, St. Croix, Virgin Islands, in 1935. The Pirates became the major league leaders in scouting Latin America. They demonstrated a stronger commitment than other teams, and much of that was attributable to the passion, devotion and hard work of one man, scout Howie Haak.

Haak had worked with Rickey in Brooklyn, and when "the Mahatma" moved on to Pittsburgh he brought the savvy talent evaluator with him. Haak had his eye on Clemente for some time, and when the Dodgers made their error in arrogance feeling no one would find Clemente, the Pirates pounced and swiped him in a supplemental draft.

In many ways, Haak was the stereotype of a baseball scout in the 1950s. He was a loner, working on the road by himself much of the year. He punctuated his conversations with profanity, and he chewed tobacco. Legend has it that Haak could simultaneously park a wad of tobacco in his cheek while eating a scrambled eggs breakfast and then somehow discern which substance to swallow and which to spit.[1]

Haak, who hit the road more often than a traveling salesman, scouted Clemente during his season playing for the AAA Montreal Royals in the Dodgers' chain. Sometimes Haak and the other Pirate super scout, Clyde Sukeforth, who had scouted Jackie Robinson for Rickey, journeyed to Montreal only to see Clemente in practice as the Dodgers played hide-and-seek with him during games by benching the outfielder. After one such trip when Clemente didn't play, Haak met him after the game and told

14. Speaking Spanish

him the Pirates wanted him and would draft him. The Haak speech told Clemente to keep quiet because "the Dodgers might not bleeping want him" but the "bleeping Pirates bleeping wanted him."[2]

There may have been a general language barrier between the disheveled Haak with his brutally straight-forward English and Clemente's Spanish, but the scout got his message across.

Rickey's days in Pittsburgh were numbered and he was no longer affiliated with the franchise after 1956. But his successor at general manager, Joe L. Brown, if anything, extended and expanded the team's efforts to sign top Latin players in countries that were baseball mad. In the ensuing years, among others, the Pirates added infielder Jose Pagan from Puerto Rico, Manny Sanguillen and Rennie Stennett from Panama, Vic Davalillo from Venezuela and Jackie Hernandez from Cuba, to the major league roster. This was not just token hiring. The Pirates were in the forefront of what in the following decades could be termed a revolution.[3]

Haak was the team's representative, the face of the Pirates, throughout the Caribbean, for decades, until he died at age 87 in 1999. Former Pirates white third baseman Richie Hebner said Pittsburgh's commitment to racial equality was not just skin deep. The numbers were large. "Howie used to go down and sign Dominican, Venezuelan, and Puerto Rican players," said Hebner, who is from Massachusetts. "It was not just with our big league club. You go down to Pirate City back in the early seventies. There were a lot of Latino kids and a lot of black kids. Hey, white, black, yellow, brown, whatever, we're gonna try to get the best players."[4]

On September 1, 1971, as the natural outgrowth of putting together a color blind roster, a combination of circumstances (pitching turns, players tired, hurt and the like), led manager Danny Murtaugh to put the first all-black lineup on the field in Major League Baseball history. Not all were African American, since some of the players were black Latinos, but in its days of discrimination the sport had not differentiated between dark-skinned Hispanics and U.S. blacks.

For the game against the Philadelphia Phillies at Three Rivers Stadium in Pittsburgh, Murtaugh's batting order read this way: Rennie Stennett at second base; Gene Clines, center field; Roberto Clemente, right field; Willie Stargell, left field; Manny Sanguillen, catcher; Dave Cash third base; Al Oliver, first base; Jackie Hernandez, shortstop. The starting pitcher was Dock Ellis.

After the game a sports writer asked Murtaugh if he had used the lineup by design to cross a rubicon. Murtaugh replied, "Did I have nine blacks in there? I thought I had nine Pirates out there on the field. Once a man puts on a Pirates uniform, I don't notice the color of his skin. When it comes to making out the lineup, I'm color blind and my players know it."[5]

Bob Robertson, a white player who was a regular first baseman, would ordinarily have started but was nursing a minor injury. Hebner was also injured. And if the roulette wheel had stopped on another pitcher's number, the starter would have been white.

Gene Alley, another white player, said a little while later that he really did believe Murtaugh had not deliberately fielded an all-black lineup so much as adjust to the situation. "It was typical of him," Alley said. "That day he happened to start nine blacks in a game with the Phillies, he had hadn't even thought about it or realized he had done it. They were, in his opinion, the nine best men available that day. And that's all that's ever important to him."

Even Al Oliver, one of the top Pirate hitters at the time, said later that he didn't notice that the team put nine blacks out on the field until the third or fourth inning. He said Cash told him. "Hey Scoop, we got all brothers out here," Oliver reported Cash saying. Oliver paused, perhaps counting, and said "We sure do!"[6]

The occasion is not well remembered, certainly not nearly so well as Jackie Robinson's color-barrier-breaking appearance for the Dodgers integrating the National League in 1947, or Larry Doby's appearance for the Indians later that year integrating the American League, but it was a landmark occurrence for major league baseball.

Baseball might be classified as one of the United States' greatest exports. The game spread where American soldiers played it on duty. The game spread to nearby countries where it insinuated its way into the blood of the inhabitants. During the 1920s, 1930s and 1940s, Latin American countries threw open their doors in winter to the great players from the Negro Leagues. Future Hall of Famers like Satchel Paige, Martin Dihigo, Buck Leonard, Cool Papa Bell and dozens of others were at least as well known in Cuba, Puerto Rico and throughout the Caribbean and were likely more appreciated than they were in the U.S.

Many white ballplayers took the cue and responded favorably to invi-

14. Speaking Spanish

tations to play winter ball in Latin American nations, as well. They improved their game to increase their chances of making the big-league club. They worked on skills that would hone their abilities. And at a time when ballplayers' salaries were much more in line with the American earning average, they made some additional cash needed for car and house payments.

Cuba was a coveted destination only 90 miles from Florida. With a scorching night life that highlighted wine, women, song and gambling, playing baseball in the balmy weather while it was snowing back home proved irresistible for many young Americans. Right up until Fidel Castro's Communist revolution, playing baseball for pay in Cuba seemed as much vacation as job. Cuba had a distinguished record of sending its best players to the U.S. to compete in the majors. Minnie Minoso, Tony Perez, Mejias, and other popular players made it to the big leagues.

Usually, the first American scout to lay eyes on a Cuban prospect was Haak. Haak never took formal Spanish lessons, counting on the universal language of baseball to make his way and friends to tip him off with information. However, he did develop a certain rudimentary linguistic skill in Spanish. It was not the type that tourists learned in travel guides that stressed ordering the right thing from the menu and asking where the bathroom was. "I know enough Spanish to run tryout camps and get the good guys' signatures on contracts," Haak said.[7] He traveled by planes, trains and automobiles, as well as boats, to wherever rumor led him to a talented player in a remote village.

When Haak, who worked as a scout for more than 50 years, first spotted Clemente, the future Hall of Famer with the cannon arm was playing in Puerto Rico. He informed Rickey, "We gotta draft him. He's better than anything we have."[8]

Rarely was Haak's judgment questioned. Haak became a familiar sight to young Latino players. He was opportunity personified. If Haak came to watch you play and you played well, he could sign you, he could give you a chance, and by doing so uplift your family from poverty. Over time, the extra-large Haak came to be nicknamed "Big Daddy" by Hispanic players. "We thank God for him," said Panamanian Manny Sanguillen. "He opened the door for us."[9]

Another Haak find for the Pirates was outfielder Joe Christopher, who made his way into the minors and by happenstance made his Major

League debut as a late-inning substitute in Haddix's masterpiece. Christopher's father was an overseer on a mango and cane plantation in the Virgin Islands and at the time Christopher was a shortstop. Christopher, who eventually played for championship teams in Puerto Rico, the Dominican Republic and Venezuela, was a member of the Virgin Islands team that traveled to Wichita, Kansas, for the annual end-of-summer National Baseball Congress tournament. The venerable NBC, representing the championship of non-professional baseball, dates back to the 1930s. It was once a showcase for a young Satchel Paige and from the 1960s on became the season-ending goal for the best teams from the Alaska Baseball League and other summer leagues displaying college-age talent.

Christopher hit well in the Virgin Islands team's short appearance and Haak signed him. Christopher played for the Pirates between 1959 and 1961 before moving on to the New York Mets in the expansion draft, but never was a regular. Joe L. Brown classified the player as someone who "could run like the dickens, was a good outfielder, and a decent hitter."[10]

A story that has made the rounds repeatedly—because it represents a what-if situation that could have changed history—is the tale that suggests if Castro's fastball was a little bit faster he would have stuck in the major leagues and never become dictator of Cuba.

Various sources give credence to the idea that Castro was at least worthy of a minor-league look-see. One account relays that the bearded guerilla fighter worked out for a group of Major League scouts after he had established himself as a star pitcher at Belen College and while he was at the University of Havana. That report reads Castro "attracted the attention of several Major League scouts with his wicked curveball. He turned down a $5,000 bonus from the Giants to pursue his law degree."

The same limited report states that Castro never pitched in official winter ball leagues, but once threw to future Pirate third baseman Don Hoak. Castro graduated from law school, went to prison for preaching socialism and revolution, and took off for the jungle to lead an uprising against the government instead of working on his pitch location.[11]

Some years later, Hoak collaborated with Pittsburgh sportswriter Myron Cope on a magazine article about the time he batted against Fidel Castro. This occurred after Castro had finished law school and before he became a full-time revolutionary, a few years before he assumed power. Hoak said the seeds of the revolution were being sown by University of

14. Speaking Spanish

Havana students who sometimes demonstrated at the ballpark during games played by Cienfuegos, Hoak's team. Castro was a well-known figure already, was a regular in attendance and described by Hoak as "a baseball fan; he belonged in the nut category."[12]

Hoak called Cuba an "American baseball player's paradise" in the 1950s, saying he received $1,000 a month in salary, $350 more for expenses and had a reduced-rate apartment that was both spacious and attractive. After games he could wander over to nearby coral reefs to fish.[13]

The way Hoak remembered his confrontation with Castro on the field, the game Cienfuegos was playing against Marianao was interrupted by about 300 students rushing onto the field around the fifth inning and demonstrating against the government. In the middle of the hubbub, Castro took the glove and ball from the Marianao pitched and annexed the mound. Castro began loosening up and after a while shouted, "Batter up!"[14]

"What the hell," Hoak recalled thinking, and he stepped in. Castro was not wearing glasses and had the beginnings of a beard, one of his future long-time trademarks. "He wore a long-sleeved white shirt. It had pleats like a formal dress shirt and a square bottom which was worn outside the trousers. Castro also wore tight black slacks and black suede shoes with pointed toes. His footwear was almost dandy, and as I see pictures of today's Castro in army fatigues and combat boots and I am amused by the contrast."[15]

Castro glared when he called for Hoak to bat. "Castro gave me the hipper-dipper windup and cut loose with a curve," Hoak wrote. "Actually, it was a pretty fair curve. It had a sharp inside break to it and it came within an inch of breaking my head."[16] Castro threw inside on Hoak a couple of times. Hoak purposely fouled some pitches over the heads of the demonstrators and then, irritated by the situation, demanded that the umpire clear the field and the game resume. And that's what happened. The duel ended with the count 2–2. "Looking back on it, I think with a little work on his control, Fidel Castro would have made a better pitcher than prime minister."[17]

Another story that makes the rounds among older baseball observers is the tale that Howie Haak once sought out Castro for a tryout. Indeed, Haak noted, the young pitcher (then 21) had a terrific curve and could throw a good sinker, but he did not have a fastball worthy of the name.

Haak sent a telegram back to Pittsburgh, to his mentor Branch Rickey, with the following analysis of what he saw: "The kid has some command of breaking pitches. (Stop). Has nothing on the fastball. (Stop). Double AA talent at best. (Stop).[18]

Right then and there the Pirates apparently stopped recruiting Fidel Castro. In another account of Haak's examination of Castro's skills, albeit retold in 1989, 30 years after Castro took power, Haak was more effusive. He called Castro "a big kid who threw a wicked bleeping curveball—nothing amateur about his pitches. He was a good prospect because he could throw and think at the same time, a rare talent in a young pitcher."[19]

Sports Illustrated's Frank Deford once took a scouting trip with Haak to Puerto Plata, Dominican Republic, and described what he saw. He wrote, "His [Haak's] bad knee, pummeled in some forgotten minor league plate collision years ago, had been hurting again, but he had taken some pills and now strode purposefully across the diamond, releasing a spray of tobacco juice that dampened the infield. The local teenagers there to try out for the Pittsburgh Pirates huddled in the shade of the dugout and eyed the stranger, who was the liege lord of their hopes. Perhaps none of the boys would admit it flat out, but if this man rejected them this afternoon they might never again have an honest chance to dream." The first thing Haak did was pull a stopwatch out of his pocket and ask the hopefuls to run a 60-yard dash."[20]

As Haak drove from place to place, it was apparent that he was well known. Regularly, some wizened local pulled him aside and whispered, "Howie, I've got a good one I'm saving for you. The boy's only 15 and the mother will only let him go where I tell him." And Haak would answer, "Good, I'll see the kid next time I'm through."[21]

Los Angeles Dodgers' Hall of Fame manager Tommy Lasorda witnessed the best and most dangerous of Cuban baseball in the 1950s when he was a young player trying to make it to the big league club. Lasorda, who played for Marianao and Almendares in the Cuban League, was playing ball on the island in 1952 when Fulgencio Batista overthrew the government of Carlos Prio. And Lasorda was also playing baseball on the island when Castro's rebels overthrew the Batista government. "The American players were treated outstanding," Lasorda said. "The fans were just tremendous, diehard, energetic fans. They sang at games. It was fun, really exciting."[22]

14. Speaking Spanish

Batista abandoned the seat of government at the very end of 1958 and Castro and his joyful supporters assumed power on New Year's Eve as the calendar turned from 1958 to 1959. Lasorda said he was attending a New Year's Eve party with players Art Fowler and Bob Allison and their wives. When they emerged into the street at 3:30 A.M. he saw three planes flying overhead and mused, "Geez, who in the world is flying at this time of night?" Lasorda said he heard later it was Batista and all his cabinet members getting out of the country. "When Castro came into Havana on New Year's Day, I can remember horns blowing. I came back from church and they were celebrating."[23]

The celebration was not about the speed of Castro's fastball, but about the speed of the takeover. Because of his long-time connection to winter ball in Cuba, as well as his outgoing personality, Lasorda was a visible figure. Not long after Castro took over the government he sent word that he wanted to talk to Lasorda. Lasorda, accompanied by Haak, met with Castro in his suite in the Havana Hilton—and talked baseball. "Howie enjoyed that, as I did, too," Lasorda said. "Everyone thought he was the savior of the country."[24]

Lasorda changed his mind about that as soon as other Americans did. After Castro clamped down on freedoms in Cuba, including the right of ballplayers to go to the United States to make a living in the majors, the source of top talent from the island dried up except for the occasions when players defected from international travel teams.

Cuba became the world's best amateur baseball team, routinely winning gold medals in the Olympics and Pan American Games. In a bit of symmetry, Lasorda was chosen to manage the United States' team for the Athens Summer Olympics in 2004. Under Lasorda's tutelage, in an Olympics when Cuba was upset, the U.S. won the gold medal. Lasorda said he cried when the National Anthem was played to celebrate the victory and said he had only one more goal in life with regard to his old association with Cuba. "I hope before the big Dodger in the sky calls me, that I would see a free Cuba," Lasorda said.[25]

15

Seventh Inning

When the Pirates led off the seventh inning, by normal, 9-inning standards, the game was officially entering the late innings. It was likely two-thirds over and the score was still stuck on 0–0.

The leadoff hitter for Pittsburgh was first baseman Rocky Nelson. Glenn Richard "Rocky" Nelson was born in 1924 in Portsmouth, Ohio, and was 24 when he broke into the majors with the St. Louis Cardinals in 1949. He never played more than 98 games in a season during his nine-year major league career, and 1959 was the season when he appeared most often. Nelson, who swung from the left side of the plate, performed more spectacularly in winter ball than he ever did in the majors, where he compiled a .249 lifetime average.

Reggie Otero, a Cuban who briefly played for the Chicago Cubs in 1945 but also became a Major League coach, liked Nelson when he hit for Otero's Havana Sugar Kings. He always felt Nelson would hit more consistently in the majors if he ended up on the right team that had a manager who would be patient with him. Otero's talent judgment seemed on the mark when Nelson won the International League Triple Crown twice in the 1950s, battering AAA pitching as if it was of Little League caliber.

Nelson assumed almost legendary status with AAA Toronto by leading the league in homers, RBIs, and batting average while being chosen Most Valuable Player. Years later he was selected for the International League Hall of Fame and the Canadian Baseball Hall of Fame.[1]

By comparison, during Nelson's early years in the majors he bounced from team to team. One season he was with St. Louis, part of the next with Pittsburgh. He kept his suitcase packed throughout the Fifties, stopping with the White Sox, Dodgers, Indians and Cardinals again before the Pirates put Nelson back to work in 1959. That year he batted .291 while splitting first-base duties with Dick Stuart, another minor league legend. In 1960, when the Pirates won the World Series, Nelson again appeared in more than half the games and hit .300, his best major league year.

On a misty night in Milwaukee, however, when it would have been

15. Seventh Inning

possible to break up the game, Nelson could do little with his seventh-inning at-bat. He grounded to Burdette, who had an easy toss to Adcock for the first out. Left fielder Bob Skinner succeeded Nelson in the batter's box. Skinner, who was called "Skins" by broadcaster Bob Prince,[2] was a hard-nosed Pirate who had been with the team since 1954. Skinner, who was 22 when he broke into the Pirates' lineup that season, playing in 132 games, has spent more than a half century in baseball.

A left-handed hitter with above average power, Skinner's best season, when he was chosen for the All-Star game, was 1958, batting .321 and driving in 70 runs. Skinner, who grew up in La Jolla, California, and returned to the West Coast in his later years, spent 12 years in the big leagues as a player, but stayed in the sport as a coach, manager and scout.

"Skins" forced the Pirates to keep him on the big-league roster in 1954 when he tore up spring training in Sarasota, Florida. Skinner had spent the preceding two years in the Navy and wasn't expected to crack the roster. At that time the Pirates viewed the 6-foot-5 Skinner as a first baseman, and with only days to go before breaking camp, then-manager Fred Haney was pleased by the predicament Skinner thrust upon him. "He can hit that long ball and swings his bat with authority," Haney said, "and that's what I like."[3]

Once the Pirates promoted him to a major league spot, Skinner kept up his torrid pace. In his first seven games he batted .455 and smacked four safeties against the Giants in one game. By then Pirates brass were looking up fresh adjectives in the dictionary to apply to Skinner's start and gushing about his future. "He's absolutely the best natural hitter I've seen in years," general manager Branch Rickey said. "He does not seem to go for too many bad balls. The boy has a tremendous future."[4]

This was not the first time Skinner had made a good first impression. In 1951, when he broke into pro ball, Skinner was assigned to the Class D Mayfield, Kentucky, team and hit .472 in 29 games before being promoted. Even if the compliments proved to be a tad premature, similar to Rickey's effusive commentary, Haney added, "He's destined to be one of the great hitters in baseball."[5]

Although he did bat .300-plus three times for the Pirates, a combination of injuries and debilitating allergies helped prevent Skinner from living up to the promise outlined by those baseball men.

Besides appearing for the Pirates in the 1960 World Series, Skinner competed in the 1964 World Series with the Cardinals. After retiring, he started managing in the high minors immediately, in 1967 taking over the old AAA San Diego Padres when they were part of the Pacific Coast League. Running that club, operated by the Phillies, Skinner was named minor league manager of the year. Before the next year was over he had replaced Gene Mauch in Philadelphia.

Eventually, Skinner coached for the Pirates, the Padres when they joined the National League, the California Angels, and the Atlanta Braves. After leading the Astros Pacific Coast League team on the field between 1989 and 1992, Skinner became a Houston scout. Skinner's son Joel became a big leaguer in 1983, breaking in with the White Sox.[6]

Skinner was a friend of Harvey Haddix, a rapport built in part by all the time they spent on the road together in hotels sharing a room. But teamwork and winning the game for the Pirates was in the forefront of Skinner's mind, not friendship, when he swung at a Burdette offering in the seventh. Skinner timed his swing correctly and connected solidly with Burdette's pitch. But he also timed his swing poorly because for one of the brief periods during the game, the weather escalated from damp to determined, from bothersome to downright interfering. "A big storm came in," Skinner said. "Wind and dark clouds. The sky didn't open up, but it sure looked like it was going to."[7]

Skinner's hit propelled Braves right fielder Hank Aaron back to the County Stadium wall. Aaron watched the white ball against the backdrop of the black sky and to Skinner it seemed as if the fielder knew he wasn't going to catch it, that the ball was going to soar into the seats for a home run. Skinner was running to first and watching the outfield.

"That wind was blowing," he said, "and Aaron looked up and the ball was coming back into play. He caught it right at the wall. If that ball had gone out it would have been just a nine-inning game."[8] The hit turned into a simple out.

Not much was simple for the Pirates that season. The team that had been the dregs of the National League in the early 1950s was being improved by Joe L. Brown's moves. He kept a core of guys like Skinner and added to the roster. By 1958, Skinner said, there was a feeling that things were on the upswing. That feeling grew stronger in 1959 with the trade that brought Haddix to the team. Yet the Pirates didn't quite jell, finishing fourth with a 78–76 record. The players knew, however, they

15. Seventh Inning

were now better than that and regrouped. "We kind of slacked off in 1959," Skinner recalled. "But the team was actually coming together a couple of years prior to 1960."[9]

The time Skinner and Haddix spent together while traveling turned them into something akin to brothers. They developed that type of bond by spending so much time together, but also sharing time doing simple things. "We knew each other so well we could be at opposite ends of a room and we knew what the other was thinking," Haddix said in the early 1990s. "They don't have roommates today. Bob and I used to order newspapers and coffee to be sent up to our room at the hotel, and then a while later we'd go down and have breakfast together. Today, most of the guys eat in their rooms, probably to avoid signing autographs in the hotel restaurant or coffee shop. In our day, maybe someone like Willie Mays had to do that, but that was about it."[10]

Haddix said he recalled getting into a comfortable rhythm quite early in the game against the Braves and that included his dugout routine. Yes, he said, Dick Groat did light a cigarette for him each half inning, but the other Pirates, well aware of the no-hitter superstition, treated him as if he had a contagious disease. "No one would talk to me," Haddix said. "They didn't want to jinx me."[11]

What was clear to Skinner on the night of the Braves game was that Haddix was pitching the type of game to which he had always aspired. Haddix, said Skinner, was a one-pitch-at-a-time guy who never got ahead of himself. He was careful with each batter, relying on control to set up the hitters. In the Milwaukee game, Haddix simply never got himself into trouble by falling behind in the count.

"Harvey's attitude, if I've heard it said once, I've heard it said many times, that the way to win every game you pitch is to shut them out and you hit one out," Skinner said. "That was his thing. He never got behind [to the hitters]. I think he got behind once to Mathews, 3-and-1. The rest of the batters, he was right on top of them, ahead of every one of them. And as a teammate, playing defense, you were just ready. When we were on defense, we weren't on defense very long."[12]

Haddix said much the same thing years earlier. He felt weak because of the flu, but everything he did on the mound fooled the Braves. Being ahead in the count kept the Milwaukee hitters wondering. "Every batter, it was zip, zip, two strikes," Haddix said. "I've had better stuff than I had that night. I only threw two pitches, the fastball and the slider. But I never had control like that."[13]

Skinner was right that the Pirates weren't on defense very long, but they weren't on offense very long, either. Burdette gave up hits, but showed no hint of wildness. The Pirates were being shuffled back to the dugout with their bats at their sides at nearly the same rate Haddix was frustrating Braves. Skinner earned no more than a pat on the back for a good try as his fly ball nestled into Aaron's glove.

He was followed in the order by second baseman Bill Mazeroski, a 17-year fixture in the Pirates' lineup who eventually was chosen for the Hall of Fame. He did not have a Hall-of-Fame at-bat in the seventh inning, merely a mortal one, flying out to Pafko in center field.

The Braves got their seventh crack at Haddix next, but the results were similar. He continued to plow through the lineup, reducing the big bats to toothpicks, reducing the star hitters to baffled observers.

On his third time up against Haddix, Johnny O'Brien hit a grounder to Hoak at third and the throw easily reached Nelson in time for the first out. Eddie Mathews, the brawny third baseman who before retiring joined the elite 500-home-run club, may or may not have been swinging for the fences, but the result is what is often produced when a slugger misses out on his main objective—a strikeout.

Hank Aaron stepped in. The man who years later broke Babe Ruth's all-time home-run record with 755 was the type of all-around hitter pitchers hated to face. Aaron, who also became the Major League all-time runs batted in champ, was hardly one dimensional. Yes, he could beat you with a homer, but he was just as likely to ignite a rally with a double. Aaron completed his career with 3,771 hits. One thing Aaron showed in his 23 seasons and 3,298 games was steadiness. He was rarely injured and maintained a sleek but sturdy physique. "Did you ever look at his waist?" Mickey Mantle noted once. "Lean and tough, and he's durable. He's the sort who never gets hurt."[14] Haddix just wanted to make sure that none of Aaron's hits came on that night in County Stadium.

By the seventh inning, even if they did not realize Haddix was pitching a perfect game, the Pirates, the Braves, and the fans were all aware that he was pitching a no-hitter. The scoreboard told that tale. The ones who might have been in the dark were the Pirate radio listeners. Bob Prince weighed the superstition argument against the information argument.

Prince, feeling he was providing a service to his audience, voted in favor of information.

"I mentioned the perfect game at the end of the fifth inning," Prince said. "People say you shouldn't talk about a no-hitter, but with all those zeroes on the board, I had to. The fans in the ballpark knew what was happening. The funny thing about it, in the sixth inning they were all pulling for Haddix. It was electrifying. Especially in the eighth and ninth."[15]

A no-hitter, or a perfect game, would be just about the only occasions when home fans might root against their own team.

16

The Boss

All but a tiny bit of Danny Murtaugh's major league playing career was spent at second base between 1941 and 1951. He was a player standing 5-foot-9 and weighing a less-than-muscular 170 pounds, who had to scrap for any successes he achieved. He worked his way into a regular's role with the Phillies and Pirates only four times during the nine seasons that produced a .254 lifetime batting average.

He was the type of player who sage baseball insiders would look at, nod, and say, "He'll be a manager some day." And indeed, Murtaugh made those thoughts reality, becoming more accomplished as a big-league manager than he had ever been as a player. But teammates from the early 1950s did not necessarily see Murtaugh in the same light. They thought of him as a fun-loving guy not stern enough to command a ship.

"As a ballplayer, Murtaugh was a hard-nosed second baseman, who could run with a body that didn't figure to be able to run," said Ralph Kiner, the dominant player on those Pirates teams. "He was one of the most subtle pranksters I ever met. He could spit tobacco juice better than anybody. He could hit your shoes from 30 feet away. He had a lot of fun on the train rides. He would have been the last guy I'd have thought would be a good manager. He was an Irishman's Irishman."[1]

Murtaugh was a more reliable fielder than hitter during his playing days, with a lifetime fielding mark of .975. In 1948, he led the National League with putouts, assists and double plays at his position. The only other time Murtaugh led the league in anything, however, was as a rookie when he stole 18 bases. Except for a three-game foray to the Boston Braves, Murtaugh, who was born in Chester, Pennsylvania, just outside of Philadelphia, spent his entire professional life associated with Pennsylvania teams. That included 29 years in the employ of the Pirates.

When Murtaugh retired from playing, the Pirates immediately named him manager of the club's AAA New Orleans Pelicans farm team. But he was quickly promoted back to the big club as a coach. In 1957, Murtaugh began his unusual managerial career. Between that season and 1976 Mur-

16. The Boss

taugh was the field boss of the Pirates four different times totaling 15 seasons.

His career was complicated by his health—primarily heart problems—but each time the Pirates fired another manager they turned to Murtaugh again. Murtaugh experienced more retirements than Michael Jordan and Cher combined. Somehow, Murtaugh never wore out his welcome in Pittsburgh. Both management and fans seemed comforted whenever he was at the helm and the team's record whenever Murtaugh was in charge gave them that confidence.

Murtaugh's personality was a good fit, too. He could display toughness, but he also smiled easily and told stories that entertained. He was of Irish heritage and did not keep that a secret. In Chicago, the feeling is that the football-playing Bears are the mirror image of the fans that support them, the blue-collar multitudes described by poet Carl Sandburg in "the city of big shoulders." Pittsburgh was built on steel and coal, not runway models and professions that emphasized blow-dried hair. Murtaugh fit. If Murtaugh went Hollywood it would be to play a character like Sergeant Rock from Easy Company. Myron Cope wrote a magazine story that described Murtaugh as the type of fellow who would have been found in a foxhole and in one of cartoonist Bill Mauldin's every-GI illustrations.[2]

One thing Murtaugh had in common with former general manager Branch Rickey was his thick eyebrows, and one thing he had in common with many of the players of his day was that he chewed tobacco incessantly. Murtaugh walked around with one lopsided cheek seemingly half the time he managed, and when he wasn't in the dugout he smoked cigars. Many of Murtaugh's stogies came from a friend, Pittsburgh Steelers owner Art Rooney, a kindred smoker.

A *Washington Post* writer once gazed at Murtaugh's face and wrote that he was "a man with the face of a basset hound encompassing a leprechaun."[3] Murtaugh was married and raised two sons and a daughter with wife Kate and talked about his family as often as he did baseball strategy.

One of Murtaugh's boyhood friends in Pennsylvania was Mickey Vernon, the long-time slugger with the Washington Senators. They stuck together even after they broke into pro ball. When the pay was meager enough to require off-season winter jobs, Murtaugh and Vernon went to work in a hat store back in Chester. "Mickey and I knew Harry Truman started in a haberdashery," Murtaugh once said, "but somehow we never made it to the White House."[4]

A paratrooper during World War II, Murtaugh later said he disliked violence and that even during baseball brawls he preferred the kind where there was more yelling than punching. He told a story about one Pirate brouhaha with the Phillies where he actually was knocked down twice before deciding to retreat. "Don't you guys know the rules?" Murtaugh said he shouted. "We're supposed to talk for a while and glare at each other—but no punches."[5]

Popular Pirates manager Danny Murtaugh was the team's skipper four different times in his career. Managing Pittsburgh on the night of Harvey Haddix's fateful game, he evidently gave no thought to taking the hurler out.

Murtaugh's first run as Pirates manager began in 1957, after the grim days of the early 1950s passed and produced some keeper ballplayers. He took over from Bobby Bragan partway through the season and finished 26–25. In 1958 the Pirates were 84–70. The finish 14 games over .500 seemed sweet to a deprived fan base.

On the evening Murtaugh wrote out his lineup for Harvey Haddix's scheduled start against the Braves in County Stadium, he was a bit hamstrung. He definitely was not playing with a full deck that night. Roberto Clemente, soon-to-be acknowledged as an all-time great, couldn't go because of a sore throwing arm. He felt Dick Groat needed a break. First base, as it had been much of the season, was a bit of a conundrum. Rocky Nelson or Dick Stuart? The coin landed on Nelson.

It was not a full-strength lineup that day, but that is something that would have passed under radar and never been examined if Haddix had not thrown such a gem. As it so happened, the player who had the best offensive game for the Pirates that day was Dick Schofield, playing in place of Groat, and who contributed three hits. And yet that was the day — with no warning, no hint, no reason to expect anything of the sort when they woke — that the players would be involved in a game remembered forever. "It just shows you what can happen," outfielder Bill Virdon said. "I was in the game for 50 years and I know you're liable to see something new tomorrow."[6]

Murtaugh maintained much of the same attitude he had as a player. Although he didn't drink, he liked to have fun and indulged in practical jokes on occasion, memorably going out to the golf course with a pocketful of cherry bomb fireworks and setting one off now and again when a partner was ready to tee off.[7]

Not one for hanging out in bars, Murtaugh liked to extend his time at the ballpark, especially before home games. He installed a rocking chair in his office and engaged in card games. He said the office was the best place for him to think. More than once Murtaugh stepped down from his position for health reasons, but he always returned from the rocking chair when beckoned by the Pirates. "Managing a ballclub is like getting malaria," he said. "Once you're bitten by the bug, it's difficult to get it out of your bloodstream."[8]

Murtaugh had the touch to keep his clubhouse content (never will there be a team when every single player is satisfied), and general manager Joe L. Brown appreciated the artistry of keeping things humming along without dissension. "He's been able to keep a fairly happy ship," Brown said.[9] "He's not a flashy manager, but he always has a reason — a sound reason — for everything he does."[10]

It is important for a manager to please his boss if he wants to stick around, but the manager must also accommodate the 25 different personalities in the locker room to help make the team click. Some players must be yelled at to do their best, some need no motivating of any sort, and some get depressed if they are criticized. The end result justifies the means. "He'd go to each of us, and get the most from all of us," said Smokey Burgess.[11]

The Pirates were a maturing team in the late 1950s when Murtaugh took over for the first time, and some of the players had survived the depths of the franchise's performance. They had learned and they sensed a different environment and developed a feeling that they had the right players they needed to become winners.

Harvey Haddix felt the Pirates of that era were the loosest group he had played with. "Danny Murtaugh was just a part of it," Haddix said. "He's overlooked. He looked at all the things and then we just went out and played. We put out on the field and that's what counted. Danny didn't have to go after our guys. Our own players would go after one another. If we thought somebody didn't quite hustle enough after the ball, two or three of the players would go after the guy."[12]

One player who had a sneak preview of how Murtaugh would manage was Pirates backup catcher Danny Kravitz. Kravitz was with the Pelicans when Murtaugh managed New Orleans, and he said Murtaugh was an entertaining guy to be around there and even under the brighter spotlight later in Pittsburgh. "He was a good manager," Kravitz said. "Geez, he was a good sport, always joking around with you, talking double talk and all kinds of stuff. He brought me up to New Orleans, then I went back to Hollywood. But the next year I came up and stayed with the Pirates."[13]

Murtaugh was a baseball man through and through, and what that meant in the 1950s was exhibiting loyalty to your organization and your players, not spending too much time outside the stadium on another hobby. It also meant being vocal in defense of players who might be attacked from outside the club when they were in a slump. Once, the Pirates were taking heat for playing poor ball all around and Murtaugh offered verbal retaliation. "I'd like to have that fellow who hits a home run every time," Murtaugh said, "who strikes out every batter when he's pitching, and who never makes a mistake in the field. The only trouble is getting him to put down his beer and come down out of the stands."[14]

Willie Stargell, a later Pirates great who joined the team near the end of Murtaugh's tenure, said the boss was helpful to him as a young player with his patience. Stargell referred to Murtaugh as "the perfect manager" for a rookie trying to find his way because he allowed the player time to find himself.[15]

Murtaugh's heart problems led him to retirement several times, and he often stated that he wanted to spend more time with his children. In between Brown's summonses for help to take over with fresh starts as manager, Murtaugh worked as a Pirates scout. He used to joke about the role and how easy it was to be a scout compared to being a big-league skipper. "Scouting is the golf tour of baseball," Murtaugh said. "Easy traveling, out in the sun, real enjoyable."[16]

Murtaugh made the lifestyle sound pleasant and easy, but it has never been easy to judge baseball talent accurately. Perhaps he meant that there was less pressure than in trying to make the right move in the middle of a game when the action was underway and a manager had only seconds, or at the most a minute or so, to make a decision.

Once Murtaugh posted his starting lineup for the May 26, 1959, game against the Braves, he didn't have decisions to make for quite a while. The innings zipped past as Haddix kept recording outs. His guys were playing flawlessly in the field. Unlike his counterparts managing in the 2000s who are governed by pitch counts and worry about pitchers throwing too many innings, it is unlikely Murtaugh ever gave a second's thought to how many pitches Haddix was throwing or whether there would come a time oh, around the 15th inning or so, that he would have to warm up a reliever.

In 1963, the San Francisco Giants' Juan Marichal won a 1–0 duel with the Braves' Warren Spahn that lasted 16 innings when Willie Mays socked a solo homer. In 1954, the White Sox's Jack Harshman was victorious in a 1–0 game against Detroit's Al Aber that also lasted 16 innings. Complete games and throwing until you begged to be taken out was the thinking of the times, not yanking a pitcher while he was pitching a shutout. It probably never penetrated Murtaugh's thoughts that he might need a relief pitcher on Haddix's night.

"Pitchers of the generations up until Marichal had a belief that 'This game is mine,'" said Elias Sports Bureau executive vice president Steve Hirdt. "The idea of doing permanent harm to a pitcher's arm didn't come into anyone's mind."[17] If strategy came into play as the innings mounted up, moves like choosing a pinch-hitter or substituting a better fielder at a position might come into play for Murtaugh.

17

Eighth Inning

Although Harvey Haddix was not aware he was pitching a perfect game, he was aware that he was pitching a no-hitter. Fans in Pittsburgh, informed by broadcaster Bob Prince in an excitable way, knew that Haddix was perfect. Fans in County Stadium were reminded constantly, just by shifting their heads to gaze at the scoreboard, that Haddix was pitching a no-hitter and those paying the closest attention, who kept their own scorecards, knew they were watching perfection.

"All of us around me knew, and he was pitching against such a great ballclub," said Roland Hemond, the long-time baseball executive in attendance in his capacity as the Braves' assistant farm director. "That's what makes our game so special. You're not fighting the clock. You've got to fight the outs. You can't freeze the ball. You have to face the hitters. I think that's what makes our game so dramatic. Each inning you've got to get the three outs."[1]

The tension was building as the game wore on and Haddix sent batter after batter back to the dugout empty-handed and Lew Burdette foiled every Pirate attempt to push across a run.

The leadoff batter for the Pirates in the eighth inning was third baseman Don Hoak. Burdette struck Hoak out with the bat resting on his shoulder. Roman Mejias, in the lineup replacing the sore-armed Roberto Clemente, came up.

As the innings wore on, the Mejias out at third base in the third inning retroactively loomed larger. Mejias had ill-advisedly tried to advance from second base to third on a single back to the pitcher off of Haddix's bat. Dick Schofield had followed up with a single that would certainly have scored Mejias for a 1–0 lead since the shot to right sent Haddix safely to third. But the Cuban runner had been erased from the basepaths, keeping the score 0–0 at the time. It was early in the game and the play didn't make much of a ripple at the moment. Later, players talked about the throw-out as a what-might-have-been. More than 35 years later, when Haddix recalled the details of the game, he remembered the play when

17. Eighth Inning

Mejias was gunned down at third. "There was a base-running mistake by Mejias," Haddix said. "He was on first base and he hesitated rounding second to third and he got thrown out."[2]

This time up, Mejias hit a grounder to Mathews at third and was thrown out at first. That brought Haddix to the plate with the opportunity to provide Pittsburgh with the lead. As he stepped into the batter's box on the left side to face Burdette, Braves catcher Del Crandall took note of the circumstances. By then the 19,000-plus fans in County Stadium were rooting for Haddix. "From the seventh inning on, every time I'd appear on the field, either going to the mound or to bat, or wherever, the people would stand and cheer me," he said. "The hometown [of the other team]. It made me feel pretty good."[3]

Byplay between batters and catchers is generally subtle, with only the home-plate umpire aware of the conversation. Crandall glanced at Haddix and said, "Harve, you've got a pretty good ballgame going." He did not, as Haddix put it, mention "the magic word" of no-hitter. Haddix responded, "Yeah, I have."[4] Nobody in the Pirates dugout breathed a word about a no-hitter, but the only way Haddix could have been unaware of that progression was by ignoring the scoreboard and he did not do that. "Every inning, walking in and out [to the mound], there's the big scoreboard right up there in front of me, so you can see exactly what's going on," he said.[5] Haddix grounded out third to first to end the Pirates' half of the eighth.

The mood in the stadium had changed since the start of just another regular-season game on a weather-threatening night when fans hoped not to be rained out and not to get too wet. There was an air of understanding that witnesses were watching a special baseball game. But teammates in the Pirate dugout remained mum, letting the game take its course without any of them admitting what the picture was.

"There wasn't much said," noted pitcher Vernon Law. "Nobody said, 'Hey, Harve, you still got a no-hitter going' or anything like that." Law said Haddix exhibited no sign of nerves, but as the game aged, its stature increased. So often pitchers breeze through three or four innings without incident, Law said, but getting to the eighth without surrendering a hit or base runner is much rarer. Senses begin to tingle.

"It's just another ballgame to a guy when he gets going," Law said. "But I'm sure he felt some pressure going into the last couple of innings, the eighth and ninth. When it got beyond that I'm sure he didn't give it an awful lot of thought because he already had a no-hitter, a perfect game through nine. He was just hanging on and hoping for a win."[6]

It was a tricky point in the game. The Pirates wanted to cheer their own on, but according to baseball superstition and standard practice, they had to be careful what to say. "You don't put any additional pressure on a guy just because he's got a no-hitter going," Law said, "but we kept encouraging him to 'Hang in there now, we're gonna get you a run.'"[7]

First baseman Joe Adcock led off the eighth inning for the Braves and he struck out. No disappointment in County Stadium. Next up was Wes Covington. He flied out to left field.

One thing about the 1959 Braves was obvious to their opponents. They didn't rattle easily. In 1957, the Braves interrupted the New York Yankee dynasty of the period by winning the World Series. The Braves were 1958 repeat National League pennant-winners and led the Yankees three games to one before dropping the seventh game of the World Series.

The Braves felt they had the goods for a third straight pennant. It was their time, their era, and with the core of the team the same they felt they could hold off contenders like the Dodgers and take another run at a world title. They could not know it in May, but the Braves would very much need this victory over Haddix come the end of September.

Burdette, the indomitable pitcher on the mound facing Haddix, beat the Yankees three times with complete games in the 1957 Series. He would have to be nicked by more than a single or two here and there to motivate Braves manager Fred Haney enough to remove him from the double shutout. Known as a pitcher who issued few walks, Burdette did have the habit of permitting several hits, then bearing down and eliminating the threat. The fact that the Pirates hit the ball often enough to compile 12 hits was nothing too much out of the ordinary against Burdette.

"He was a competitor," Eddie Mathews wrote about Burdette. "Lew would do what he had to do to beat you. Burdette pitched tight. He had to—that was his way of pitching. He never had a great fastball, an overpowering fastball. Lew beat you with control and by keeping you off the plate. He'd put one under your chin if he had to, and occasionally one would get away."[8]

There was none of that head-hunting, brushback stuff in the Pirates' game, but Burdette's worries were of his own making, allowing routine hits. "Lew had to pitch with men on base almost every inning," Mathews said. "He never gave in."[9] Neither did Haddix.

The third man up in the home half of the eighth was catcher Crandall, batting sixth in the order. It was a testimony to how much power the Braves had because Crandall was a dangerous swinger in addition to being regarded as a top-flight fielder.

Pirate left-fielder Bob Skinner said that it was easy for pitchers to overlook Crandall and make a mistake throwing to him. The Braves were so loaded, by the time the pitcher reached Crandall in the order, he would take him for granted just like Pafko because he had survived encounters with Hank Aaron, Mathews, and Joe Adcock. "When you got down to Crandall, down at the bottom of the line," Skinner said, "you know we were kind of relieved. He wasn't as good a hitter, but he had a lot of power. He could really mess you up."[10]

While he was working his way to the majors, the Braves considered Crandall a good fielding prospect, but he surprised officials in spring training when he was just as competent with a bat. Crandall was just 19 years old when he broke into the majors with the Boston Braves in 1949. His career was interrupted by military service, but he became the Braves' full-time starter in 1953, the first year he was a National League All-Star. That was one of eight times he was chosen as one of the circuit's best. When people asked him where his sharp hitting had come from, Crandall credited marriage.

"I think having a more settled home life is the big reason," Crandall said, without elaborating on how he spent his nights as a bachelor. "I haven't changed my stance at all, and as far as I can tell I'm not doing anything at the plate I didn't do before." Crandall had the type of power that fit right into the Braves lineup, eight times smacking at least 10 home runs in a year. He was the type of hitter who could give Haddix heartburn with one swing of the bat, though he was unable to do so that night.

"County Stadium was a good place to play," Crandall said. "It was a fair ballpark. It was fair for hitters and for pitchers." The passion Milwaukee fans and fans from all over Wisconsin brought to the park to root for the Braves was unprecedented, Crandall felt, and that made it surprising to hear them cheering on Haddix. "Those people loved us."[11] The love of the Braves was never in doubt, but those knowledgeable about baseball realized they might be watching a once-in-a-lifetime occurrence. They may have suspended their allegiance for an hour or so.

"We had a feeling as the game went on that we were going to catch up to Haddix," Crandall said. "But he had our number. When it got past nine innings, you had to take your hat off to him. They had so many hits, it was a wonder they didn't score."[12]

Crandall grounded to third base and was thrown out by Don Hoak. On to the ninth inning.

Although the fans were applauding his performance to remind him that he was cruising along with a no-hitter, Haddix said he did not let that excite him very much. Some years before, he had taken a no-hitter into the ninth inning of a game against the Philadelphia Phillies and lost it on a hit by Richie Ashburn leading off.

"I had been through this thing before," Haddix said, "and I did not try for the no-hitter. I just kept right on going, one up, two up, and three up and down all the way through to the ninth inning. And then I said, 'I've been this close before. I'm going to go for it.' The game was 0–0 of course and that was the only inning of that ballgame that I really meant to try to throw a no-hitter and I gave it my all at that time."[13]

In the 2000s, managers get an itchy trigger finger by the eighth inning no matter how well their starting pitcher is performing. They've got a bullpen full of live arms that can throw 95 mph and they feel derelict when they don't use them, and they get criticized for leaving their starting pitcher in the game too long.

Given the habits of the day, Danny Murtaugh was not going to replace Harvey Haddix throwing a perfect game if he had thrown 180 pitches. The irony in that was the best relief pitcher in the game was seated a few feet away from Murtaugh in the dugout. Roy Face was re-defining the job of late-game reliever, bailing the Pirates out of tough situation after difficult crisis day after day in 1959. But Face was just as much a spectator as the paying customers at County Stadium that day. The bullpen was only a few yards away, but it might as well have been located in Chicago. "I never left the bench," Face said. "I stayed on the bench and never went to the bullpen."[14] He had one of the best seats in the house to watch Haddix and Burdette and watch is what he did that night.

By the end of the eighth, Haddix had faced 24 major league hitters and retired them all in a 0–0 game. His kingdom for a Pirates run.

18

Ninth Inning

It was the ninth inning. This was supposed to be the last inning. It should have been the end of a regular, normal baseball game that was not tied. But as the ninth inning began, the game was tied. The scoreboard read 0–0, the same as it had when the first pitch was thrown.

By the ninth inning, the players knew this was no average day. While fans might perk up and start rooting for a no-hitter or a perfect game (quietly) as early as the third inning, Major League players rarely let their minds drift in that direction until a few more innings are in the bank. They are used to seeing pitchers come out and go a couple of times through the order without permitting even a scratch hit. "If you get past the fifth inning and a guy's throwing a no-hitter, then people start looking at each other," Pirate pitcher Bob Friend said, jokingly making musical sounds that connoted increasing drama such as just before the shark attacked in the movie *Jaws*.[1]

But if the pitcher keeps it up and the game is entering the ninth inning, then the prospects are much more likely. Players start thinking more like fans in the sense that they are genuinely rooting a teammate on because they think he is close enough to accomplish something special. "It was an exciting night," Friend said.[2]

As was to be expected, no one was making no-hitter small talk with Haddix while he was in the dugout with the Pirates at bat, but when he returned to the mound, the players on the bench tried to improve his luck. Dick Groat said those who were not in the game that night had come into possession of a green peanut and passed it back and forth along the bench as a good-luck charm. With no rabbit's foot in sight, they had to make do. At one point, Groat said, the players placed the peanut on the top step of the dugout with the idea it would jump-start a rally. So-called peanut luck did not produce, however.[3]

In the Pirates' case on this cool night, the result of the game was also at stake. They wanted to win, not only for Harvey Haddix, but for themselves. They understood Haddix was carrying more than his share of the burden and they wanted to pay him back with a run, so he could win the darned game.

"We were struggling," Pirate pitcher Vernon Law said. "I was just hoping somebody could break out for him. It was not a good thing to think of a no-hitter and perfect game going down the drain for him after the ninth inning. We could not get a danged run across. That's what irritated me."[4]

The tension in the dugout, among the players who watched but were not in the lineup that night, increased as the game went on, according to shortstop Groat. The players wanted to see Haddix pull off the perfecto, record the no-hitter, and that made them nervous as each Braves hitter took his licks. But they were also frustrated because of all nights, the Pirates could not score a single run.

"It was just the most methodical performance I think I've ever seen," Groat said of the way Haddix blew through the Milwaukee lineup. "There were only a few balls hit hard all night. In the first inning he went to 3-and-1 on Eddie Mathews, got him out, and was not behind another hitter all night. The rest of the next 11 innings were perfect. It was just an unbelievable performance."[5]

Entering the visitors' half of the ninth inning, the Pirates had not worked Lew Burdette for a base on balls. He had not hit a batter and no Pirate had reached base on an error. At that point, Pittsburgh had totaled six hits, all singles. They had not put together any type of serious challenge. The only thing that came close to classifying as a threat was the third inning when the Pirates knocked three singles off Burdette. "We passed up numerous opportunities with men on third and just couldn't get a hit," Bill Virdon said.[6]

The Pirates had not loaded the bases and had not struck an extra-base hit. By Haddix standards, Burdette was far from perfect, but by everyday baseball standards, Burdette was also pitching superbly.

When the Pirates led off the ninth inning, they felt the pressure. The attitude was: "Got to score." But the reality was, it was going to be harder than wishing and hoping. The first batter facing Burdette was Dick Schofield. He grounded out second to first, Johnny O'Brien to Joe Adcock. The second batter was Bill Virdon. The Pirates' centerfielder singled to center.

Smokey Burgess got decent wood on the ball, but flew out to center

18. Ninth Inning

Southpaw Harvey Haddix, nicknamed "The Kitten," pitched nine perfect innings without a win to his credit. The game would go into extra innings.

for the second out. When Rocky Nelson singled to right, sending Virdon to third, there was some excitement on the Pirates' bench. The situation represented the team's best chance to score since the third inning. Could the Pirates take advantage of the big chance? No. Bob Skinner grounded the ball back to Burdette, who threw him out at first base, ending the inning.

Years later Haddix speculated on how the Pirates' offense might have been more productive with Groat and Roberto Clemente in the lineup that night. "It might not have gone 13 innings if their bats were in the lineup," Haddix said.[7]

The comparatively less powerful Braves bats were on schedule to meet Haddix in the bottom of the ninth inning. Quite conscious of pitching a no-hitter, Haddix wanted to finish the nine innings in style. He did something unusual, changing his approach and what had worked for him all night long. He adopted a more risky approach of trying to blow strikes past the batters and rather focusing on location and teasing them into hitting weak grounders or soft flies, Haddix sought to rack up "K's."

"It was the only inning I tried for the no-hitter," Haddix said. "I wanted to strike everybody out. I got two of the three on strikeouts and then went back to pitching my normal game."[8]

First up was outfielder Andy Pafko. On Haddix's 70th pitch of the night, Pafko stood still for a called strike. On the next offering, Pafko swung and stroked a foul ball to the upper deck in right field. He was quickly in an 0–2 hole. Haddix wasted a ball low and outside, then induced Pafko into a swing and a miss. One out. Eight and a third innings perfect.

Shortstop Johnny Logan took his turn in the box, but didn't give Haddix much of a chance to strike him out. Logan took a whack at the first pitch and hit a fly ball to Skinner in left for the second out. Eight and two-thirds innings perfect.

That brought the pitcher Burdette up to face Haddix in the position of being the one man left who could mess things up, to spoil Haddix's perfect game, no-hitter, and win the game for himself. Haddix threw a ball low and outside. 1–0. Strike called, 1–1. Burdette got his bat on the next pitch, grounding it into the Pirates' dugout on the left side, 1–2. Then Haddix did what he set out to do. He whistled a pitch past Burdette, who swung and missed for the strikeout. Three outs. Nine innings

18. Ninth Inning

perfect. It was great cause for celebration for Harvey Haddix and the Pirates, yet the game wasn't over. Baseball had never confronted such a situation. The Braves had sent 27 men to the plate and Haddix retired them all. Perfect game. But now Haddix had to be more than perfect, or keep on being perfect, depending on how one looked at it.

In the Pirates' minds, even though the game was continuing, and the won-loss result was not determined, the game had gone into the books as a no-hitter. Haddix had recorded his 27 outs in a row over nine innings, so he had recorded a perfect game. That's what the players believed at the time. "For a guy to pitch that long and that perfectly, you shouldn't have any question about what it was," Friend said.[9]

Haddix had cruised through the Braves lineup three times by throwing 78 pitches. He was still perfect after nine. Major League perfect games come along only slightly more often than once a decade, and by May of 1959 there had been just six thrown and none in the National League since 1880. Seemingly, Haddix had joined a strange mix of baseball company, from little-knowns to the most famous of hurlers.

On June 12, 1880, Lee Richmond, a left-hander pitching for a Worcester, Massachusetts, team defeated Cleveland, 1–0, for the first recognized perfect game. Richmond, who won 32 games and lost 32 games that season, spent six years playing Major League baseball. He finished 75–100 and evaporated into the mists of time.

Only five days later, baseball experienced its second perfect game. On June 17 of the same year, the much better remembered John Montgomery Ward, pitching for Providence, shut out Buffalo, 5–0, also without allowing a base runner. The losing pitcher in that game was Pud Galvin, a Hall of Famer who won 364 games and who has been rather cutely described as the first baseball player to employ performance-enhancing drugs because he admitted to using monkey testosterone.[10]

The season before his perfect game, Ward had won 47 games, by far his best showing in a seven-year career that concluded with 164 wins and a 61.4 winning percentage. Ward was given credit for developing the curveball, and when injuries curtailed his pitching, he switched to the outfield. Ward was elected to the Baseball Hall of Fame in 1964.[11]

The irony of two perfect games hurled in the same week did not mean they were going to break out all over like a rash. Twenty-four years passed until baseball's next perfect game, this time thrown in the young American

League. Cy Young, whose monstrous lifetime statistics put pitching records out of sight for all time, tossed a perfect game for the Boston Red Sox on May 5, 1904, beating the Philadelphia Athletics 3–0. Young won 511 games in his 22-season career and the perfect game was the second of three no-hitters he pitched. Young won 94 more games than Walter Johnson, the second biggest winner in baseball history. After his death in 1955 Major League Baseball named its most coveted individual pitching award after him.

Addie Joss of Cleveland turned in the next perfect game on October 2, 1908, topping the Chicago White Sox 1–0. Joss was a 6-foot-3 right-hander who won 17 or more games seven times in a nine-year career that was cut short by his untimely death in 1911 from tubercular meningitis. Joss won 160 games and 62.3 percent of his decisions, and decades after his demise in 1978 was voted into the Hall of Fame.

Baseball went 14 years without seeing another perfect game, and the pitcher who threw it was not destined for Hall of Fame consideration. He essentially was a Hall of Famer for one day. White Sox righty Charlie Robertson caught the stars in alignment on May 30, 1922, when he shut out the Detroit Tigers 2–0 without allowing a base runner. Robertson, however, did not even post a winning record that season, finishing 14–15. He managed an eight-year major league career and finished with a 49–80 mark. No major baseball awards were named after him.

As an illustration of how rare major league perfect games are, no other perfect game was recorded for 34 years after Robertson's fling. The next one was the most celebrated of all perfect games because a journeyman pitcher named Don Larsen chose the biggest stage under the brightest lights for his memorable performance.

Larsen was a fun-loving player who according to all legends stayed out late and drank hard. Casey Stengel, Larsen's Hall of Fame manager with the Yankees, said of his often wayward player, "The only thing he fears is sleep." And when Larsen was caught out after curfew during spring training because he crashed his car into a light pole, Stengel said, "He must have went out to mail a letter."[12]

Larsen, who pitched for eight teams (a couple of them twice) in a 14-year career between 1953 and 1967 that produced an 81–91 lifetime mark, was on the mound for the New York Yankees during the 1956 World Series. With the eyes of America on the showcase of the sport on October

18. Ninth Inning

8, 1956, Larsen slammed the door on the Brooklyn Dodgers, throwing 97 pitches in a 2–0 victory. "I had great control," Larsen explained after he completed the magical feat. "I never had that kind of control in my life."[13]

When Haddix wrapped up his nine innings, matching the heroics of the past, Larsen's—if not the others'—effort was fresh in baseball fans' minds. What set Haddix apart from the other perfect game pitchers was that his day at the office was not finished. He had more to do, like get ready for the 10th inning.

19

Tenth Inning

The Pirates were without Dick Groat and Roberto Clemente on the night when Harvey Haddix made history, but the starting second baseman was a future Hall of Famer. Bill Mazeroski was a major element in the core of the Pittsburgh Pirates of the era, with fielding that constantly drew raves and a reputation for clutch hitting.

Mazeroski was the leadoff batter in the top of the 10th inning as once again the Pirates sought to strike a match and ignite an offensive flame that would carry Haddix to victory.

Mazeroski, who was nicknamed "Maz" for short, grew up in Tiltonsville, Ohio, and signed with the Pirates at age 17 in 1954. By 1956 the converted shortstop was playing half of the games for Pittsburgh and by 1957 he was the full-time starter at second, a place he resided for 2,163 games.

"I sure would hate to be a second baseman in the Pirate farm system with Maz hanging around," Pittsburgh manager Danny Murtaugh said in 1959. "This boy is good for 15 years and any other second baseman simply doesn't have a future. He's young, strong, clever, ideal temperament and his future is unlimited."[1] Murtaugh's estimate was pretty close. Mazeroski was the Pittsburgh second baseman for 17 seasons.

The young Ohioan was such a spectacular fielder that broadcaster Bob Prince simply referred to him as "The Glove." At times it did seem as if the leather mitt was merely a natural appendage, an oversized hand, so naturally did Mazeroski scoop up ground balls. A seven-time All-Star, Mazeroski won his first Gold Glove in 1958, led the National League in assists nine times, and set an all-time league record for participating in double plays.

By the early stages of the 1959 season, Mazeroski was established, but he later felt the year was one of his weakest and most disappointing. In the off-season between the end of the 1959 campaign and 1960 Mazeroski dropped his weight from 195 to 178 through exercise and diet.

"I didn't exercise last winter," Mazeroski said of the 1958–59 off-sea-

19. Tenth Inning

son and subsequent batting average drop of 34 points, "and perhaps I grew too complacent. I went to camp too heavy and never was able to get untracked."[2] Mazeroski did not get untracked hitting against Burdette, either. He hit a ground ball to second and was thrown out at first base for the Pirates' first out.

The second batter up, third baseman Don Hoak, lifted the Pirates' hopes with a single to left. With one on and one out, this was one of the rare chances in the game that looked promising for either team to score a run. Right-fielder Roman Mejias was due up, but Murtaugh scanned the personnel on the bench and went for the big bat.

The man least likely to be chosen as a late-inning defensive replacement was in the majors for one reason—he could hit the cover off the ball. Dick Stuart shared first base with Rocky Nelson and others, mostly because the Pirates had to put him somewhere in the field. Stuart was a tailor-made designated hitter, but two things stood in his way of fulfilling that destiny. Stuart was born too soon, since allowing teams to employ an extra swinger who didn't field was not written into the rules for another 14 years, and he was playing in the National League, which still doesn't use the DH.

As the man whose lack of inspiration with a glove on his hand inspired the nickname "Dr. Strangeglove," Stuart was not going to see action out in the field during this spinetingling game because of the risk of his committing an error. But with his tremendous power he was a legitimate pinch-hitting choice. And with his cavalier attitude, Stuart wasn't likely to feel any particular pressure.

Stuart was a baseball character, the sort of which came along perhaps once a decade. The big ego, the handsome head of hair, the outgoing personality, the kinship with Hollywood actors more than Cooperstown hitters were ingrained young. Stuart was 18 when he signed with the Pirates in 1951, and scout Bob Fontaine thought he had just inked a budding superstar worth every penny of a $10,000 bonus.[3]

When Stuart signed the contract binding him to Pittsburgh it was noted that his middle name was "Lee," but it just as well could have been "Cocky." When Fontaine handed over the check, Stuart said, "The guy who breaks Babe Ruth's record [of 60 homers in a season] will be worth a fortune. They better save up. I'm going to want it all in cash."[4]

Branch Rickey, Jr., who worked as an assistant to his father in the Pirates' front office, saw some vintage Stuart early on in the minors while scouting. Fans cheered Stuart when his turn at bat was announced, but when the slugger hit a feeble ground ball to shortstop, he tossed away his bat and ran only a few steps down the first-base line instead of legging out the play. "Thank the Lord my father never saw that," Rickey said. "They would have had to take him away in an ambulance."[5]

During his journey through the minors, Stuart, who stood 6-foot-4 and weighed around 215 pounds, made a legendary 1956 stop in Lincoln, Nebraska, of the Class B Western League. He blasted 66 home runs and took to signing autographs "Dick Stuart—66."[6] He indeed exceeded Ruth's one-year mark, even if the feat was accomplished in minor-league obscurity.

When Stuart reported to the Pirates in 1958 he had the number "66" stenciled on his suitcase. Stuart believed his own hype and swashbuckled through the minors and majors forevermore, a playboy on the move (he bragged about the homers, whether waitresses, airline stewardesses or hat check girls knew what he was talking about or not), inhaling cigars, keeping late hours, and confident that he was just one pitch away from his next home run. "Anybody can field," Stuart said. "They pay you to hit those home runs."[7]

He didn't attempt to improve his fielding, apparently convinced that was a failing in the game he could overcome with his big bat. During one spring training camp in Florida in 1959, Stuart stunned onlookers with his fielding incompetence, yet shrugged it off. "Dick Stuart hit .750 yesterday," one report stated, "which should have been enough to beat the White Sox, but he fielded .555 and the Pirates lost, 7–5." Stuart committed four errors in the game.[8]

The season Stuart hit his 66 home runs, he also struck out 171 times. The Pirates liked his power, but considered the ratio unacceptable. Near the end of the 1958 season, the team turned Stuart over to George Sisler for private coaching. Sisler, who at the time owned the record for most hits in one season, retired with a .340 lifetime average, a number impressive enough to sway Hall of Fame voters in his favor.

Though quite out of character, Stuart applied himself seriously to the pointers Sisler offered and the older man liked what he saw about Stuart's new stroke. "He's a very fine hitter," Sisler said. "There were two or three things I thought he did wrong and I corrected him. This boy has so much power he doesn't have to aim for the fences. He can bring the fences down to his size."[9]

19. Tenth Inning

Although Stuart seemed to have all the potential in the world to actually equal Babe Ruth in the majors, his actions when he was anywhere but the batter's box annoyed Pirates officials and sometimes left them agape, bragging about how great he was included. It was suggested by one writer that instead of Stuart being able to make a reservation in the Hall of Fame, he would put team officials "connected with him into a semi-private room."[10] If interpretation is needed, this means he was likely to drive them into a mental hospital.

To say that Stuart didn't fit the mold of what type of player and teammate Danny Murtaugh wanted to manage was like saying that the *Titanic* was a big boat. "A baseball player should have dignity these days," Murtaugh said in 1959. "After all, the kids in the Little League look up to them."[11]

Just like the wildly hyped ocean liner that sailed into catastrophe on its maiden voyage, many would bet Stuart was headed for a collision with disaster. Stuart visited ticket sellers and without providing a name told them he would improve business for them once fans clued into his home-run bashing. He dressed impeccably and smiled at his reflection in the mirror often in the Pirates' locker room. "This is a major occupation for Stuart," a writer noted. "In all of sport no one ever looked at himself in the mirror as hard as Stuart does. Next to looking at his reflection in a mirror, the best thing Stuart does is comb his hair, something he does as if it was part of his contract. Stuart believed that never should a star appear disheveled."[12]

Pinch-hitting in the 10th inning provided Stuart with the opportunity to be a star, to be the savior, to live up to his own beliefs about just how great a hitter he was. He eyed Burdette. Burdette eyed Stuart. When Burdette let loose what Stuart took to be a friendly pitch he swung. The ball carried to center field, where Andy Pafko gathered it in for the second out. Then Stuart returned to the bench. Two outs.

The next batter was Haddix. No pinch-hitter for him. Murtaugh was riding the lefty's arm all the way. With a runner on, if Haddix could hit safely, or even walk, the top of the order would be up and might be able to generate a run. It didn't happen. Haddix grounded back to Burdette for the second time in the game.

It was the Braves' turn again. For the 10th time they were going to send batters up to see what Harvey Haddix had. Was he tiring? This was uncharted territory. Nobody had pitched more than nine perfect innings. How could he keep it up? The odds were against it. The Braves were due for a hit, for a base-runner, at least.

"What more could you do now other than win?" Braves backup infielder Mel Roach said of what was left for Haddix.[13]

To start the bottom of the 10th, the Pirates had to make a change in the field. Stuart had had his chance at the plate, but Murtaugh was not going to put him into the lineup full-time and count on him to chase down fly balls in the outfield. To replace Mejias in right field, Murtaugh turned to a rookie who had just been brought up earlier in the day to fill in on the roster for the injured Clemente. Joe Christopher, originally from the Virgin Islands, and one of the fruits produced by Pittsburgh's exhaustive Latin American and Caribbean scouting programs, was inserted into the lineup, appearing in his first Major League game. "That was the first game that I played with a Major League uniform on," Christopher said. "Quite a way to make a debut, wasn't it?"[14]

Christopher was playing in Columbus, Ohio, when he was summoned to the Pirates the day before Haddix's game. He joined the team on the road in Milwaukee, but after being used to back up Mejias in the Haddix game, Christopher was injured after playing 15 games and his season ended with a .000 batting average, going 0 for 12.

Much as Murtaugh had, Braves manager Fred Haney tried to shake things up and present Haddix with a new challenge. He called upon backup catcher Del Rice to pinch-hit for Johnny O'Brien. Rice was an old pro who had been in the National League since 1945 when he broke in with the St. Louis Cardinals.

Rice did not have the hitting credentials of a Hank Aaron or Eddie Mathews (who did?), and was mostly used to give catching regular Del Crandall a periodic rest. Rice, whose lifetime batting average was .237 spread over 17 years, was a fresh face, a new right-handed hitter for Haddix to contend with, and with all of his experience he was less likely than a youngster to be rattled by the situation.

Rice could be patient at the plate, working Haddix hard to get the count in his favor, and just maybe find a way to get on base. The first pitch was right over for strike one called. Rice liked the look of Haddix's second pitch better and swung, but he missed it for strike two. Just as most of the other Braves batters were all night long, Rice was immediately

19. Tenth Inning

behind in the count. The next pitch was a ball outside and Rice was not tempted to go after it.

On Haddix's 82nd pitch of the evening, Rice connected solidly. The ball soared deep to center, driving Bill Virdon back towards the County Stadium wall. Some players remember the swat as one of the most dangerous threats to the no-hitter all night. "There were only a few difficult plays all night and that was one of them," Dick Schofield said.[15]

If Stuart stretched sports writers' imaginations to dream up ways to describe his awful fielding, Virdon was the opposite, grabbing balls he had no right to reach and putting them away for outs. His work could favorably be compared to Van Gogh as quality art. From his perspective, Virdon did not think the Rice hit was a challenging play, only that the ball was hit sharply. "It was well hit, but it was not a tough chance," Virdon said. None of the fly balls hit off Haddix that day were in his mind, he said. "There were fly balls, but they didn't have a chance of going out of the ballpark. They were easy to get to and, you know, routine catches."[16]

Mathews followed Rice to the plate and also hit a fly ball out to Virdon. The always-dangerous Hank Aaron was next. It was the fourth time around for Haddix facing the man who would become the most prolific home-run hitter in baseball history. Aaron grounded out to short.

Now Haddix had retired 30 men in a row with no hits, walks, errors, hit batsmen, or, given the way the game had played out, runs. Ten innings gone and Pirate Harvey Haddix was still perfect. The players in the dugout on his side, in the lineup or just watching, shared one thought. "Let's hurry up and get it over," said backup catcher Hank Foiles.[17]

20

Eleventh Inning

After Braves manager Fred Haney's futile attempt to jump-start his offense by pinch-hitting Del Rice for Johnny O'Brien, he needed a fresh second baseman. Haney turned to Felix Mantilla, who had seen sporadic action, mostly off the bench since his 1956 rookie season.

Mantilla, from Isabella, Puerto Rico, would appear in 103 games for the Braves in 1959, the most to that point in his career, but for his first several seasons he was regarded as a good glove man with very limited hitting skills. Although Mantilla's best hitting days were ahead of him in the American League, his .215 average during the 1959 season made him no better a prospect than the pitcher to reach base.

Although there were never any worries about Mantilla's fielding prowess, he had made an impression in the minors with his bat. Barely turning 18 during his first season of pro ball, Mantilla tore up the Three-I League for Evansville in 1952, hitting .323 with 11 home runs and adding 28 stolen bases. Mantilla, who was a skinny 6-foot, 160 pounds as a young player, struggled off the diamond that year because his first language was Spanish. "I didn't speak English that well," Mantilla said. "Culturally, it was very different."[1]

After a season of winter ball, Mantilla was assigned to Jacksonville in the South Atlantic League, where he first met Hank Aaron. For much of the summer, they were the team's double-play combination, Mantilla manning short and Aaron at second. By the next year Aaron was an outfielder. Aaron, Mantilla, and Horace Gardner were the first black players in Jacksonville and Mantilla said race was an obvious issue in the South in 1953.

"I guess I was a guinea pig at that time," said Mantilla, who said he and Gardner also broke the color barrier in Evansville, though the racial discrimination they encountered occurred mostly with Jacksonville. "We had to play in Columbia, South Carolina, Montgomery, Alabama, and some of those places were pretty tough."[2]

During four more years of minor league apprenticeship, as he moved

20. Eleventh Inning

on to tougher competition, Mantilla always hit in the .270s, good enough to encourage team officials.

By 1956, it was up or out for Mantilla, and his 35-game trial with Milwaukee produced a .283 average. No one anticipated the years-long slump that followed. Yet one play in the field almost ruined Mantilla's big-league career. In a July 1957 game against the Pirates, Braves center field Bill Bruton had his eyes on a sinking fly ball stroked by Bill Virdon at the same time Mantilla watched the hit. Both men ran at full speed trying to field the ball and collided hard on the outfield grass. Mantilla rolled over several times from the impact while Bruton lay prone. Initially, a stretcher was brought onto the field for Bruton, but he waved it off. Both players were shaken up by the scary crash, though there were no long-term effects.

Mantilla had trouble cracking the Braves' set infield that included Johnny Logan at short and Red Schoendienst at second, and later called his six seasons in the majors with Milwaukee "wasted years." [3] In an 11-year career, Mantilla enjoyed himself most with the Boston Red Sox, where one season he batted .315, one season he hit 30 home runs and a third season he played in 150 games and made the American League All-Star team.

The idea of pinch-hitting Rice for O'Brien was a sound one, although it did not work out, because Haney knew he could insert Mantilla at second. It was that move rather than the pinch-hitting strategy that later proved pivotal in writing the history of the Harvey Haddix game.

The Pirate leadoff man in the top of the 11th inning was Dick Schofield. Once again the shortstop did his best to make people forget Dick Groat wasn't in the lineup, stroking a single to left field. There was a man on base again, offering a fresh chance for the Pirates to rescue Haddix. Life stirred in the dugout. Players could sense that this was their moment to score that one lousy run that was needed. Pitcher Bob Friend, watching with his hands in the pockets of his Pirates warm-up jacket, said, "C'mon."[4] It was a simple exhortation, but it was probably on the lips of all his teammates.

Backup catcher Danny Kravitz in the very quiet Pirate bullpen said he was thinking the game had gone on long enough. "I was hoping in my mind that we would win sooner or later there," he said. "Everyone was on edge, I'll tell you that. It sure was a remarkable game. Oh, geez, I was hoping that Harvey would win that game."[5]

For the moment, opportunity rested in Bill Virdon's hands. Over his dozen years in the big leagues, Virdon hit .267. He was more frequently praised for his fielding than his hitting, but he was always a calm ballplayer, a trait that later served him well as a manager with the Pirates, Houston and especially with the New York Yankees when he worked in the pressure cooker atmosphere created by owner George Steinbrenner. Virdon might not have been another Paul Waner at the plate, but he got his share of hits.

Years later Virdon expressed admiration for Lew Burdette's ability to squirm out of trouble time and again and said Haddix's game was something he was proud to play in. "It's a special game to know you were there and saw it and took part in it," Virdon said. "I don't think there's any question about that."[6]

But Virdon couldn't end it, or even give the game a little nudge towards resolution. He hit a ground ball to Mantilla at second base and Mantilla threw to second, where shortstop Johnny Logan was covering for the force out on Schofield. That left Virdon standing on first and the menacing Smokey Burgess with the same percentage of a chance to knock in a run that Virdon had. The lefty swinging Burgess grounded to first. Adcock scooped up the ball, threw to Logan covering second to eliminate Virdon, and then Logan's throw beat Burgess back to the bag to complete a double play. Once again Burdette was less than perfect, but not truly reachable.

Haddix had retired 30 straight batters and everyone in the Braves lineup (and one fresh face) was able to watch his motion, his approach, study his fastball, his curve, and his adjustments to speed, location and delivery, and none of it had made the slightest difference. One way or another, for 10 full innings, Haddix prevented every single opposing hitter from getting as far as first base. "We realized what Haddix was doing," said Milwaukee catcher Del Crandall. "We didn't know how, but he was doing it to us."[7]

Joe Adcock was the first Braves batter due up in the home half of the 11th inning. During his prime power years in the late 1950s and 1960s, Adcock made pitchers as nervous as Hank Aaron and Eddie Mathews did. He did not have their longevity, but Adcock blasted 336 career home runs, so he was a fireworks exhibition waiting to happen, too. In 1956, he slammed 38 homers.

20. Eleventh Inning

Like so many of the early Milwaukee Braves, Adcock was popular in a community smitten with baseball. Away from the park, he sought to capitalize on that familiarity by lending his name to a restaurant. He was not a day-to-day operator of the establishment, but "Joe Adcock's" did a nice business using his name as a free ad until a 1955 fire devastated the building with $100,000 worth of damage.[8]

It was a new era for ballplayers who could trade on their names in a manner only a very few could in the past. The connection worked in the home city as long as the player wasn't traded (which he wasn't very often if he was good) and kept producing. Before he was married, Adcock, who later raised thoroughbred horses in his home state of Louisiana, got more than his share of fan mail from females.[9] And before he perfected the swing that delivered the most productive day for a hitter ever (four home runs and a double, or for poker players, four aces and a king high), Adcock's weakness was the change-up. Some days he was lucky he didn't dislocate his back swishing the bat through the air at off-speed pitches. "I was lunging, especially at that slow stuff," Adcock said, "breakin' my back. I still do it once in a while, but I'm waiting more. You've got to see the ball before you go for it."[10]

Adcock walked into the batter's box in the 11th inning ready to hit. Haddix had worked him carefully and this time, Haddix's 85th pitch of the night, Adcock swung immediately. Adcock liked the first pitch well enough to swing, but didn't get all of it. The ball was hit hard and drove Dick Schofield deep into the hole at short, but he fielded it cleanly and his throw to Rocky Nelson was accurate. One out on the board for the Braves.

Wes Covington, who had had a quiet night at bat and in left field, also came out swinging. He recorded a swing and a miss for a strike. The Braves must not have believed Haddix was tiring because they did little in terms of waiting him out. Covington swung at the second pitch, too, and this time the bat met the ball. He flied out to Virdon in center field.

Up came catcher Del Crandall, with two quick outs recorded. Crandall took all of two pitches. He accepted a first-pitch called strike and then passed up a ball low. Crandall took his best cut at the third pitch and also lofted a fly-ball out to Virdon. Another inning of perfection in the record books for Haddix. That made 11 complete, 33 men up and down. No one else had been so stingy with base hits or base runners as Harvey Haddix since baseball went professional with the Red Stockings in Cincinnati in 1869. Few had approached Haddix's achievement.

On July 4, 1908, Hooks Wiltse, hurling for the New York Giants, was victorious, 1–0, over the Philadelphia Phillies by throwing a 10-inning no-hitter. Wiltse was a solid pitcher who won 23 games that season and compiled a .607 winning percentage in 12 seasons.

On May 2, 1917, when Fred Toney of the Cincinnati Reds edged the Chicago Cubs, 1–0, it was also a 10-inning job and was part of one of the most extraordinary games in major league history. Cubs twirler Hippo Vaughan matched Toney for 9 and one-third hitless innings in the only double no-hitter of its kind.[11]

Prior to Haddix's performance, there had been nine times in Major League history, five in the National League and four in the American League, when a pitcher had thrown at least nine innings of no-hit baseball but later surrendered a hit.[12]

On August 1, 1906, pitching for the Brooklyn Superbas, Harry McIntyre carried a no-hitter into the 11th inning against the Pittsburgh Pirates. McIntyre gave up a two-out single that inning and then allowed three more hits and lost the game 1–0 in the 13th inning. It was the grandest showing of McIntyre's career—in nine seasons he piled up a 71–117 record.

On April 15, 1909, opening day of the season, Red Ames of the New York Giants brought a no-hitter into the 10th inning before giving up a single to the Superbas and then being touched for six more hits in a 13-inning, 3–0 loss. Ames had a 17-year major league career and won 183 games.[13]

Almost certainly the way baseball is played in the 2000s, as soon as McIntyre and Ames surrendered their first hits of their games, they would have been removed by managers fretting over pitch counts—if they had been allowed to stay in that long in the first place.

Exactly three years prior to Haddix's game—to the day—on May 26, 1956, Johnny Klippstein, then of the Reds, pitched a no-hitter against the Braves through seven innings, but was removed from the game and replaced by Herschel Freeman for one inning. Freeman preserved the no-hitter, and in turn was replaced by Joe Black. The game continued into extra innings. Black gave up the first Milwaukee hit in the 10th and then lost the game, 3–0, in the 11th inning.[14]

20. Eleventh Inning

One pitcher who kept his opponents hitless longer than Haddix was Johnny Vander Meer, also pitching for Cincinnati in 1938 when he completed consecutive, no-hit, nine-inning games, the only time the feat was accomplished in baseball history. On June 11, Vander Meer blanked the Boston Braves, 3–0. Four days later, on June 15, Vander Meer shut out the Dodgers, 6–0. No-hitter followed by no-hitter, but in neither case, nor in any of the other long no-hitters' cases, were they perfect games.[15]

In an interview many years after his special game, Haddix was told that Vander Meer said there had only been a couple of close calls in each game, one a line drive that the pitcher knocked down. "You never know what can happen," Haddix said of the flukes and bounces of the game. "You never know what can happen."[16]

After 11 innings of pitching the finest baseball the world had ever seen, Haddix had no idea what was going to happen. He didn't know how long he could keep up posting those zeroes on the scoreboard. He didn't know if manager Danny Murtaugh might yet pull him out even though he had thrown just 90 pitches. He didn't know if the Pirates would mount a big rally in the 12th. And he didn't know if he would make a mistake and allow a big hit to a Braves slugger.

Haddix never displayed any sign of nerves during the game, except sticking to the routine of lighting up a cigarette periodically. At the time he smoked three packs a day, so inhaling puffs between innings for 13 innings really wasn't out of the ordinary for him.[17]

One thing Haddix discovered about being perfect during the course of the game was that he never had to bother pitching from a stretch because there was never anybody on base who could steal on him.

The predicted rain never proved bothersome during the game, never graduating beyond the drizzle stage. The Braves fans who sat out the evening at home because of dire weather forecasts likely second-guessed themselves the next day. In Pittsburgh, where all communications during the event were electronic and brought to fans by a candid Bob Prince, word spread that Haddix had a no-hitter going for him.

Entering the ninth inning, Haddix's mother telephoned his wife, Marcia, to inform her that her husband was on the cusp of throwing a no-hitter. Marcia Haddix was at home in Springfield, Ohio, however, located more than 200 miles from Pittsburgh. The Haddixes' permanent home was not within the normal orbit of KDKA's broadcasts and mostly she picked up fuzz.

Reception, she learned, through the less crowded air waves of the night sky, was better outside on the car radio. So Marcia Haddix spent the rest of the game sitting in the family auto listening to her husband make history.[18]

21

Twelfth Inning

When Harvey Haddix struck out Lew Burdette to end the ninth inning, broadcaster Bob Prince erupted with enthusiastic gushing about the pitcher's accomplishment. By pitching perfectly through the end of baseball's standard distance, Haddix had joined rarefied company.

The listeners in the Pittsburgh area were glued to their radios, wondering if Haddix could pull off the no-hitter, and when he did so, Prince led the cheers. It was a notable moment, even if it was not a complete game, and Prince effusively described the conclusion of the Braves ninth, simultaneously talking to his audience and his broadcast partner Jim Woods.

"Anything that Jim and I have witnessed in this season absolutely at this moment pales into insignificance and we have had some thumpers," Prince said on his KDKA broadcast. "Here's the windup and the 1–2 pitch to Burdette. Fouled off to the left out of play. And Burdette has shortened up the grip on that bat and really is trying to hang in there. And don't forget he is quite a threat with the long ball. Two men down. Last half of the ninth inning. No score. I can't repeat it enough.

"The 1–2 pitch. He struck him out swinging! Haddix pitches a perfect, nine-inning, no-run game." At that point Prince was shouting into his microphone a little bit hoarsely, but loudly enough to pop the buttons on one of his plaid sport coats. "A standing ovation." Prince went silent and let the sounds of County Stadium fans' applause and cheers for Haddix carry across the airwaves. "Ladies and gentlemen, Harvey Haddix has just become the seventh pitcher in the history of all baseball to pitch a perfect, no-hit, no-run, nine-inning ballgame.

The final out was a strikeout on Lew Burdette. It was the eighth turned in by Haddix and at that moment he became the seventh pitcher in all of baseball to pitch a perfect, no-hit, no-run game."[1]

Fans dotted around the Pittsburgh area who might have been doing some paperwork, late-night cooking, ironing, or other chores with a divided attention span had been won over by Prince by then, hanging on each Braves batter's result. The main reason Bill Kennedy, Sr., the Bell engineer, was listening that evening, besides his devotion to the Pirates, was that he had the evening off from night school. The game otherwise would have conflicted with classes and he would have missed the whole thing.

The only problem with Prince's narrative was that the game wasn't over. Yes, Haddix had done something rare and unusual by setting down all 27 Braves hitters he faced, but because the score was 0–0, the teams weren't going anywhere. Haddix had recorded a nine-inning perfect game, but he wasn't finished. He hadn't recorded a complete game because the game was incomplete. Just like any other scoreless game even at the end of nine innings of regulation play, this game was going into extra innings.

Years later, well into the future, in a ruling that outraged survivors, the fact that the game was not over, that Haddix's perfection was still in motion, so to speak, after nine innings, would prove very significant. Neither Haddix nor any other Pirate player could look into the future and they were rather preoccupied with the present, still trying to eke out a run and the victory.

Although Prince's declarations had the sound of finality, they were in fact being applied to a work in progress. Of course, Haddix kept progressing, setting down the Braves in the 10th and 11th innings with ease.

The leadoff man for Pittsburgh in the 12th inning was first baseman Rocky Nelson. Nelson studied Burdette and was served up the same old stuff; whether it was a fastball or a spitter, no one would ever prove. Nelson laid the wood on the ball and sent it soaring to center field, but the chance was no strain for Andy Pafko and one out went up on the scoreboard.

Left-fielder Bob Skinner, who never saw any sign that his road roommate was ill once he began pitching, stepped into the box thinking of one thing—get on base and somehow circle the bases for a run. He had the commitment, but not the wisdom to beat Burdette on this at-bat. Skinner crushed a pitch down the first-base line but it died in Joe Adcock's glove. Two outs for the Pirates.

It was second baseman Bill Mazeroski's turn to hit. At the end of the 1960 season, about a year and a half in the future, Mazeroski came to the plate in an even more dramatic situation. At stake was not winning a perfect game for a teammate, but winning the World Series for his team. In

21. Twelfth Inning

the bottom of the ninth inning of the seventh game, Mazeroski teed off on a Ralph Terry pitch and smacked a home run into the left-field stands at Forbes Field as a disconsolate Yogi Berra watched the ball soar over his head. Mazeroski's blast became one of the most famous hits in baseball history. As he ran around the bases, he triggered a massive, city-wide celebration that was in full flower before he reached home plate. The play remains one of the most dramatic in all World Series play and one of the most revered sporting moments in Pittsburgh sports history, if not the most revered. The home run made Mazeroski a hero for life in Pittsburgh.

His plate appearance in the top of the 12th inning in County Stadium against the Braves could not match it, but Mazeroski shook things up with a single to center field. Was Burdette weakening? Could the Pirates reach him for a blasted run? Of course, they had been down this road before, all night long, in fact. Burdette might spring a little leak, but he always recovered to put his finger in the dike.

Third baseman Don Hoak came up. Hoak had had a fairly quiet night, both at bat and in the field. He was never really quiet in the sense of being silent, however. Hoak was his usual self, urging his teammates to pick up their game, get some runs, finish off those darned Braves. He knew they could do it, he said. That was Hoak's way, always talking, always pumping up the rest of the lineup. Baseball was no tennis match where officials would run around going "Shush!" all the time. Talk it up, seemed to be Hoak's perpetual attitude. It was almost as if he believed the more a player talked about hitting, the better he would be able to hit.

"It's encouraging to know that Hoak's behind me," pitcher Bob Friend said of the player's presence in the lineup. "In a spot, he may come up to me and say, 'You can get this guy out with a fastball low and away.' I may have the same idea myself, but Don telling it to me makes it that much more certain."[2]

No one anointed him, but Hoak took charge when he thought it was necessary. Dick Stuart got on his teammates' nerves with lackadaisical fielding play and Hoak told him off, bluntly saying, "You're not hustling. If you can't give us 90 feet, why don't you go back to bed?'" Hoak always understood that you had to play the game hard and give it your all. He also understood the team dynamic, that someone had to be willing to speak out in various circumstances, sometimes making unpopular comments. Dick Groat said. "The way he gets on the rest of us should peel the skin

Hard-Luck Harvey Haddix and the Greatest Game Ever Lost

Pirates second baseman Bill Mazeroski, later elected to the Hall of Fame, was the anchor of Pittsburgh's infield for 17 years and retired as the holder of numerous fielding records.

off our backs. But when you're trying to win a pennant, you need someone whose tongue can lash you like a whip. For us, Hoak is the one."[3]

Only a couple of hours earlier, in the clubhouse, Hoak had teased Haddix by saying if he pitched to the Braves' hitters according to the game plan he would throw a no-hitter—and there they were. What Hoak wanted to do more than anything with that time at-bat was lash another hit to send Mazeroski to second or beyond, but it was no dice. Hoak hit a ground ball to Johnny Logan at short and Logan flipped the ball to Felix Mantilla covering second for the force out on Mazeroski.

On to the bottom of the 12th inning. How long could Harvey Haddix keep up his perfection? The Braves' batting order had not been disrupted. One, two, three, side out, over and over again 11 times, for 33 straight outs. Although the number of innings being played was reaching into the category of extraordinary, Haddix's perfect control meant he had not required very many pitches.

21. Twelfth Inning

The low-and-outside first pitch to Milwaukee center fielder Andy Pafko was Haddix's 91st of the game. Haddix was so sharp that when he followed up with another ball, also low and outside, there was a low murmur in the Braves dugout. There was no reason to think the Braves couldn't pull out a win.

"Everyone went oh-for-four that day," Pafko said years later with a laugh, "and that was the best group I ever played with." Yet for all his success as a solid hitter, Pafko admitted that was one day he felt helpless as a batter.[4] Sure enough, the 2–0 count batter advantage proved to be an illusion. Pafko took a swing and missed on the next pitch, then fouled the fourth Haddix toss into the left-field bleachers. It was 2–2. Pafko swung again and trickled a grounder to the mound. Haddix fielded it and threw to Rocky Nelson for the easy out.

Johnny Logan came to the plate with one out in the 12th for the Braves. Logan was a player who liked to get the games over and then cool off with a cool one. He drank beer in the clubhouse to celebrate wins and drank beer in taverns around town in Milwaukee, which he made his permanent home, after he got out of the sport and moved into broadcasting.

Much like Don Hoak, Logan had a pugnacious attitude and he brought that attitude to the batter's box, an outlook that said to the pitcher he would have to work to get him out. Once, Logan had a fight with a teammate, Vern Bickford, outside a restaurant, and the two were pals again before manager Charlie Grimm even found out about the altercation. Bickford ended up with a lump over one eye. More publicly, Logan engaged in on-field fights with the Dodgers' Don Drysdale, after a pitch came in too close for comfort, and brawls with the Reds' Johnny Temple and Jim Greengrass. Logan seemed to be in need of a referee as often as an umpire.

If Haddix had hit Logan with a pitch the fiery shortstop would have been the first player to charge the mound, and he would have expected his teammates to back him up. In the 1990s, Logan disdained the way modern players had drifted away from the hard knocks of the sport. Pitchers waited for manager's instructions to throw inside, he said, and some players wouldn't help out a fighting teammate because they felt it wasn't "their" fight, he said. "Back in those days, we had pride," Logan said of the 1950s and 1960s.[5]

Those are the type of incidents Major League baseball was determined to eradicate as the years passed. A fight on the field was bound to get a player fined or suspended. As Logan aged, he seemed to mellow some. Milwaukee fans got to know a different side of him as a banquet speaker and Brewers broadcaster. For Milwaukee, he became a Harry Caray–type of figure, with fractured English streaming from his mouth. After being presented with an award, Logan once said, "I will perish this trophy forever." He once told the wife of Braves owner Lou Perini, "You have a very homely yacht." He also ordered dessert once by directing the waiter, "I'll have pie a la mode with ice cream."[6]

Any kind of hit off of Haddix would have been dessert with a cherry on top by the time Logan came to the plate for the fourth time in the game. It was not a time for jokes, serious or unintended, but neither Logan nor his bat had much to say. There was a 2–1 count on Logan when he struck the ball into short center field. Bill Virdon caught it with no trouble.

Burdette was matching Haddix with zeroes in the line score, even if he couldn't quite keep as many Pirates off the bases. When he came to the plate in the bottom of the 12th Burdette was once again presented the personal opportunity to do something about Haddix's perfection. Burdette came out swinging and swung and missed for strike one. He took a ball low and outside and then a second ball low. On the next offering, Burdette took the bat off his shoulder and swung and missed. It was 2–2 in the count when Haddix served up another tempting pitch. On Haddix's 104th pitch, Burdette swung and hit a grounder to Hoak at third, who then threw him out at first.

Three more men had been crossed off of Haddix's checklist. His total of consecutive outs recorded was up to 36. After his excited ninth-inning close-out description, Pirates announcer Bob Prince kept the information coming, completely disregarding any superstition about not discussing a no-hitter. "He then went on to get them in the 10th, the 11th, and the 12th," Prince said, "retiring 36 in a row."[7]

Haddix had been perfect for 12 innings, an outing never approached in baseball history. Yet for all of that, the Braves and Pirates were still playing, the score frozen at 0–0. At the end of each half inning of Haddix pitching, the fans in County Stadium cheered his effort. They admired what he was doing, even if it involved shutting down their favorite team.

By their actions, the fans had transferred their allegiance from the

21. Twelfth Inning

Milwaukee Braves to the Pittsburgh Pirates' pitcher Harvey Haddix. In most walks of life, perfection is unattainable. Confronted with an example of perfection in the works, the fans chose to root for this singular rendezvous with destiny, putting their emotions on a higher plane than simple everyday support for their club. The Braves would play another game the next day and another one the next. For one tiny slice of time the fans could call time out from the regularly scheduled and embrace the extraordinary.

Braves fans at home also had their own version of the broadcast to listen to as Haddix progressed through the lineup, though likely with more mixed emotions than Pirate fans had. Earl Gillespie was the Milwaukee play-by-play man whose familiar voice was the link between the team and the fans cruising on the highways of Wisconsin in their cars, taking care of shopping, or simply sitting at home.

Gillespie had played minor-league baseball for the Green Bay Blue Jays in the early 1940s, but served in World War II as a firefighter instead of on the diamond in the mid–1940s. He decided on a career change to sports broadcasting during the war because his re-creation of overseas football games proved so entertaining to his fellow troops. By 1953, when the Braves shifted from Boston to Milwaukee, he was the new team's main baseball broadcaster.

Much like Harry Caray and Phil Rizzuto, as well, when he was broadcasting for the New York Yankees, Gillespie made the exultant phrase "Holy Cow!" a personal trademark. Milwaukee sent Gillespie cow figurines by the box load. Selected as the Wisconsin sportscaster of the year eight times, Gillespie, who handled Green Bay Packers games, Marquette University basketball and University of Wisconsin sports after the Braves abandoned Milwaukee for Atlanta, was probably the most recognizable voice in the Dairy State. When the Braves won their only World Series in Milwaukee in 1957, it was Gillespie who informed the radio audience.

When Gillespie was installed in the Wisconsin Sports Hall of Fame, he cracked a joke. "I only hit .286 with Green Bay Blue Jays of the old Wisconsin State League, so I know it wasn't for that reason," Gillespie said. Johnny Logan summed up Gillespie's career: "He was a lousy hitter, but a good talker."[8] After Gillespie's death in 2003, fellow baseball announcer Merle Harmon described Gillespie's voice as "smooth, ice cream smooth."[9]

This is how Gillespie saw the final out of the 12th inning in the Pirates game: "Haddix into the motion. 2–2 pitch. A swing, a ground ball to the third baseman's left. He [Hoak] nabs it. Here's the throw to first base. He's out and that retires the side. And Harvey Haddix now has 12 perfect innings of a brilliant, simply magnificent, pitching performance. Another standing ovation."[10]

Like so many others whose memories were less than perfect, it was impossible to know just how many of the 19,000-plus fans in County Stadium recognized that Haddix was still pitching a perfect game. They knew he was pitching a no-hitter, however. The one big zero on the scoreboard on the Braves' line score told them that any time they wished to glance at it.

Periodically, Haddix did. He looked at the other zeroes on the scoreboard, too, the ones that went straight across in a line and added up to the game score—still zero for the Pirates and still zero for the Braves. They made for interesting reading for the man on the mound, especially since he admitted later that after he made it through the ninth inning for a regulation no-hitter, the 10th, 11th and 12th blurred in his mind.

"I knew that I had a no-hitter, but I was never a stat man," Haddix said. "I never worried about stuff like that. I knew I had a no-hitter, but I didn't let it affect my pitching."[11]

22

Thirteenth Inning

Joe Christopher had a chance to be a hero, to register an unforgettable at-bat in his first time at the plate in the major leagues. He had the opportunity to strike a game-settling home run in the greatest game ever pitched when he led off the 13th inning. He had a chance to start a rally that would blow Lew Burdette off the mound and force Fred Haney to his unused bullpen. Christopher, a rookie about 24 hours removed from the minor leagues, had a chance to author some special history in what, due to circumstances, would be just about the flashiest debut at-bat in baseball history.

Only the newly minted Pittsburgh right-fielder did not. Christopher hit a grounder back to the mound and was thrown out at first by Burdette. One out.

Next up was Harvey Haddix, the man of the hour, recipient of vigorous applause from the Braves fans who admired his gumption, staying power, and remarkable one-night ability to get everyone on the planet out. Once again, Haddix had a chance to help himself with a big hit, to bash a ball over the fence, or at least work his way on base. If he was weary from the stress of being perfect all night, Haddix never showed it. Pirate manager Danny Murtaugh never made a move to use a pinch-hitter, or a move to the bullpen. It was not clear if he would have had an insurrection on his hands from Haddix, his teammates, or the fans, but Murtaugh was not warming up anyone to replace Haddix and he was not going to bring up Dick Groat or any other available player to hit in Haddix's stead.

Haddix took his own hacks against Burdette. This time he connected and lofted a fly ball to center for the Pirates' second out.

For the third time in the game, shortstop Dick Schofield, trying to inspire teammates with a follow-me approach, cracked a single. That was the 12th hit for the Pirates off Burdette, and they still couldn't fathom how the righty could be both so generous with hits and Scrooge-like with runs simultaneously. Sure enough, Schofield died on first base in the 13th when Bill Virdon hit a ground ball to second base and was retired on the easy throw by Felix Mantilla to Joe Adcock.

Hard-Luck Harvey Haddix and the Greatest Game Ever Lost

There was no indication, other than the law of averages, that the 13th inning would be any different for the Braves than the first 12 had been. Southpaw Harvey Haddix would sling the ball in and the hitters would be mostly baffled. Braves would strike out. Braves would ground out. Braves would fly out. And another inning of perfection would be in the books and it would go on like that, inning after inning until the sun came up, Haddix's arm rested limply on his left hip, or the umpires sent everyone home because the game lasted too long.

At least that was the way it looked. Haddix had retired 36 Braves in a row and nothing that had occurred in the game thus far hinted that he wouldn't be able to retire another 36 in a row, other than it had never been done before. No one had pitched 12 perfect innings in a Major League baseball game. The adage that the players knew so well from familiarity and what Braves assistant farm director Roland Hemond lived by to keep his love of the game fresh was so true that night—no matter how many times you go to watch a baseball game, there is a chance you might see something you have never seen before. The unknown, what's going to play out on the diamond stage each time the umpire yells "Play ball!" is what Hemond believes is so great about baseball.[1]

The first batter for the Braves in the bottom of the 13th inning was Felix Mantilla, who had not been in the game when it began. Haddix's 105th pitch of the night was a called strike. Mantilla got hold of the second pitch and fouled it to left. The third pitch was outside, a ball. The count was 1–2 when Mantilla hit a routine grounder to third base. Don Hoak, as he had so many thousand times before, scooped up the ball easily, and threw to Rocky Nelson at first base.

Only the throw was wide, pulling Nelson off the base. It was Hoak's mistake on the throw. In official scoring parlance, the play was recorded as "E-5." The Braves had their first base runner of the game. Haddix, through no fault of his own, but as an illustration of how difficult it was for all forces to come together neatly, was no longer perfect. However, he still had a no-hitter going, a shutout, and was still trying to win the danged ballgame.

Braves announcer Earl Gillespie called the play this way: "Nobody on base. Nobody out. Haddix delivers. A swing. A ground ball to the third baseman. He's in fast and the throw to first from Hoak is a low throw. There's the first base runner."[2]

22. Thirteenth Inning

If the game had advanced almost metronomically from the first inning, now there was a disruption in its rhythm. "He [Mantilla] hit the most routine ground ball to third base you could ever want, to Don Hoak," Haddix said later. "He had so much time that he picked up the ball, looked at the seams, and got the ball just right and threw it to first. Nelson didn't handle the ball so the spell was broken with that man [Mantilla] right there."[3]

In his retelling of the play for the radio audience in Pittsburgh, announcer Bob Prince commiserated with Hoak. "There isn't anybody right now sicker at this moment than Don Hoak," Prince said. "I guarantee you that he's crushed over this."[4]

By that point in the broadcast, stations around the country were calling KDKA asking if they could pick up a feed, and many broadcast the closing innings. The game was not televised, however. KDKA-TV had had the option of showing the Pirates from the road that night and chose instead to televise a speech by Vice President Richard Nixon.

"He [Haddix] had good stuff," said Mantilla, who watched the early innings from the dugout before entering the game. "He was not a Sandy Koufax, but he was around the plate all his life. He had good control and he kept us off balance. We knew we were in trouble around the fifth inning. We were doing nothing. Then the sixth, seventh, eighth. We could tell we were in pretty deep against him."[5] It was Mantilla's shovel that began to dig the Braves out of difficulty.

Haddix used the word "spell" in a way that made it sound as if magic had been employed and the magic had died. In a way it had, because abruptly, what had felt like a cocoon of perfection gave way to what felt more like everyday baseball. With a man on base, and it being somewhat of a fluke at that, the Braves sought to pounce quickly.

Manager Fred Haney gave slugger Eddie Mathews a rare order. The third baseman who hit 512 home runs in his career was told to bunt. On Haddix's first pitch, Mathews squared around, caught a piece of the ball and laid down a sacrifice attempt. Haddix fielded the ball and threw to Mazeroski covering first to retire Mathews. The play put Mantilla in scoring position, however.

With one out, Murtaugh devised his counter strategy. A perfect game was off the table, so he had no hesitation in telling Haddix to intentionally walk Hank Aaron. So the Braves had runners on first and second, needing one run to win. The Pirates hoped for a Joe Adcock infield grounder that would give them a shot at a double play to end the 13th inning. Adcock was most definitely the type of hitter who could end the game with one swing. A home run would be a lot to ask for, a double more attainable, but even a well-placed single would have Mantilla running full speed ahead to the plate. Pirate pitcher Vernon Law had studied Adcock and felt he knew his strengths.

"He was a first ball, fastball hitter," Law said. "I'd throw him a straight fastball, but I would take enough off from it that he would be out in front and I could get a nice little ground ball out of him. Normally he'd be looking for something straight on the first pitch and be cutting away."[6]

Haddix's first offering to Adcock was outside for ball one. "Ball one and no strikes on Joe Adcock," Gillespie intoned. "The winning run on second base in the last half of the 13th inning."[7]

Adcock, the power hitter who had once hit a major league-tying four home runs in a single game, was ready for the next Haddix pitch. Adcock coiled and swung and the ball shot into the air.

"A swing and a high fly ball going deep to right-center field," Gillespie said. "Back, back, and it's a home run for Joe Adcock. And the ballgame is over."[8]

Prince's take on the same play went this way: "There's the pitch. There's a fly ball deep to right-center. That ball may be on through and over everything. It's gone. Home run. Absolutely fantastic."[9] It was not completely clear if Prince meant the home run, the ending, the Haddix effort, or the entire night, but "absolutely fantastic" seemed a fair enough description of the proceedings.

Pirate players watching the ball leave Adcock's bat had an uh-oh moment, recognizing instantly the hit had legs. "He hit it well," Bob Friend said of Adcock's shot. "That was the best hit ball all night. He really cranked it to right center."[10]

Haddix did not think Adcock had hit a mistake pitch. He gave the big swinger praise. He had kept the first pitch out of Adcock's reach and the batter didn't bite. "The second pitch to him I got a slider a little bit up and out from the plate," Haddix said. "It wasn't a bad pitch. It wasn't a good pitch. It was just good enough to hit and I have to give him credit. He didn't try to pull the ball. He went with it and hit it over the right-center field fence as a right handed batter."[11]

22. Thirteenth Inning

Braves first baseman Joe Adcock was just one of several sluggers in the Milwaukee lineup, and he poled the home run that sent Harvey Haddix to defeat.

The Braves fans who had supported Haddix's masterpiece in the making throughout the night cheered just as lustily for the Adcock home run that ended the game with an apparent 3–0 Milwaukee victory.

However, the unusual night was not yet over. There was no debate that the Braves had won the game, but immediately there was confusion over the final score. Mantilla had followed the progress of Adcock's shot and saw it leave County Stadium. Barely. The ball landed only a couple of feet beyond the fence. Joe Christopher made a game try leaping for it, but his glove could not climb as high as the ball.

Mantilla kept running and crossed the plate with the winning run. That was not in dispute. Hank Aaron also watched the ball soar out of play, but instead of running the bases, touching second and third, he figured the game was over the moment Mantilla crossed the plate. So Aaron cut across the pitcher's mound and ran off toward the clubhouse. Adcock, who knew he had hit a home run, planned to run all of the bases.

The Braves knew one thing for sure. They had won the game. The Pirates knew one thing for sure. They had lost the game. On a night that would go down in baseball history for other reasons, neither team was fixated on the final score. When the Braves exited the field, most of them believed they had won the game 2–0, which is what the umpires were initially proclaiming. After an umpire conference, the score was adjusted to 1–0. No one polled the fans about what they thought the final score was. It was a peculiar ending to an unprecedented game. "We were just happy we won," Milwaukee catcher Del Crandall said.[12]

That was a lot to ask since Haddix had pitched the greatest game of all time. To many the Haddix performance combined with the ending made for strange baseball watching. "We knew we won, but that was the most bizarre game I've ever been through," said Mel Roach, the Braves' backup.[13]

It was a game that lasted into the 13th inning, but only lasted 2 hours and 54 minutes. Most nine-inning games in the majors in the 2000s lasted that long, and with years of perspective on the speed of the game participants and observers were amused at how quickly the night had passed. "Wow, two hours, fifty-four minutes for 12 innings," Roland Hemond remarked. "They didn't have all the commercials between innings. The marketing side of the game adds to the length."[14]

Pirate backup catcher Danny Kravitz is one of the 1950s players who

22. Thirteenth Inning

laughed at the notion of a 13-inning game being completed in less than three hours in the 2000s. Such a game, he said, would likely take much longer, even with the dearth of base runners. "The way some of these guys move around out there [so slowly on the mound], it probably would take four hours," he said.[15]

Skinner, who remains a scout for the Houston Astros, joked that it would take a modern day manager four pitchers to get to 13 innings, even if they weren't giving up hits and runs.[16] It is possible he is right about that, but pitch count often dictates the current removal of starters, and while facing 40 batters Haddix threw only 115 pitches.

Once the Pirates retreated from the dampness, from the immediacy of the excitement, from the three-hour drama they had just acted in, they were subdued in the visitors' clubhouse. The sound of water hitting tiled floor in the showers was louder than conversation as players peeled off their black and white uniforms. "It was quiet, real quiet," Bob Skinner said. "The rest of us kind of had our heads down. We lost and we didn't score any runs for a guy who pitched his heart out. The only people talking were the sports writers who had gathered around Harvey. I felt for him."[17]

Haddix had not known he was throwing a perfect game when it was happening, so he had not digested that news by the time the newsmen came around asking questions about it. He did know he had pitched a no-hitter and that it had gone on well past nine innings. He also knew that he had lost the game and that was the fact that his thoughts rested on. Haddix didn't throw any tantrums, didn't shout or moan, whine or complain. He stoically answered questions from the assembled media, calmly admitting disappointment, but in no way blaming his teammates or anyone else for the defeat.

Headline writers at the nation's newspapers were spinning the story in tight phrases for the masses that had missed seeing, hearing, or even hearing about Haddix's pitching that night. He would wake up to newspapers proclaiming the tale of the "greatest game ever pitched" in a variety of ways. A sampling of headlines read, "Haddix Earns Tag—'Hard-Luck Hurler," "Bucs' Harvey Haddix Makes Baseball History With 12 Inning No-Hitter, but Loses, 1–0," "Haddix's Perfect Game For Naught As Milwaukee Wins It In 13th Inning," and "Haddix Loses 'Greatest Game.'"

"I knew I had a no-hitter because the scoreboard is in plain view," Haddix said in a post-game interview. "But I wasn't so certain about it being a perfect game. I thought perhaps I might have walked somebody in the early innings. But going down the stretch my main idea was to win."[18]

Haddix was 33 and he looked all of his years. Haddix had a towel over his shoulder and sipped a soft drink as he answered reporters' questions. "It's just another loss, but it hurts a little more," he said. "When you go that long it's hard to remember the base runners. After the third inning, I knew I had something. My control and stuff were good. Sliders were my best pitches."[19]

Initially, there was more disbelief among other Pirates that the team had lost such a game. At first, manager Danny Murtaugh wouldn't even comment. Then he said, "It was a damn silly one to lose."[20]

With the repeat questions, Haddix went back and forth with his answers about should-haves and could-haves about pitches thrown in the 13th inning. He said a ball called on Mantilla should have been a strike and that the ball that came in high enough for Adcock to cream was intended to cross the plate lower and a bit more out of reach. "I guess I made a mistake on Adcock," he said. "I was tired. I wanted a low pitch and came in high with a slider. He really walloped it. Maybe I should have walked Adcock," he said.[21] Haddix actually smiled when he said that.

As officials huddled by telephone and telegram to sort out the final score, others compiled information about Haddix's pitching that placed the game in historical perspective. At the time, the way perfect games were measured, the Braves-Pirates contest was the eighth perfect game in Major League history (not seventh as Prince said). It was the longest group of perfect innings recorded by a pitcher, and it was the first extra-inning perfect game in National League history.

For Haddix to make history—even though in the immediate aftermath the Pirates weren't sure exactly what type of history he made—bugged his teammates. "You're always disappointed when you lose," Bob Skinner said, "but I think the disappointment after that game was such that I don't think any other game but losing a World Series game could match that. I always think of that game as being part of something special and I'm pulled in [emotionally] when I think about Harvey. That's part of it."[22]

The locker room was subdued afterwards, but for those who really thought about what Haddix had done, there was more a mix of emotions.

22. Thirteenth Inning

Yes, he had lost the game, but he had pitched so well that people would remember his game forever. "The ending, that was definitely unfortunate," Dick Schofield said. "But it was a fantastic game. Naturally, you want to win the game, but I think everybody realized what a fantastic job he had done. So I don't think you could be too sad about that."[23]

Schofield was still in the locker room when the clubhouse phone rang and the call was for Haddix. It was Lew Burdette on the other end of the line, calling from the home clubhouse. After the short conversation, Burdette told the writers in the Braves locker room what he had said. "I told him, 'I realize I got what I wanted, a win, but I'd really give it up because you pitched the greatest game that's ever been pitched in the history of baseball. It was a damned shame you had to lose.'"[24]

Burdette had taken time out from reveling in the emotion of his own hard-won game to have a serious moment with Haddix, but not long after, when he was trying to negotiate a new contract with the Braves, Burdette, true to his fun-loving, out-sized ways, exhibited more bravado. "I'm the greatest pitcher who ever lived," he told Braves administrators in the context of asking for a $10,000 raise. "The greatest game that was ever pitched in baseball wasn't good enough to beat me, so I've got to be the greatest."[25]

Although Muhammad Ali, as Cassius Clay, was a year away from bursting onto the world stage, Burdette's phrasing would have done the boxer proud. No one caught Harvey Haddix calling himself the greatest pitcher who ever lived or boasting about that night throwing the greatest game ever pitched. He didn't see it that way. "I have to give Harvey credit," Skinner said. "He took it like a man. He was upset we lost as a team. That's the kind of guy he is. He's a real pro."[26]

The clubhouse gradually emptied. Sports writers retreated to their typewriters to file their stories. Pirate players cleaned up, dressed, and headed back to the hotel. Haddix was slow to strip off his sweaty baseball uniform and to shower. When he buttoned his shirt cuffs and tied his shoes, Haddix realized he was the last Pirate left. But when he walked out of the locker room, ready to hail a cab, there was Don Hoak waiting for him to share it.

Hoak had made the error that allowed Mantilla to take first base, ending the perfect game and igniting the Braves' brief rally to win the game. As the taxi rolled through the night to the Schroeder Hotel, Hoak said to Haddix, "I've booted 'em before, and I'll boot 'em again. But I'll also make some good plays for you, Harve." "That was it," Haddix said. "No apologies and I didn't want any."[27]

Haddix was ready for a rest, to take time to think, but it wasn't that late and when he got back to his room he was restless. The phone kept ringing, from all over the country. People wanted to know how he had done it, wanted to hear his words and feelings about throwing the greatest game ever pitched. Everyone wanted to relive the last moments of the 13th inning. Tell us all about it, Harvey, they said. Are you mad at Hoak? No. Are you mad you lost the game? Yes. How ironic is it that Felix Mantilla, a player who didn't even start the game, scored the winning run? Do you wish you had that pitch to Joe Adcock back? Of course.

Haddix had not even sorted out his own feelings yet and he was being asked to divulge them over and over again. Haddix was no novice, no rookie player, but the attention was still all a bit overwhelming. In 1959, there were fewer reporters from newspapers covering games, especially away games. There were fewer radio stations covering games and sports talk radio wasn't even a glimmer in program directors' minds. The game hadn't even been televised. So the focus, the attention, was a fraction of what it would be in the 2000s, but it was still plenty for Haddix, the Ohio farmer at heart who liked the peace and quiet of large acreage more than the horns blasting and sirens howling in a big city.

Everyone kept telling Haddix he had done something great, but he didn't really feel that he had. He couldn't separate the uniqueness of throwing 12 perfect innings from ending up with a loss on his pitching record.

Nobody seemed to be aware of the time as the clock crept past midnight, on towards 2 A.M., and nobody seemed to care. There was no way that Haddix could go to sleep with the incessant phone ringing and his adrenaline still flowing. After an hour or more of the racket and the questions, Haddix went for a walk with some teammates.

The heavy rain threat had evaporated and if it was cool and damp at all, they hardly noticed it. The dead hours of the morning were as dead in Milwaukee as would be expected, pedestrians invisible and just about all cars parked for the night. There was no commercial traffic. There was just Haddix and a couple of guys walking the night until the sun was about to rise. They came to a 24-hour eatery, a greasy spoon, the type of

22. Thirteenth Inning

place that catered to the people of the night who could not tell time and didn't care what it said anyway.

Haddix said it was about 6 A.M. when the restaurant was discovered and he felt it was time to give his feet a rest. Right away, from the next table, he overheard the conversation. The patrons were talking about the Braves-Pirates game, how the Braves had pulled it out and how that Harvey Haddix guy had pitched a whale of a game. It was the first time after May 26, 1959, that Haddix listened to others commenting on his pitching that night, but after that it seemed to never stop. There were 19,000 or so fans in attendance at County Stadium for the game, but in his lifetime, Haddix bet that he must have had 100,000 people tell him they were there that night, or even more recklessly say they saw a game on television that wasn't televised.[28]

Bob Friend was eating bacon and eggs with Haddix and he said the magnitude of his game had not truly penetrated Haddix's consciousness. "It hadn't sunken in yet with Harvey," Friend said. "He was just kind of down because we lost the game."[29] The morning papers were soon to hammer home the message that Harvey Haddix had pitched the greatest game of all time, but before he read the big type, he was more preoccupied by defeat.

23

Aftermath

As Bill Kennedy sat by the radio in his home, mesmerized by Harvey Haddix's pitching, Bob Prince's voice, and completely forgetting about any other paperwork he had hoped to finish that night, he was never more involved in rooting for a Pirates victory. "I was a big Pirates fan that night," he said. "I just thought this was the most wonderful thing that had ever happened. Here we were in the 12th inning and he hadn't given up a hit yet."[1]

Upstairs in his bedroom, a younger Bill Kennedy, just shy of eight years old, and the family's only son, was supposed to be asleep. He was in bed, with the door closed, but unlocked, the blankets pulled up over his head. Instead of going to sleep, as was his habit Bill was reading under the covers by flashlight.

Somewhere along the way that evening, as his father listened to a compelling story on the radio, young Bill's flashlight batteries flickered out. Still unwilling to call it a night and give up on the compelling story he was reading, he grabbed the lamp on his night table, and with its 60-watt bulb burning brightly, shoved that under the covers instead of the flashlight. That way he could continue to read and a parent passing by the door would not be alerted by the light.

At an unknown time during the evening, the younger Kennedy passed out in the middle of a page, falling asleep with the lamp light still on. When the Pirates game ended, Haddix losing in spectacularly stunning and odd fashion, Bill the elder decided to share the story of the game with his son and walked up the stairs to the second floor. A little bit gloomy because of the result, he planned to talk about what he termed "how awful things became."[2]

Bill Kennedy opened the door and saw smoke coming from his son's bed. Rather quickly, a man who had been immersed in Haddix's game for hours had his attention diverted. The light bulb was on the verge of igniting a fire and was smoldering under the covers. Father rushed to his son's bedside, woke him up with a shout, yanked him from the bed and trickily

23. Aftermath

hauled up and maneuvered the smoking mattress out the window and watched it thump to the ground in the back yard.

Neither Kennedy was injured in the incident (though the older Kennedy wonders what would have happened if he hadn't arrived on the scene when he did), nor did the mattress burst into flames and damage the grass as they viewed it from above. The time was approaching midnight so everyone went to bed on father's instructions and nobody even bothered to telephone the fire department. It was no harm, no foul, except for the mattress' suffering. After the threat of conflagration, the younger Kennedy was more careful about his late-night reading.[3]

"Fortunately, it just charred a little bit of the bed," the older Kennedy said. "I didn't see any open flame."[4] Bill Kennedy has always associated the night he listened to Haddix's try for a perfect game with the night he rescued his son from death by mattress fire.

The nation's sporting press put Harvey Haddix in the limelight the next day. In newspapers, on television, he was the story of the day. Most writers couldn't get over the fact that Haddix had been great for so long, but lost the game.

"You never complain, Harvey Haddix. You're an Ohio dirt farmer," wrote Sandy Grady, one poet of the sports pages. "You've never questioned the seasons, the soil, the weather. You forget bad luck, the way a gambler forgets bad dice." When he gave up the winning hit to Joe Adcock in the 13th inning, Haddix's mood struck Grady as benign, or resigned. "'I was tired and I made a bad pitch,' you said so typically. 'It's just another loss.'"[5]

Of course, it was not just another loss. If Haddix was playing the stoic, the good teammate, or his pulse rate was genuinely that far below normal was not easy to read. Grady, who had met Haddix before, felt it was the real Haddix on display, calm, accepting of the reality rather than raging against it. "You have the instincts of a club fighter," Grady wrote. "You've never been a thoughtful man. You'd rather talk about bass fishing, or rabbit hunting, or your kid, or the 430-acre farm your dad has at South Vienna, Ohio."[6]

The analysis was widespread and the questions that poured in for Haddix revolved more around the notion of "How do you feel?" After a while it became clear how Haddix felt—he didn't want to be bothered talking about the game any longer the next day after his sleepless night. One sports writer showed up at Haddix's hotel room door and was greeted by a "Do Not Disturb" sign hanging on the door knob.[7]

Other reporters ferreted out Marcia Haddix, who reported the story of being alerted by telephone about the game her husband was pitching and her efforts to listen in her car in Springfield, Ohio. "We can't get KDKA very plain down here," she said, "so we generally don't bother listening to the games." When she found the right spot to capture the radio waves in extra innings, Marcia Haddix said, "Miraculously, the last part of the game came in perfectly."[8] Perfectly. That was the word she used.

Without even knowing for sure that her husband's hotel phone was swamped by callers with questions or congratulations and that she would likely have been greeted by a busy signal, Marcia Haddix said she skipped trying to telephone him late after the game. She still hadn't heard from Harvey Haddix by 11 A.M. the next day, but also postulated correctly on his whereabouts. "I guess he's still sleeping," she said.[9]

Some of the sports writers had asked Haddix if he called his wife right after the game and he told them no, he hadn't, because he didn't want to wake her up. That was dutifully reported in Milwaukee papers. "He wouldn't have wakened me. We didn't get to sleep all night," she said. With a distinct sense of baseball historical perspective, Marcia Haddix said when she was listening she was focused more on how long her husband could pitch without surrendering a hit than whether or not he would get a win or a loss. She knew that someone, some time, would have to get a base hit.[10] "It didn't really matter (if he won or lost)," she said. "We just kept waiting for that first hit. Wondering when it would come and who it would be. Harvey pitched well. As long as he pitched well, we were all satisfied down here."[11]

The who was Joe Adcock. He was neither the biggest name in the Braves lineup, nor the weakest hitter by a long shot. It was a regular habit of opposing teams to walk Hank Aaron intentionally with the theory that anyone who was up next was going to be less of a threat. But Adcock often made those hopeful strategists pay. "I just knew they were going to walk Aaron in that situation," Adcock said. "It was nothing new to me. I made my living hitting behind (Eddie) Mathews and Aaron. I had worlds of opportunity to break up games."[12]

Years later in an interview, Haddix admitted he was starting to tire. "I had managed to fan him three times during this game," Haddix said. "He was out for the kill."[13]

23. Aftermath

Adcock was a hitter that a pitcher had to watch out for every time through the order, and when he got his fifth at-bat against Haddix he was ready. "He knew what he had in mind when he let the ball loose," Adcock said. "The wind had been blowing in all night and maybe it was a freak because when I came to bat the flag in center field was still. I was thinking he'd been keeping the ball away from me all night and maybe he'd do it again and he did and I hit it."[14]

Adcock hit the ball far enough to end the game, but while no one questioned the legitimacy of his home run, the brouhaha over the rest of the Braves' on-field shenanigans continued into the next day. It was all because of Hank Aaron's base running. Adcock's home run was clean, and Felix Mantilla's jog across the plate after touching third base gave the Braves the only run they needed. But Aaron's failure to touch third and his running off the field while Adcock circled the bases mixed up everything.

After the cockamamie play, Frank Dascoli, chief of the four-man umpiring team handling the game, ruled that the final score was 2–0. It was apparent that Adcock's hit cleared the wall for what should have been a three-run homer. Mantilla ran to third, touched the base with his foot, and stepped on home plate. Aaron, however, left the base paths, believing the game was over when Mantilla scored. When Adcock crossed second and made his way to third, Dascoli said, that meant he was out for passing Aaron. Told he had made a mistake, Aaron ran back to second base to get back behind Adcock, and resumed circling the bases, touching third and home.

"Mantilla's run counted," Dascoli said. "Adcock was automatically out for passing a runner on the bases. But since Aaron had not left the base paths to avoid being tagged, he could go back to third, then score, and his run counted. That makes it 2–0."[15]

Aaron refused to address the media on the topic after the game, but the score made less difference to either team than the decision. Braves teammates did rib Aaron about the gaffe, however. "For the kind of money they pay you, Henry," an unnamed teammate said, "you ought to be able to run 360 feet around the bases on a cool evening."[16] For serious Hank Aaron fans who might consider him to be the example of the perfect ballplayer, this was evidence that at least once during his long career he made a mistake.

Hard-Luck Harvey Haddix and the Greatest Game Ever Lost

After National League President Warren Giles reviewed the weird game-ending circumstances the next day, the final score was declared to be 1–0, instead of either 3–0, which it should have been if everyone ran the bases, or 2–0, which had been mentioned.

"The play is specifically covered in the league's handbook of instructions to umpires," Giles said. "If the bases are full and a man hits a ball out of the park, but passes a runner on the bases, he is automatically out. If the game is in the last half of the ninth inning, or the last half of an extra inning, only the runs necessary to win are counted. I think it all boils down to simple reasoning. Since the hitter cannot be credited with a home run, it is unreasonable to treat the base runner or runners as though he had hit a home run."[17]

It was only by coincidence that the umpires had that instruction to call upon, however. The information was given to the arbiters following an incident in spring training that was similar to the ending of the Haddix game. Cincinnati Reds outfielder Vada Pinson passed a runner after hitting a home run in the bottom of the ninth of an exhibition game. "It was then that we discovered there was no provision in the playing rules for such a situation," Giles said.[18]

Adcock's home run was changed, as well, and officially ruled a double. So to top off everything unusual about a perfect game that ended with a loss, and a no-hitter that extended for 12 innings, was a game that had the final score changed a day later when a home run was wiped out of the books and recalibrated as a double. Officially, Haddix retired 36 straight men, 12 full innings' worth of batters, and gave up one hit and one unearned run.

"Joe was mad because they took away his home run," Braves catcher Del Crandall said with a laugh.[19] Adcock had run around the bases with his head down and at first wasn't really aware of the controversy. Only in the clubhouse, when the team had cleared the field, did he realize he was going to be credited with a double. "Hank came over to me in the locker room later to tell me he was sorry he cost me a homer," Adcock said.[20]

Although Haddix maintained his refrain that the most disappointing aspect of the night was that the Pirates lost the game, others sensed more keenly he had done something truly remarkable in pitching 12 innings of perfect ball. Pittsburgh Mayor Thomas J. Gallagher sent Haddix a telegram the next day to let him know that. "On behalf of all the

23. Aftermath

Pirate fans and every citizen of Pittsburgh," the telegram read, "may I extend congratulations on your spectacular pitching performance against the Milwaukee Braves. Your skill and personal courage, although exerted in a heartbreaking losing effort, is an inspiration to all of us who dearly love our national game. You have scaled the heights of immortality in your chosen profession, a goal few men rarely attain. All of us in Pittsburgh are thrilled and proud to share in your hour and glory, the luster of which no loss will ever tarnish."[21]

When Haddix spoke after the game and said he was not quite sure he had had a perfect game going in the first place, he most certainly did not understand the nuances of what it meant to pitch a perfect game that went on for longer than nine innings. He had to be informed of the uniqueness of his achievement and took a day or so to come to grips with the words "never before."

One writer informed Haddix that no pitcher in Major League history had ever retired more than the 27 straight he had reached in the ninth inning, never mind 36. "You're kidding," Haddix replied. "You mean nobody? Not even guys like Cy Young and Walter Johnson and Christy Mathewson, or any of those old fellows? Well, what do you know about that?"[22] Haddix was also unaware that the last regular-season perfect game in baseball history dated to 1922. "Gee," he said, "it took me three years after that to be born."[23]

Almost lost in the hubbub of the phenomenal game and Haddix's soulful walk around the city was how exhausted and ill he was before he took the mound. He admitted his throat still hurt when the game began and that he still even felt a little bit queasy. "I sucked on throat lozenges the whole game," Haddix said. "I was sick to my stomach. If I wasn't scheduled to pitch, I never would have gotten out of bed that day."[24]

The quest for the no-hitter and the perfect game had kept the Pirates pretty quiet in the dugout during the game and the loss kept them pretty quiet immediately after the game. Only later, in short conversations among themselves, and with Haddix, did the players talk more freely about the night. Typically, they shook their heads in disbelief that such a showpiece of a game did not end up in the Pittsburgh win column.

"Disappointment" was the primary emotion, Dick Groat said. "Of course we did talk about it later. We had 12 hits and that's a lot for a shutout. We just couldn't get a big base hit when we needed it. You can't believe you lost a game like that, but it happens in the game of baseball. The ending was bizarre, but there wasn't any doubt when Adcock hit the ball it was going to go out. It was hard to take. Very much so. We were all so disappointed for Harvey, more so than for the team because he had put on, in my opinion, the greatest pitching performance of all time."[25]

Some fans had more extreme reactions. Gene P. "Two-Finger" Carney, who became a baseball book author later in life, wrote about being moved when "God Bless America" was being sung in a Mexican restaurant. "I'm a fairly stoical person, although I cried when Harvey Haddix lost his perfect game in 1959."[26]

Warren Spahn, who won 363 games and is the winningest left-handed pitcher of all time, was a witness in the Braves dugout and said what stood out was how "The Kitten" made things look so routine. "I was embarrassed for all left-handed pitchers because he made it look so damn easy," Spahn said. "I don't think he had to throw a whole lot of pitches that night. He threw strikes and we kept popping up and beating it into the ground. It was like, when is this going to end? ... Our ballclub felt very, very lucky that we came out on top."[27]

Don Larsen's perfect game for the New York Yankees against Brooklyn in the 1956 World Series is the only post-season perfecto, but a much earlier perfect game had a kinship with Haddix's, primarily because it was a round peg being stuffed into a square hole.

Babe Ruth, to that point in his career more stalwart pitcher than power hitter, was the starter for the Boston Red Sox on June 23, 1917, in the first game of a doubleheader at Fenway Park between Boston and the Washington Senators. In the top of the first inning, the southpaw walked Washington leadoff man Ray Morgan. Ruth was infuriated by the call of ball four and argued long and loud with umpire Brick Owens. Ultimately, Owens banished Ruth from the game. Ruth's behavior was so egregious he was fined $100 and suspended for 10 games.

Boston needed a hurry-up reliever and called upon Ernie Shore. After Shore's quick warm-up, Morgan made a dash for second on an attempted steal and was thrown out. Shore proceeded to retire the next 26 Senators without giving up a hit. There was considerable debate about how to classify the game, but it was eventually termed a perfect game because Washington sent just the minimum of 27 hitters to the plate. At the time of

23. Aftermath

Haddix's unusual perfect game, Shore's effort was considered the most unusual perfect game.

Haddix's magnificence aside, it is far from an everyday occurrence in major league baseball for the final score of a game to change overnight. "No, you don't see that," Pirate pitcher Vernon Law said.[28] Law said that Haddix generally seemed unaffected by the brilliant showing and quirky ending and just went back to work pitching every fourth day in the rotation.

"I pitched a game that went 18 innings," Law said, "and I got as much publicity from not winning it as I would have from winning it. Same with Harvey. He probably got as much publicity for not winning as he would have for winning. Either way, what the heck, it's another game. You either win or lose. You just accept that. He was not mad. He could kid and joke around with the best of them and he did. He joked about it, as we all do. It was a situation where he just accepted it and the next game he went out to win that one, too."[29]

The day after Haddix's gem, the Pirates and the Braves met again. Milwaukee won, 4–3, defeating Law with the venerable Spahn. The three-game series wrapped up a day later when Bob Friend blanked the Braves on four hits for the 3–0 win.

Haddix's next start for the Pirates occurred on June 2, 1959, against the St. Louis Cardinals. It was another fine day for the southpaw. He pitched another complete game, this time going nine innings, and shut the Cards out on eight hits as the Pirates won 3–0. Haddix's season record after that was 5–3.

Haddix was definitely made aware that his no-hitter, perfect game, the heartbreaking loss, touched people. Commissioner Ford Frick wrote to Haddix. So did Giles, the National League chief executive. Broadcaster Harry Caray, then with the Cardinals, wrote Haddix a note, too. It was a strange experience to be offered so much hearty congratulations for a game that he lost. Haddix had difficulty getting beyond that fact. Wasn't winning the object of the game?

There was a certain emptiness that came with being praised so vociferously for not winning. Haddix could understand it to some degree because no-hitters were prized moments for pitchers, and pitching a perfect game was beyond the dream of most major league hurlers. Yet any time Haddix had ever seen a photograph of a pitcher who had thrown a no-hitter the guy was smiling. That's because the pitcher had won the game. Haddix's result was more of a good-news, bad-news deal, like the joke.

In the midst of all the praise that cascaded down on Haddix with letters, postcards and telegrams came a telegram of a quite different sort from some college students in Texas, at a school Haddix couldn't remember when he later told the story. "All it said was, 'Dear Harvey, Tough shit,'" Haddix said.[30]

Rather than be offended by the discordant message, Haddix thought it over and decided that maybe the unidentified college kids had it right, that they were more clear-eyed assessing the situation than anyone else.

"It was short and sweet, but it summed up everything pretty well," Haddix said. "And I told my wife Marcia, 'You know what? That's exactly what it was.'"[31]

It is not likely that the college guys meant the note as a compliment, but the brutal honesty of their comment appealed to Haddix. He said if they had included their names and addresses he would have sent them an autographed baseball or some other type of acknowledgment. When Haddix showed the telegram to Bob Prince, he guffawed and had it mounted and framed.[32]

What Haddix learned from the Texas telegram, he said, was that win or lose, perfect game or not, life was going to go on. "Losing that game in 13 innings actually may have given me more notoriety in the long run than if I had won in nine," he said.[33]

If Haddix had "only" pitched a nine-inning perfect game, then it is certain the next day's headlines would not have read, "Greatest Game Ever Pitched." But the effort still would have been on the short list.

24

The 1959 Season

The almost-perfect game lingered in the atmosphere around the Pirates for some time because newcomers to the scene who were not eyewitnesses wanted to hear what Harvey Haddix thought about it all.

Teammates who hadn't uttered a peep in the dugout while Haddix was throwing wanted to exhale with their own observations. Yet the way baseball works there is little time for reflection or rehashing. Pittsburgh and Milwaukee wrapped up their series and then went right on to another series without break. Major league baseball is an everyday sport. There are no weeklong gaps as there are in pro football, where a team can wash the results out of its hair gradually.

The Pirates played on and Haddix took his turn in the rotation, but Haddix's Braves game performance was still a topic for discussion. "Haddix just roamed the streets all night," said reliever Roy Face, telling the tale of how difficult it was for the pitcher to go right to sleep on the night when he fell to the Braves in the 13th inning. The Pirates talked among themselves, Face said, about "what a great game it was. I thought I had seen the greatest game ever pitched."[1]

Sports radio personalities wanted to talk to Haddix. Visiting newspapermen wanted to hear Haddix's thoughts. He received various honors, plaques and certificates all to commemorate this so-called greatest game, the one he couldn't get over losing, the one that no one could get over him losing.

There was no video evidence of Haddix's showing since it was not televised. There were no highlights shared by ESPN, which wasn't even a thought in creative sports broadcasters' brains at the time. So everyone who stopped by went to the source. What was it like? They kept asking. "There was nothing close to being a hit," Haddix said. "They hit some balls hard, but they were right at guys. There were no running, diving catches, or anything like that."[2]

The downpour that was expected never arrived. The air was damp and the field was wet from earlier rain, but when Haddix described the scene as featuring a mix of thunder and lightning in the distance and calling the night weird,[3] it almost sounded as if sorcery was involved. In the future, a film would be made out of Bernard Malamud's novel *The Natural* and critics called the style "magic realism." Haddix almost made it sound as if he was a character in such a production.

Someone thought to snap a photograph of Haddix and his catcher, Smokey Burgess, glancing at the front of a newspaper called *The Sun-Telegraph* the morning after his effort. The headline, in declaration-of-war-sized type, read "HADDIX HURLS GREATEST GAME OF ALL TIME." A picture was posed of Haddix and Joe Adcock smiling at one another and shaking hands. It would have been more realistic if Adcock only was smiling, though Haddix never expressed any anger towards the hitter.

If anyone listened to Haddix's wife, they would likely conclude that Haddix's was a phony, if obliging smile for a photographer when he grasped Adcock's hand. He was happy to set down 36 hitters in order, but he was not happy about losing the game. "He felt that game was a loss for his team and he didn't play to lose," Marcia Haddix said.[4]

Don Hoak's throwing error was the official play that ended Haddix's perfect game, but Lew Burdette, the opposing pitcher, wondered if the miscue shouldn't have been charged to first baseman Rocky Nelson. "They gave Hoak the error," Burdette said, "but Rocky could have stretched and caught the ball."[5]

No one connected to the Pirates, least of all Haddix, ever criticized Nelson. The attribution on the play had not mattered in the long run. The Braves still would have had their base runner and still would have had their run regardless of which infielder was charged with the error.

The bizarre ending to the game did provoke deep thought among sports writers who traveled the path of what-if. A New York sports writer began a column this way: "Supposing the Pirates had lifted Harvey Haddix for a pinch hitter after 12 innings of perfect ball, then rallied for a winning margin (in the 13th), and the reliever had proceeded to hold the Braves in check, who would have been the winning pitcher?"[6]

In 1959, relief pitchers assigned to close out games were still a novelty; the word "closer" was not in baseball's vocabulary. Starting pitchers throwing a shutout were almost never removed from the game in the late innings unless something unexpected happened. The "save" statistic did not come into vogue for measuring relief effectiveness until a couple of years later, in the early 1960s. The modern day baseball fan would have no difficulty sorting out the ruling since such similar events have occurred many times over the years. The win would go to the reliever, the pitcher of record.

The sportswriter actually took the question to Warren Giles, National League president, whom he described as sighing deeply when he answered, "Your repulsive bull penner, that's who." "It would have been his game to win or lose. Haddix would have been erased as a consideration after the 12th inning, at which stage it was 0 to 0."[7]

Some might have cried out with a retort that it would be an injustice, but that was the rule and still is the rule. If Haddix was treated unfairly as the game played out, it was an unfairness decreed by fate, not archaic rules. If the Pirates had scored a run, such discussions never would have taken place.

Haddix maintained his graciousness and calm as the world peppered him with questions. His fellow Pirates exhibited a little bit more emotion on his behalf than Haddix ever did in public. "A pitcher does this once in a lifetime—once in baseball history—and we can't win the game for him," outfielder Bill Virdon said.[8]

When Haddix walked off the diamond as the Braves fans cheered behind him and umpires conferred on how to sort out the score, the first to greet him near the dugout was manager Danny Murtaugh. Murtaugh gave Haddix a hug. A little later the team's field boss said, "What a shame to lose a game for a fellow like that."[9]

Pirates on the 1959 team who had long memories still considered the terrible teams of earlier in the decade to be haunting reminders of the distance required to become pennant contenders. Dick Groat, Bob Friend, Vernon Law and a few others had been around for several years. After Branch Rickey gave way to Joe L. Brown as general manager and some of the younger players started climbing through the farm system, they realized the Pirates were no longer the worst team in baseball, that they were building something. The off-season trade that brought in Harvey Haddix, Smokey Burgess and Don Hoak gave the 1959 team high hopes.

When the Pirates arrived in Milwaukee for their three-game, late–May series, they had a 21–19 record. They were above .500, a rare enough circumstance for Pittsburgh in the 1950s, but not quite jelling. The Pirates lost two out of three to the two-time defending National

League champs and left Milwaukee with a 22–21 record. A six-game winning streak soon after put the Pirates six games over .500, but an immediate stretch of losing six out of seven dropped them right back where they had been. That was pretty much the Pirates' story that season. The ingredients for a blue-ribbon-winning dish seemed to be on hand for the cook, but there was still some experimentation needed. The Pirates finished fourth in the NL with a 78–76 record. "We didn't have a great year that year, but then we turned it around," Groat said.[10]

Although the 12-inning perfect game stood out like a beacon flashing against the night sky, Haddix did not have a great all-around 1959 pitching year, either. He finished with a 12–12 record and a 3.13 earned run average while throwing 224⅓ innings. For one night his pitching defied compliments, but the rest of the season it was middle of the road, just like the Pirates as a whole.

The Pirates did not have a .300 hitter for the 1959 season. Smokey Burgess and Dick Stuart tied for the team high by batting .297. Hoak hit .294, Skinner, .280 and Groat, .275. Clemente batted .296, but only played in 105 games. That could have been the difference in the comparative level of the Pirates' success. At that point in a career that had begun in Pittsburgh in 1955, Clemente had hit over .300 just once. He was on the cusp of fulfilling the greatness Branch Rickey had felt as strongly was within him as Clemente himself believed. Soon enough, many others would see it. Before the 1960 season, backup catcher Hal Smith told Clemente, "If you play in 140 games, we'll win the pennant."[11]

Among the starting pitchers, Vernon Law was the big winner with an 18–9 record. However, Roy Face's 18–1 record was the best ever compiled by a reliever. If Murtaugh felt any one of his starters was in trouble he waved for Face. Often, Face wouldn't even watch part of the Pirates' games. He retreated to the clubhouse to lie down. When the game advanced into the later innings, or if it looked as if Murtaugh was going to call upon him earlier than usual, a messenger would seek him out and even wake him up if he was napping.

"In Pittsburgh, our right-field bullpen was right near the tunnel that went into the clubhouse so we could go back and forth into the clubhouse," Face said. "They'd come in around in the seventh inning and tell me it's my turn. I relieved from the seventh inning on. They wouldn't even have a save today if they had to do it like we did. It was not like it is these days with one pitch or one batter. I would go into the game in the ninth and if it was going to extra innings I might still be pitching. I won a lot of games that year, but I could have lost six or seven of those games, too. We came from behind and got a couple. They [the other team] would tie it up and then we'd get a couple of runs and win it."[12]

Face felt so strongly that he had been a fortunate observer of baseball history being written on the night Haddix pitched his special game that he made sure he got himself a souvenir. He collected copies of the box score of the game and then asked all of his Pirate teammates and members of the Braves to autograph them. He got broadcaster Bob Prince's signature, too, then he had the package laminated.

The Haddix game was one night during the 1959 season that Danny Murtaugh never looked Face's way. The most difficult challenge Face faced that night was deciding when to switch his left arm from top to bottom and move his right arm from bottom to top as he folded his arms in the dugout. "That was the easiest game I ever worked," Face joked.[13]

The Braves of 1959 were in a very different position. Treating their frenzied fans to the ultimate prize, Milwaukee had captured the 1957 World Series and then returned to the October classic to play the Yankees again in 1958. The Braves lost the rematch, but in 1959 they were angling for a third straight pennant, prepared to ride those big bats and the arms of Lew Burdette and Warren Spahn. Milwaukee was a savvy, experienced team and utility man Mel Roach felt Fred Haney was just the right manager for the group. "He would say, 'Here's the balls and gloves, just go play,'" Roach recalled. "'If you need me, let me know.'"[14]

Roach saw Haney as a hands-off manager, but then what was he going to tell Hank Aaron, Eddie Mathews and Joe Adcock about hitting? The chemistry, too, was outstanding, Roach felt. "It was a really good, close-knit group of guys," he said. "Henry Aaron was a super guy and Spahn, they were all just good guys, as well as great ballplayers."[15]

Roach only saw sporadic action for the Braves, but he was thrilled to be part of such a superb team and work as teammates side by side with some of the greatest players in history. Spahn pitched a no-hitter during the 1960 season against the Phillies and then added a second no-hitter to his resume on April 28 of the 1961 season, defeating the Giants.

Roach was in the lineup for Spahn's next start against the Los Angeles Dodgers. Inning by inning went by with Spahn again pitching a no-hitter.

He seemed on the verge of matching Johnny Vander Meer's feat of pitching two straight no-hitters.

"Junior Gilliam, the second baseman, hit a ball off the end of the bat," said Roach, who was in the outfield, "and I took three steps back. Then the ball fell in front of me for a base hit. That was the only hit of the game until two outs in the bottom of the ninth inning.

"Tommy Davis got a hit, but if I had caught that fly ball, he would never have come to bat. And Spahny would have thrown consecutive no-hitters. Of course, I was in tears afterwards and he came over to me and said, 'Look, I never beat the Dodgers anyway. I'm just happy to be a winner.' He was so gracious. That's what made it a great team."[16]

The Braves could not best the Dodgers in 1959, however. The Braves fought to the end, led by Aaron's stupendous season. He batted .355 with 39 home runs and 123 RBIs. Mathews smacked 46 home runs and drove in 114 while batting .306. Spahn and Burdette each won 21 games.

The Dodgers and Braves tied with 86 wins and 68 losses at the end of the regular season, the Braves' pennant hopes still percolating as the leaves on the trees turned orange and red. A best two-out-of-three playoff was scheduled, but the Braves lost two straight and missed the Series. Trailing 1–0 in the playoff, Haney turned to Burdette to be his Dodger killer. The manager delivered a fiery speech to his team in the locker room and then handed the ball to Burdette in front of the players. "Come on, what are you waiting for?" Burdette announced. "There's a bunch of Dodgers we've got to go through if we want to be in that Series."[17]

Haney went around the room, thanking his players for their contributions during the regular season, and stopped in front of Burdette. "Chew them up, kid," Haney exhorted Burdette. "We're counting on you."[18]

Haney removed Burdette from the game after eight innings with a 5–2 lead, but with the bases loaded for L.A. The Dodgers ended up winning the game, 6–5, in the 12th inning. Unlike the last time, five months earlier at the end of May, when he had pitched so long into the night, Burdette was not victorious. His long season ended with the Braves going home and the Dodgers going on.

Soon enough the glorious love affair between Milwaukee and the Braves began to fade. By 1966, the Braves who had brought such joy to Milwaukee were transients again, making their debut in the new Major League city of Atlanta.

24. The 1959 Season

Eddie Mathews, a future Hall of Fame third baseman for the Braves.

As the 1959 season wore on and the Pirates seesawed through the campaign, the excitement over Haddix's 12-inning perfect game receded into the background. People who saw it said they would never forget it. Teammates agreed it was the greatest game pitched of all time. But they were also busy trying to win a pennant, trying to win as many games as they could and make something special out of 1959 for themselves.

After weeks and months passed, they didn't talk much about the night Harvey Haddix was perfect through 12 innings and the game got away from him and them, though the memory was not far beneath the surface. "We're happy to be teammates of a man who pitched the greatest game in history," said Bob Friend. "We were breathing with him on every pitch."[19]

After living through, playing in, and dissecting such a game, the Pirates had no idea that they were a year away from experiencing another baseball drama that for most of them, including Haddix, eclipsed the story of the southpaw's magnificent game.

25

The Year All Pittsburgh Went Crazy

A year to the day after Harvey Haddix pitched 12 perfect innings of baseball for the Pittsburgh Pirates, a sports writer checked in with the southpaw to see how he was commemorating the moment.

The writer discovered that on May 26, 1960, Haddix was doing nothing at all to either celebrate or take note of the greatest game ever pitched. For one thing, he had completely forgotten the anniversary. During the long major league baseball season, if teams are given days off by the schedule makers, they are typically Mondays or Thursdays. Those days break up series and allow for travel.

As it so happened, May 26, 1960, was a Thursday and the Pirates had the day off from competition. That meant Haddix didn't even stop by the ballpark and had to be ferreted out for comment. The pitcher's answer about how he was reflecting upon his year-old milestone game surprised the questioner. "This is the first I've thought about it since you mentioned it," Haddix replied. "I didn't realize the full impact of what I did until later when I began receiving plaques, gifts, and invitations for banquets."[1]

In the minutes and hours after what turned into a 1–0 loss to the Milwaukee Braves in 13 innings, Haddix was continuously surprised by public reaction. While the baseball world and the world at-large praised him for setting down 36 men in order, a feat never before approached by a major league pitcher, in his own mind Haddix was stuck on the fact that he lost the game.

As with any achievement or event, gradually Haddix's game faded into the rear-view mirror. The pennant races were completed. The Pirates finished a disappointed fourth in the National League. Winter passed. And a new season, the 1960 campaign, began. This time the Pirates felt they had all of the ingredients to make a run at their first pennant since 1927.

The Pirates appeared in the first World Series in 1903, losing to Boston. They won the World Series over the Tigers in 1909 and they defeated the Washington Senators in the 1925 World Series. Given their

25. The Year All Pittsburgh Went Crazy

tradition, employment of famous players from Honus Wagner to Lloyd Waner, neither Pirate team administrators nor fans could imagine that when they played in the 1927 World Series, fodder for the New York Yankees, one of the most powerful assemblages of talent ever, the club would disappear off the championship map.

By the time the Pirates gathered at spring training in Fort Myers, Florida, in the late winter of 1960, it had been 33 years since Pittsburgh was represented in the World Series. This year, Murtaugh and his now-veteran cast vowed, would be their year. "Growing up in Pittsburgh, I was aware we hadn't won for 33 years," said Dick Groat. "Winning a World Series is really what it's all about."[2]

By the next spring, a year after throwing his benchmark game, Haddix had moved on in the way American society did, anxious for new experiences, to fulfill new goals, and to appreciate new Pirate developments. "It was nice while it lasted," Haddix said of his run of fame engendered by the greatest game ever pitched. "But I'd like to do something this year to let people know I'm still around."[3]

The Pirates brought the same attitude to the 1960 season, one that perhaps was the most pleasurable in the existence of the franchise. Just two days after Haddix talked about his year-old pitching performance, the Pirates made a trade to solidify the pitching staff, acquiring David Wilmer "Vinegar Bend" Mizell from the Cardinals while surrendering young second baseman Julian Javier.

Mizell, whose nickname stemmed from representing the neighborhood of Vinegar Bend, Alabama, and who later became a U.S. Congressman from North Carolina, had been a steady performer in the National League for most of the 1950s. Although only 30, the southpaw was nearing the end of his productive years, but was the perfect complement to the Pirates' staff at the time. Mizell went 13–5 in a Pittsburgh uniform.

Vernon Law, Bob Friend, and Haddix were the other key starters. Smokey Burgess (who batted .294) and Hal Smith were the main catchers. The infield, with Rocky Nelson and Dick Stuart sharing first, Bill Mazeroski at second, Groat at short, with Schofield backing him up, and Don Hoak at third, was essentially the same as it was in 1959. Bob Skinner, Bill Virdon and a healthy Roberto Clemente were the regular starting outfielders.

Groat was a vocal leader, batted .325 to lead the National League, and was voted Most Valuable Player. Dick Stuart struck out 107 times, but also contributed 23 home runs and 83 RBIs. Hoak drove in 79 and Skinner knocked in 86. It was a lineup that had no weakness. Clemente emerged as a star, batting .314, hitting 16 home runs and driving in 94 runs. His fielding drew gasps. Clemente played in 144 of the 154 games, making Smith's prediction of Pirate success based on his appearance in 140 games come true. Clemente was a distant also-ran in the MVP voting and was often overlooked in the discussion for most valuable Pirate.

The *Pittsburgh Press*' main Pirates writer, Les Biederman, publicly backed Groat for the award, but also told other sports writers that Clemente did not even deserve to be considered. When Clemente heard that gossip he became quite upset and confided in teammate Nelson. Nelson felt the entire campaign going on behind Clemente's back was unfair and spoke up to Jack Hernon, the Pittsburgh *Post-Gazette*'s Pirates writer. "There's one thing I can't understand," Nelson said. "I've read many stories about who is the most valuable player on the Pirates, but I never see the name Roberto mentioned. I don't know how he can be overlooked when you talk about players on the club, but he doesn't get a call. He's been consistently around .320 all season. He has hit more home runs than ever. And certainly he is the best right fielder in the league. If Roberto beefs about not being mentioned, I wouldn't blame him."[4]

Law finished 20–9 and won the Cy Young award as the best pitcher in the league. Friend won 18 games, going 18–12 after a horrible 8–19 season in 1959. In one 1959 newspaper account of a game in which he got knocked out in the second inning, Friend was called "the flop of the year."[5] He blamed himself for the Pirates' drop-off in play between 1958 and 1959. "It's pride, and prestige, but that's minor compared to other ways that it hurts," Friend said of his off year. "We've come so close in this darned thing and if I had anything approaching last year's record [22–14], we would have won it."[6]

In 1960, Friend threw 276 innings and Law 271. Face, just about the only one around throwing a fork ball, was not quite as untouchable as he had been in 1959, but won 10 games in the bullpen. Haddix finished 11–10 with a 3.97 earned run average with 172 innings pitched. He took his regular turn in the rotation, but had no game to approach his miracle of '59. Nor did anyone expect to see a repeat. Haddix was a contributor, but not a star in Pittsburgh's 95–59 season.

The Pirates showed early signs of success with a nine-game winning

25. The Year All Pittsburgh Went Crazy

streak in April, and they also had a stretch winning nine out of 10 games in May. The Pirates won the pennant by seven games over the Braves while drawing 1.7 million fans to Forbes Field. One aspect of the team's play that the starting pitchers admired was Virdon's grace patrolling center field. "As far as I'm concerned, Virdon is the best in the field," Face said. "He's as good as Willie Mays and I can't make it any stronger than that."[7] Haddix said Virdon had great range and the Pirate pitchers put him to work proving it. "We pitchers make him chase our mistakes, but he always does the job," Haddix said. "Virdon is as good as any of them. And he does it every day."[8]

Pittsburgh celebrated the city's first National League pennant in 33 years, but the joy was tempered by the feeling that the American League opponent, the New York Yankees, might be unbeatable. The Yankees finished 97–57 during the 1960 regular season, eight games ahead of the Baltimore Orioles; their won-loss record was two games better than the Pirates.[9] However, the Yankees had just claimed their 10th pennant in 12 seasons under manager Casey Stengel, and in many minds, because of their dynasty, the Yankees of 1960 were indistinguishable from the Yankees of four or five years earlier. They were installed as 13–10 betting favorites to win the World Series.

The Yankees appeared loaded at every position. It began with the M&M boys, center fielder Mickey Mantle and right fielder Roger Maris. Mantle slugged 40 home runs and drove in 94. Maris swatted 39 homers and knocked in 114. Yogi Berra, who hit 15 homers and batted .276, was still around, shifting between catcher behind Elston Howard and left field. First baseman Bill Skowron batted .309 with 26 homers. Such luminaries as second baseman Bobby Richardson, shortstop Tony Kubek, and third baseman Clete Boyer filled out the infield. Lefty Whitey Ford was still the ace of the pitching staff, but he had had an off year, going just 12–9. Art Ditmar's 15 wins were the most in the rotation.

The Yankees were a long-ball club capable of blowing out any team with sudden impact, and once the World Series opened that became apparent to all. The Pirates won the opener, 6–4, at Forbes Field with Law getting the victory and Ditmar taking the loss. However, the Yankees pummeled the Pirates, 16–3, in the second game. A seven-run sixth inning did the Pirates in. Mantle smashed two home runs and Bob Turley got the victory as Friend was tagged with the loss.

The Series shifted to Yankee Stadium for game three and the Yankees

Pirates center fielder Bill Virdon was a renowned fielder, but he said the night Harvey Haddix pitched 12 perfect innings was just about his easiest day of work in his career.

crushed the Pirates, 10–0, before 70,001 fans. New York jumped on the Pirates immediately, with a six-run first and this game, as much as anything, gave the public the idea that the Yankees were really just toying with Pittsburgh. Ford was credited with the victory and Mizell took the loss. Mantle hit his third home run of the Series.

25. The Year All Pittsburgh Went Crazy

For the fourth game, also at Yankee Stadium, Danny Murtaugh came back with Law as his starter. Stengel started Ralph Terry. Law was back in regular-season form and the Pirates won, 3–2, to knot the Series. A three-run rally in the fifth gave Pittsburgh the win.

Murtaugh tapped Harvey Haddix on the shoulder for the fifth game and Stengel countered with Ditmar. In a game that disturbed Yankee fans that only a few days earlier had been so optimistic, the Pirates came through for Haddix. The final score was 5–2 and, with the Series shifting back to Pittsburgh, the Pirates led three games to two.

There were ups and downs, with those embarrassing losing scores to the Yankees, yet the Pirates were still ahead. Virdon said in that way the Series had much in common with the regular season. "The whole year was really kind of different because we came from behind like 30 times in the eighth or ninth innings," he said. "So you were never sure exactly what was going to happen. You always knew you had a chance, but you weren't sure you were going to do it. Everybody took part. We had a lot of consistent hitters. Everybody did their job."[9]

Going through so many close calls and pulling out victories gave the Pirates confidence, Haddix said, so when they got blasted 16–3 and 10–0 by the Yankees, the team was able to shrug off the results as just routine losses.

"This is the 1960 Pirates," Haddix said in recalling the club. "That's the way we played all year. We had a bunch of guys who would not quit. They never knew when they were beaten and, of course, if you don't give up you've got a chance at winning. That's exactly what happened in the 1960 season. We laughed on the days that they [the Yankees] kicked the tar out of us. We laughed about it. That's better than pouting, because it helped us. The game was gone and we got ready for the next day."[10]

Haddix's stuff was working in the fifth game. He went $6\frac{1}{3}$ innings, gave up two runs on five hits, and struck out six men after being staked to a quick 3–0 lead in the second inning. Maris touched Haddix for a home run, and he walked Mantle twice intentionally. Short on patience and with an eye to the long-term result, Stengel yanked Ditmar quickly, after just $1\frac{1}{3}$ innings. Roy Face relieved Haddix in the seventh and pitched the final $2\frac{2}{3}$ innings.

Despite getting clobbered twice, the Pirates were taking the World Series back to Forbes Field with two tries to wrap it up in a sixth or seventh game. Game six twisted everyone's thinking about momentum, as once again the Yankees erupted against Pirate pitching for a 12–0 win. The Yankees torched Pirate pitching for 17 hits while Whitey Ford completely handcuffed Pittsburgh with a seven-hit shutout.

The seventh game of a Series that had the country abuzz because of its peculiar scores was scheduled for October 13, 1960, in Pittsburgh. The Pirates couldn't afford another slow start on the mound. The Yankee batsmen couldn't afford another walkabout. Murtaugh started Law, who had earned the opportunity with his exceptional regular season. Stengel chose Turley to start, but when the Pirates jumped on him for four quick runs, he was banished to the clubhouse in the second inning.

Law was stingy through five innings, but when he started to weaken in the sixth, Murtaugh went to his money man, the man nicknamed "the Baron of the Bullpen." Roy Face came in to shut the door on the Yankee hitters, only on this rare occasion, he couldn't. Face pitched three innings and gave up four runs.

The score was 7–4 Yankees entering the bottom of the eighth inning, but the Pirates energized the home crowd of 36,683 with a rally that pushed them to a 9–7 lead. Murtaugh turned to Bob Friend to close things out in the ninth, but the plan fizzled. It was a 9–8 game when Murtaugh called Haddix's name.

"I was warming up in the bullpen and I came in with men on first and third and nobody out," Haddix said.

> I looked at the plate and there stood Maris. Over there [on deck] stood Mantle and following him stood Berra and following him was Skowron. With the game tied up, or that close, that's a tough situation. It was the only time I ever got nervous on the mound. I said, 'I can't pitch this way, so I've got to do something about it.' I stood out there and I laughed at myself and I cussed myself out. I did anything. It must have taken five minutes. All the time I'm trying to get this nervousness off me Maris is standing there grinding the bat. It looked like sawdust was coming out of it. He wanted to hit and the more I could delay, the better it would be for me.[11]

Haddix said Maris was so anxious he popped up an outside pitch to the catcher. Mantle hit a single and the game was tied 9–9. Berra and Skowron, Haddix said, also reached for pitches that would have been balls.[12]

The Pirates went into the home half of the ninth tied, their fans roaring for a miracle finish. Haddix joined his teammates on the dugout bench to root for a rousing comeback. Right-hander Ralph Terry was on the mound for New York. He had finished the eighth inning, getting the last out, and was ready to go longer.

The leadoff hitter for the Pirates was second baseman Bill Mazeroski, who was hitting eighth in the order, just ahead of the pitcher. Haddix was the second scheduled hitter, but his turn, or likely pinch-hitter Dick Stuart's, never came. Terry delivered and Mazeroski unleashed a perfect swing that connected with an offering about chest high. The ball was propelled over the left-field wall in Forbes Field. Fans exploded, some of them running onto the field and chasing a now-hatless Mazeroski around the bases all the way to home plate. His teammates waited there en masse to hug him and celebrate.

"With the crack of the bat I knew it was a home run," Haddix said. "I told the guys on the bench beside me, 'I've thrown enough of them out of here to know that's gone.' Sure enough, when that thing sailed over the wall, Pittsburgh went wild."[13]

Although it is little remembered, especially in comparison to his perfect game, Haddix was the winning pitcher in the clinching game and, combined with his victory in game five, was 2–0 in the Series.

The photograph taken of Mazeroski approaching home plate is one of the most famous in baseball history. The hit itself, a walk-off homer to clinch a World Series championship, is regarded as perhaps the most dramatic in baseball history. It was recorded at 3:36 P.M. Eastern time in an era when all World Series games were played in the afternoon, and it was measured as landing 406 feet from home plate.

One of the Forbes Field eyewitnesses was Bill Kennedy, the father of the boy who accidentally set his bed on fire the night Haddix retired 36 batters in a row. The older Kennedy was friendly with a group of prominent owners of a construction company who had acquired tickets to the games. For one Series game, he sent his son Bill off with his nephew Bobby; one of the games the Yankees won. It was an exciting opportunity, but he thinks the boys were happiest because they missed school to go to a baseball game.

Kennedy kept the seventh game tickets for himself and said he was sitting behind home plate, about 40 rows back, when Mazeroski slammed the Series winner. "It is indeed one of the greatest sports moments in Pittsburgh history," Kennedy said. "He [Mazeroski] was dancing he was so thrilled about the whole thing. And there's a whole horde of people gathering around to grab him."[14]

The final score was 10–9 and fans of the sport still marvel at how a team that lost three games out of seven in a World Series could have been so thoroughly crushed 16–3, 10–0, and 12–0, yet still won it all. Mazeroski's home run lives on in baseball legend as the most identifiable swing of his Hall of Fame career and the most famous swing in Pittsburgh baseball history.

Mazeroski was not a particularly renowned home-run hitter, but just one of the many Pirates in the lineup who could hit a home run. "Everyone would love to do something like that, but there wasn't one jealous person on that club," Virdon said, "because it was Maz. He's good people. Everyone liked Maz. He was good-hearted, pleasant to be around. He was a clutch hitter.... He was the Pirate. Everybody was completely satisfied that he was the one who hit the home run."[15]

Ironically, one of the most connected Pirate supporters of all, broadcaster Bob Prince, missed seeing the clout. He was in an elevator racing to get to the locker room to position himself for post-game interviews when Mazeroski hit the homer. Prince was one of the first to interview Mazeroski afterwards when they were pushed together in the crowded clubhouse, but he didn't ask the right questions because he didn't realize Mazeroski had blasted the game-winner. It made for peculiar radio. "I always wondered why he didn't ask me about the home run," Mazeroski said. "I asked him a year later."[16]

Haddix was always more proud and pleased that he was the winning pitcher in two 1960 World Series games than he was about throwing the 12-inning perfect game that turned into a loss. "That game probably gets more attention than if I had won it," Haddix said on the 32nd anniversary of the Braves contest. "But to me, my most important game was the seventh game of the World Series the next year. No one remembers I won that. I also won the fifth."[17]

Haddix voted for participation in a team achievement as the greater thrill than writing history in a team defeat.

26

Waxing Eloquent Over Haddix

Of all the tributes and flowery descriptions, verbal and written, issued about Harvey Haddix's work on the mound against the Braves on May 26, 1959, none compare to the simply named *Twelve Perfect Innings: A Pretty Good Game* for quirkiness, strangeness and sheer astonishment. So enamored, so taken with Haddix's pitching wizardy, Dr. Weldon Myers, a creative writing instructor and poet living in Lakeland, Florida, poured forth an 84-page pamphlet dissecting, reporting on, and extolling the uniqueness of the Haddix game.

Twelve Perfect Innings: A Pretty Good Game is the Iliad of baseball poetry, an ode to a remarkable night told in quite different fashion than the newspaper sports writers trying to meet deadline at the end of a 13-inning ballgame.

In its own way, the articulation in the poem is as wondrous a feat as Haddix's pitching, and nothing else like it has ever been written about the sport. Tim Wiles, who eventually became director of research for the Baseball Hall of Fame Library, wrote a newspaper story about baseball poetry in 1996 headlined, "Who's on Verse."

In that story, Wiles, who is a huge fan of "Casey at the Bat" and acts the role in public, noted that Myers' opus on Haddix appeared out of nowhere and then Myers as a baseball scribe "was never heard from again."[1] It is possible that Myers simply ran out of words or baseball ideas with the 1961 publication of "Twelve Perfect Innings" by the Commercial Press in Lakeland.

As if the poem might require as much translation as the *Iliad*, Myers left behind an accompanying list of personal notes explaining his motivation in writing about Haddix's game and what he was trying to accomplish. "It was selected out of hundreds of great baseball games this particular contest to celebrate because it was the record single-game pitching achievement in baseball history," Myers wrote. "It would be a pity if such a game were left to the sports writers who treat it today and hurry on to the next event. Only imaginative and artistic narrative can give the contest the consideration it deserves."[2]

Myers makes what seems to be a safe assumption, researched to a point by Wiles, in claiming there has never been a poem about a game quite like his. "It is unique in being the only long, sustained account in verse of a ballgame ever written," Myers said. "(I have this on good authority.) Short pieces have been written like 'Casey at the Bat,' but no writer has taken the trouble to study a game thoroughly and reconstruct the event, in verse, from beginning to end—as far as I can determine."[3]

Myers attended the University of Virginia and played shortstop on the baseball team for Bridgewater College, but that was far in his past when Haddix came along. Myers, a published poet, also had been an English professor at his alma mater and spent 25 years teaching creative writing at Converse College in Spartanburg, South Carolina.[4] Myers, living in retirement in Florida, undertook the challenge of writing the epic book soon after Haddix completed the game and finished it in 1961. His deadline was a little bit longer than the sports writers' on the scene.[5]

In his foreword, Myers outlines in painstaking detail how he attempted to maintain proper rhymes, accents, beats, and syllables and said he felt the pressure of trying to be perfect. "Whoever undertakes to write the story of 'Twelve Perfect Innings' is under a sort of contract to bring along some element of perfection in the telling," Myers wrote.[6]

Myers called his introduction "Warm-Up," and it reads as follows:

> Nine full innings of perfect ball
> With never a hit or walk were all
> That any pitcher till recent date
> Was called upon to perpetrate
> In '56 when Larsen hurled
> Nine flawless innings before the world,
> Perfect pitching meant, no doubt,
> The opposition's perfect rout.
> In '59, on Harvey Haddix
> Fell a different mathematics.
> After nine perfect innings he
> Was with his Pirates still at sea.
> From Harvey's gun the Haney boat
> Though full of holes was still afloat.
> He blasted it three rallies more,
> Pierced it, bored it to the core.
> Lew Burdette, who held the deck,
> Saved the ship from total wreck.

26. Waxing Eloquent Over Haddix

> Blasted at, he blasted back,
> Traded Harvey whack for whack.
> In the 13th battle-round
> Was fired a long and lucky shot
> Which hit an undefended spot:
> The Pirate ship was ducked and drowned.
>
> Think of Harvey how he pounded
> Nine Braves who were all grounded.
> Three dozen batters in a row—
> He stood them up and laid them low;
> Beat them back and out and down
> In their own Milwaukee town.
> Remember also Lew Burdette
> Who was the only man who met
> Haddix on the famous mound
> And beat him on that battle-ground—
> Licked the guy who that day hurled
> The topmost record of the world.
> Lost and won is every race,
> Browning said, in a lurid place.
> All human effort is doomed to meet
> Its haunting curse, the Incomplete.
> Give Lew credit for a game:
> Harvey rose to record fame.
> What to Haddix would one say
> In a fitting final way?
> Burdette his rival said it in
> Four words: He deserved to win.
> Such painstaking play should be
> Reported correspondingly.
> A game of workmanship so fine
> Deserves the tuned and measured line.
> If I put the thing in prose
> With no rhyme or rhythmic run,
> I might all the facts disclose,
> But leave the fancy and the fun
> To dry up in the factual sun.[7]

A less ambitious man might have left it at that, the introduction a worthy poem in itself standing alone to commemorate Haddix's pitching. But, as Myers wrote as the title for his introduction, he was just getting warmed up.

Right from the beginning of the poem, and the game, Myers makes it clear he is not going to be chintzy with description. Each player gets a reasonably detailed biographical treatment as he steps to the plate, starting with Braves leadoff hitter Johnny O'Brien. After noting the ground ball out to Dick Schofield, who tossed to Rocky Nelson, Myers comments on O'Brien's leave-taking from the field. "The first extinguished at the first. One, and 26 to go. See you later, Johnny O."[8]

The third batter up in the first inning for Haddix to contend with was Hank Aaron, well-respected for his hitting talents. Myers saw Aaron's first confrontation with Haddix this way:

> Inning 1 Henry Aaron 3rd Batter
>
> Hank is prince of paddle-wielders.
> All the faces of the fielders
> Take a hopeless solemn stare on
> When the bat of Henry Aaron
> Sends a shapely Spalding ball,
> Leaving little hide or hair on.
> To the woods beyond the wall.
> Few the days he could not fire it,
> Before he met a Pittsburgh Pirate,
> Harvey Haddix, a buccaneer,
> With his Pittsburgh goods and gear.
> Harvey, standing at the center
> Of the world, awaits his mentor,
> Sturdy co-conspirator,
> Smokey Burgess, wrapped for war,
> Squatting armored on the floor
> With his victim just before,
> And umpire Smith, in blue or black,
> Crouching just a little back.
>
> Smokey signaled for a charmer.
> Harvey nodded, said no more.
> Then the lefty Pirate hurler
> Lifted leg and shot a curler
> Through the front-room open door.
> Hank was tempted, nearly acted.
> Twitched and started, self-retracted.
> Straeek! Nobody contradicted
> In the bleachers or the stand.
>
> Still on trial, unconvicted,
> Still the master of his fate,

26. Waxing Eloquent Over Haddix

Hank asserted self-command,
Demonstrated self-possession,
Tapping stick upon the plate;
At the beginning of recession,
Offence-resources well in hand.
Smokey signaled new advice.
Every play is acted twice:
First idea, inner image,
Then the outer scrap and scrimmage;
Clear and confident selection,
Steady nerve and quick projection.
Harvey took what Smokey signed,
Rolled it lightly in his mind,
And let it fly with subtle crook
Sixty feet to the batter's nook.

Keen-eyed Henry kept his nerve,
Saw the motion, caught the curve,
Matched his hurried mathematics
Against the plotted trick of Haddix
And struck the rocket's underjowl
And bumped it up and back, a foul.
Strike and no. 2 at that.
Sighs, a sympathetic wheeze,
Fluttered like a late–May breeze
Over the bleachers where they sat,
Brave believers by the lake,
Hoping, praying for a break.
Next a ball and then a ripping
Foul outside the south-coast skipping.
Then a knock, a business call.
Aaron's mark was on the ball
Which he meant should go in search
Of a country school or church
Hid behind the city wall.
Henry flung his bat and loped,
Down to first he hopped and hoped.
The sphere descended through the mist
To the grip of Virdon's fist,
Like a rocket in distress
Which has lost its moon address.[9]

Periodically, after writing of the demise of a batter, Myers inserted a small story about Haddix or other participants, also in poetry, before going on to the next inning. He called one "Interinning Parable" and another one "Interinning Salute to Umpires." Myers admitted he couldn't think of much in the English language to rhyme with "Pafko," as in Andy Pafko, the Braves' centerfielder, so that's why he used "Andy" in his work.[10]

After Haddix had been through the Braves' batting order once without being scathed, Myers wrote:

> So the Pirate turned them down.
> Nine came up and stood to spell,
> Nine in order slipped and fell
> In this educated town.[11]

On and on the verse runs, much like the game, with one notable departure. Myers only dealt with the Braves hitters as they faced Haddix. With only occasional exception he did not bring the same poetic eye to the Pirates as they came to the plate each inning trying to reach Burdette. It was Haddix that Myers focused on and his effort to hold off Milwaukee, not his teammates' failure to support him with a run.

Between the fourth and fifth innings, Myers reported:

> Scoreless inning followed inning
> Four times since that bold beginning
> When the slender Pirate barber
> Welcomed to his fresh-air arbor
> And his chair Brave after Brave
> For a hair-cut and a shave;
> Not with new electric blazer
> But with old-time shears and razor.[12]

Pafko, the 25th Milwaukee hitter, led off the ninth inning and was retired. Johnny Logan followed and made an out. That brought opposing pitcher Burdette to the plate. Wielding his stick, he stood between Haddix and a perfect nine innings.

Inning 9—Lew Burdette—27th Batter
> Johnny has vanished, faded out.
> Inning 9 is all but finished.
> Haddix, with fury undiminished,
> Summons Burdette to the judgment bout.
> Lew, Milwaukee hurler-in-chief,
> Has battled through with no relief
> On the mound, but in the box

26. Waxing Eloquent Over Haddix

He is coiled in a Pittsburgh paradox.
No Brave off Haddix can raise a hit;
No Pirate, though hitting, can forge a run.
Yet a break must come, the teams must quit,
Trial over and judgment done.

Smokey through the open door
Silently signaled Burdette's doom.
Lew remembered how once before
He waited too long in the waiting room.
Harvey was kind to his fellow hurler,
Giving a ball, a low outside,
Which Lew correctly classified.
Next from Haddix a teasing curler.
Burdette interpreted both alike,
But the classification of Ump was strike.
When Lew on the mound slips a close pitch by,
Like Jackie he thinks, What a good boy am I!
But when he is fanned before all the addicts,
Does he say, What a good boy is Haddix?
The Braves with Haney incline to think
Of pennants and series yet to come.
They figure and fight for the minimum,
They challenge and charge along the brink.

The hurler must be a batting tough:
Excellent pitching is not enough
For a team which in sufficient congeries
Would pile up wins for pennant and series.
Though Lew is doomed, I hesitate
To turn him over to Haddix and Fate.
Friends of mine set their heart's reliance
On the Braves over Pirates, Dodgers and Giants.
With Lew thrice fanned, I fear the omen:
He stands for the team, the Milwaukee showmen.
But the final 9th inning fact is this:
Lew bludgeons a foul, maneuvers a miss.[13]

Haddix retired the first 36 men he faced, completing the 12th inning unscatched. Felix Mantilla, the Braves second baseman, reached base on the Don Hoak throwing error to start the 13th, ending the perfect game. In part, Myers wrote:

So the Pirate wall was lost
When the first invader crossed

> At that one unlucky spot
> Which a sentinel forgot.[14]

Joe Adcock ended the game, even if the score was unclear, with a home run, and Myers dealt with the blow this way:

> Adcock, mighty clean-up man,
> Comes forth, as any man can see,
> To stand knee-deep in the wave
> And surge of opportunity.
> With 2 on base, the hour has meaning
> For Joe at last to do some cleaning.[15]

And so, in a few more stanzas, the game was over, summed up in a way no other baseball game played before or since, ever has been. And in that sense, the poem matched the occasion, for Haddix's efforts have never been approached. No other pitcher has ever retired the first 36 men that came to the plate.

Myers gave an interview to his hometown newspaper in Lakeland when the poem was printed in its pamphlet. Myers said the majesty of Haddix's game compelled him to try to recapture the moment in verse. "It must be a verbal tribute," Myers said. "One that encompassed all the flavor, humor and drama of that day and thus I tried to capture Haddix's almost impossible accomplishment in the meter of poetry."[16]

The newspaper columnist gave Myers credit that he likely appreciated, calling the poem "a work of art."[17]

Haddix's, too, baseball fans might say.

27

Life After Imperfection

Harvey Haddix never again approached the heights of his nearly perfect game—and no one expected a once-in-a-lifetime drama to be repeated, anyway. He remained a regular in the Pittsburgh Pirates' rotation during the 1960 World Series title season, and went 10–6 in 1961 and 9–6 in 1962.

The 1963 campaign was Haddix's last in Pittsburgh, and it was an abbreviated one. Haddix became a reliever, appearing in 49 games, throwing just 70 innings and compiling a 3–4 record. The shift to the bullpen did not bother Haddix. He was 37 when the season began and he could sense that his big-league career was nearing completion. "It was something new to me and I didn't mind trying it because as time went on it became tougher and tougher for me to go nine innings," Haddix said. "I could go five or six innings, but that wasn't enough."[1]

Haddix said the shift to the pen was "quite an adjustment. The toughest thing for me was that I was the only left-handed arm in the bullpen and my arm got very, very tired."[2] The weariness came not from the frequency of Haddix's calls to the mound, but from the frequency of his calls from the dugout. He was up and down, warming up, sitting down, putting extra wear on his arm, often without playing in the game.

In December, the Pirates sold Haddix to the Baltimore Orioles. On the occasion of the transaction, long-time Pittsburgh sports writer Les Biederman wrote a tribute to Haddix, thanking him for authoring the writer's greatest thrill in baseball. Biederman was referring to the almost-perfect game and he recounted much of the action from that night. "It was without a doubt the greatest game ever pitched and yet Haddix bore up gracefully and majestically in the defeat," Biederman wrote. "He regretted the loss of the game more than he appreciated the glory of pitching 12 perfect innings."[3]

From 1963 on, Haddix was a full-time reliever. In 1964, he posted a 5–5 record with 10 saves in 49 appearances for Baltimore manager Hank Bauer. Spring training of 1965 with the Orioles was not renewing for Haddix. Just the opposite. It set him back. He pitched one inning in relief one day and then came back to pitch two innings in relief the next day. He sensed there was something wrong. He went to the manager and said, "My arm feels heavy, but I think I can continue to pitch."[4] It was probably the incorrect decision considering what followed. "After that my arm was never the same that year," Haddix said. "I had no pain, but I did not have my stuff."[5]

Haddix ended his playing days with a 3–2 season in just 33⅓ innings. He was 40 when he concluded a 14-year major league career with 136 victories and 113 losses. At the end of his career, being a reliever was more about staying in the game and being a team man than doing what he loved best, starting games. "I never liked relieving as much as starting," Haddix said. "But when you don't have the choice, you do what the manager asks of you."[6]

He actually announced his retirement before the season ended, convinced he no longer had the power in his left arm to retire batters. Haddix "The Kitten" had turned into a pussycat and he turned down a deal to complete the season with the Milwaukee Braves. "I haven't been throwing good all year," said Haddix, who knew he was at the end of his career.[7]

Haddix said he had given the decision thought for weeks and a little bit later, when a sports writer tried to catch up to him to probe his thinking, Haddix was elusive. The first time the writer rang, Haddix was out chopping corn. The second time he was out fishing. Baseball seemed to be in the rearview mirror. It was, but only on the mound.

When he retired, it was no surprise that Haddix was asked to reminisce about his gem against the Braves in 1959. He reminded writers of what he had been saying for a couple of years. Winning two games in the World Series in 1960 was a bigger thrill for him than the perfect 12 innings. "After all," he said, "I lost the one in Milwaukee."[8]

Haddix said for the moment he was going to hang out on his farm in Ohio, but he speculated that someone might come calling with an offer to become a pitching coach. Watching sunsets over the fields from a rocking chair did not last long for Haddix. The Kansas City Athletics called first and offered him a chance to become pitching coach for their AAA Vancouver team. Haddix was about to sign that contract when the New York Mets called and offered the opportunity to get back into uniform for the parent club in 1966.

Only a few months passed between Haddix's retirement and the announcement of his new job as a member of manager Wes Westrum's staff. Among other prominent names in that coaching group were Yogi Berra and Whitey Herzog. At his introductory press conference, Haddix told New York sophisticates about the incident when he shot the roaming buffalo as a favor for his neighbor. That was fresh meat for sports writers prepared to regurgitate the tale of Haddix's operatic pitching performance against the Braves in 1959. The incidents were linked in print to the then-downtrodden Mets' future. "If a 'Kitten' can kill a crazed buffalo, can't a Mets team escape last place?"[9]

Haddix and the Mets had plenty of talent to mold after years of being a franchise automatically penciled in as the worst team in the National League. Tom Seaver, Nolan Ryan, Jerry Koosman and Tug McGraw were on the way up. "Would you believe that staff that I started off with over there?" Haddix said. "Was that fun! Nolan didn't want to pitch in New York was my impression. He came to me one day and said, 'What do I have to do to get traded from this ballclub?' He was a country boy and he didn't like the big city and he wanted out of there."[10]

When Haddix assumed his new job with the Mets, someone asked him what made a good pitching coach, and he had a teacher's response. "When a guy gets to throwing wrong, a good pitching coach can detect it and correct it. Every coach I ever played for helped me in some way." Haddix was eager to impart his knowledge to a younger generation. "I can't give him [an up-and-coming pitcher] the arm or the talent," Haddix said. "He has to bring that to the big leagues himself, but there are basic things to be done and a pitching coach can show them to him. I've always had the desire to be a pitching coach. That has been in my mind since I came into the big leagues."[11]

When Westrum departed as manager of the Mets, most of the coaches went with him. Haddix returned to the Pirates' fold for the 1967 season, acting as minor league pitching coach, and then in November of 1968 he was hired as pitching coach for the Cincinnati Reds. "I believe in working pitchers hard, not to punish them," Haddix said upon his hiring, "but to get them ready physically. One reason for sore arms is that too many pitchers today don't know how to care for themselves properly."[12]

The Haddix conditioning program placed more of a premium on speed. He preferred ordering pitchers to perform 10 fast sprints rather than 30 foul line-to-foul line runs. Another aspect of the Haddix philosophy was requiring pitchers to throw between starts.

Haddix owed his job with the Mets to baseball's expansion, but he worried about how the addition of more teams would dilute minor-league play and the development of pitchers who might be rushed to the majors. "Boys with immature arms are being forced to pitch under maximum pressure too soon," he said. "There just aren't enough players to go around. We're teaching kids things in the majors right now that we had to learn in the bushes."[13]

Haddix said he learned early on during his playing career that some players have distinctive throwing or hitting styles and that making them conform to what everyone believes is pristine technique might not be the best thing for an individual. Hall of Fame outfielder Stan Musial with the Cardinals had an unusual batting stance, where he held the bat high, and Musial's success influenced Haddix to leave young pitchers alone.

"I watched him very closely and he did everything wrong as a player, but he could hit the ball," Haddix said. "So after my career, when I became a coach, I decided right then that I would not try to change anybody because he was doing something that looked wrong. If he could accomplish something with it [his style], leave him alone. Do not change him and make him fit the mold."[14]

In 1970, Haddix rejoined the Pirates as a minor league coach, and the next season he was hired to supervise the Boston Red Sox's major league pitchers. Haddix was the seventh Red Sox pitching coach since 1963 in a revolving-door job. *The Sporting News* headline when Haddix was revealed as Boston's next choice for the position read, "Haddix on Hot Seat as Red Sox Pitching Coach."[15]

Haddix's wife, Marcia, had stopped uprooting the kids and moving to his city of employment after the 1965 season with Baltimore. After the year with Boston, Haddix said she suggested, "You'd better stay home for a while."[16] Haddix left his pitching ideas on a shelf and stayed out of baseball until 1975, when manager Frank Robinson brought him in as the Indians' pitching coach. At least that was close to home, and after his hiatus, Haddix said his wife was more enthusiastic about the prospect, saying, "Go for it."[17]

Haddix stayed with the Indians for four seasons and in 1979 was a coach for the Pirates' World Series champs. This time Haddix stayed with the Pirates until 1984, when he really did retire his uniform.

"I had an enjoyable career the whole way," Haddix said. "I enjoyed

27. Life After Imperfection

every town that I played in and went to, but I would have to say Pittsburgh and St. Louis stand out for me. I wouldn't [change] a whole lot, no. I think you'd be smarter and do things a little bit different, but there are no second chances in our game so you go with what you did."[18]

That was certainly one lesson learned from throwing the wrong pitch to Joe Adcock many years before. "That's the game of baseball," Haddix said. "There's nothing perfect."[19]

When Haddix's major league baseball career ended, throwing and coaching, he returned to his farm in Ohio, and after raising one son and two daughters, he raised a large number of cattle. His one-game gem receded from everyday consciousness, but sports writers kept alive the tale of how Haddix mowed down 36 straight hitters one night in Milwaukee in 1959. The phone rang from all over the country for every anniversary. Twenty years later, sports writers wanted to talk about the game. Twenty-five years later, the calls came in.

Whenever Haddix ventured off his farm, to run errands, to watch baseball, on vacation, at a baseball memorabilia show, whenever they recognized his face or name, baseball fans also reminded him of the magical night of near-perfection. "People come up to me almost every day during the season and want to know about it," he said.[20]

Often, Haddix was asked for the play-by-play, to relive the game's important moments, to review his thoughts and feelings. The general failing memory of old age would never push aside Haddix's recall of his most famous night in baseball. When Haddix was interviewed for the 25th anniversary of the Milwaukee game, he said all types of national television shows that had had no presence at the game wanted to put him on the air to talk about the event, including the *Ed Sullivan Show*. But Haddix turned them all down, he said, because he would have had to leave the team to make the appearances.[21]

Haddix said he still owned the glove he wore in the game against the Braves, but that his Pirates uniform, the magician's outfit, had vanished. It was donated to the Pittsburgh Pirates Hall of Fame at Three Rivers Stadium, but when the Baseball Hall of Fame later requested it, nobody could find old number 31. Just like Adcock's home run, it disappeared into the mists.[22]

28

Upon Further Review

The insult to Harvey Haddix's injury was 32 years in the making. He also lived to experience it.

In September of 1991, Major League Baseball convened a committee on statistical accuracy under the supervision of Commissioner Fay Vincent. The committee rewrote the definition of a no-hitter and essentially rewrote history in the process.

Before 1991, the Major League Baseball definition of a no-hitter was "an official game in which a pitcher or pitchers, gives up no hits."[1] Upon completion of that 1991 meeting, the official definition of a no-hitter became "A no-hitter is a game in which a pitcher or pitchers complete a game of nine innings or more without allowing a hit."[2]

Altering just a few words in the definition made a seismic impact on a multitude of long completed games. Under the first definition, if a game ended because of rain after five innings, yet was recognized as a completed game and went into the record books, a pitcher who held the opposing team without a hit was deemed to have pitched a no-hitter.

Similarly, if a pitcher had completed nine innings or more of a game, yet lost the no-hitter in extra innings, and perhaps the game, his effort was considered to be a no-hitter. The new phrasing of the rule wiped games like that from the record books. It was agreed that to be considered a no-hitter, the pitcher had to keep up his no-hitter as long as the game lasted. About 50 no-hitters that had been recognized over the years were eradicated from the list of officially sanctioned no-hitters either because their authors allowed a hit later or the game they pitched in was deemed too short for acknowledgement.[3]

The most celebrated achievement wiped off the list was Harvey Haddix's 12-inning perfect performance that he lost 1–0 in the 13th inning. Under the new definition, Haddix did not pitch a no-hitter because the game continued and he ultimately gave up a hit.

It took 12 innings and less than three hours for Haddix to claim immortality in Milwaukee. It took one inning of Braves hitting to cost him a perfect game, a no-hitter, a shutout, and a win in short order. And then, after a pause of 32 years, Haddix had his no-hitter stripped from him, as well.

Haddix did not rebel against the decision. He took the news with equanimity, even if others were furious on his behalf. When the ruling came down Haddix said he understood the committee's position. "I'd probably say it wasn't a no-hitter because it wasn't a complete game," Haddix said. "When you think about it, that would be correct. It's disappointing to find out it's not a no-hitter, but it's still the record—most consecutive perfect innings, most consecutive batters retired."[4]

Haddix was right about that. His performance had always defied definition, even though everyone who saw the game realized it was a never-before, never-again showing. Major League Baseball had pretty much put a stamp on that uniqueness by refusing to even call Haddix's pitching a no-hitter.

Pirate teammates who witnessed Haddix's effort or played in the game were more incensed by baseball's declaration than Haddix admitted being. "That sure was the ultimate insult," Pirate pitcher Bob Friend said. "They [Major League Baseball] don't do everything right, that's for sure."[5]

Reliever Roy Face was annoyed by the ruling. "It was a 12-inning no-hitter, but it wasn't a complete game so he doesn't get a no-hitter out of it," Face said. "That doesn't seem right. I know I saw the greatest game ever pitched."[6] What Face was surprised to learn was that Haddix's game might have been the greatest game ever pitched, but it still somehow eluded baseball's official designation as one of 250-plus no-hitters.

Haddix never brooded over his loss to the Braves. He was more surprised than anyone else the way it was remembered and how often fans and people in the sport chatted with him about it. But once the night of the defeat passed, he didn't dwell on it, and that's because it was a defeat. In reacting to the 1991 news from the majors as "disappointing," Haddix was echoing his thoughts of 1959, that losing the perfect game and losing the no-hitter in the 13th was "disappointing." But the biggest disappointment, he repeated many times, was losing the game.

Not everyone has the same forgiving nature as Haddix, and periodically sports writers who examine the past take time to analyze that 1991 baseball decision. They have found it wanting and in their writings have scorched the sport for its seeming folly. "I'm sure there is a sillier rule in sports somewhere, but Major League Baseball's rule about no-hitters has to be near the top of the list," one scribe noted.[7]

In June of 2008, two Los Angeles Angels pitchers, Jered Weaver and Jose Arredondo, combined to pitch eight innings and allow no hits. The Angels lost the game 1–0 on a Weaver error and the game was not considered an official no-hitter. The opposition, as the home team, did not bat in the ninth. Writer Mike Celizic expounded, saying, "No matter what Major League Baseball says, the box score tells the truth, and a zero under the hits column says it's a no-hitter. Baseball doesn't have a name for these games."[8] No one had a name for Haddix's game, either, except to call it imperfect.

Haddix only lived a few more years following baseball's alteration of how it viewed his game. In January of 1994, in failing health, Haddix checked into Community Hospital in Springfield, Ohio, and there he died at the age of 68 on January 8. The cause of death given by the hospital was emphysema.[9]

Haddix had always been a heavy smoker. He smoked between innings during games. "I tried to get him to quit smoking on more than one occasion," ex–Pirate teammate Vernon Law said. "I said, 'Harve, this is gonna kill you if you don't stop smoking.' And eventually, it did."[10]

In the nearly 50 years since Haddix pitched his unnamable, almost-perfect, almost-no-hit, 12-inning beauty of a baseball game, several of the Pirates who participated in the game or watched from the dugout have passed away.

Manager Danny Murtaugh, who suffered from heart problems, died at age 59 in 1976. Catcher Smokey Burgess died at age 64 in 1991. Dick Stuart died at age 70 in 2002. Don Hoak was only 41 when he died in 1969. Rocky Nelson died at age 81 in 2006. Roberto Clemente was only 38, still on the active roster and had just collected his 3,000th hit when he died in a plane crash on Dec. 31, 1972, in Puerto Rico while attempting to deliver food, medicine and other supplies to earthquake-stricken residents of Managua, Nicaragua. Hall of Fame election rules of a five-year waiting period following retirement were waved and Clemente was quickly elected to the Hall. Second baseman Bill Mazeroski played his entire, 17-year-career for the Pirates before retiring in 1972. He was elected to the Hall of Fame in 2001.

Haddix did not have a Hall of Fame career, but he remains a player admired as a teammate and friend that is recalled fondly. "He was one of the best," said outfielder Bill Virdon.[11] "Harvey, hell, he was one of the nicest guys you could meet," said catcher Danny Kravitz. "We always talked about hunting, fishing and sports."[12] "Harvey Haddix was one of the finest people I ever played baseball with," said shortstop Dick Groat, "on and off the field."[13]

Haddix was a major league pitcher for 14 seasons between 1952 and 1965, competing for the St. Louis Cardinals, the Pittsburgh Pirates, the Philadelphia Phillies, the Cincinnati Reds, and the Baltimore Orioles. He was a three-time All-Star and he was proudest of winning two games in the epic 1960 World Series that gave the Pirates a seven-game victory over the New York Yankees. "Harvey could do it all," Virdon said. "He could field his position. He could throw strikes. He could throw breaking balls and change-ups. He was an all-around pitcher."[14]

Either as a minor-league or major-league pitching coach, he spent about 15 of the next 19 years in uniform, as well. In his free time he was a farmer, a hunter and a fisherman. And when Haddix died he was survived by his wife, Marcia, and three children.

Harvey Haddix was a career baseball man as a player, and a coach and he was respected for his mound savvy and 136 victories. For one single evening, however, he pitched the most brilliant baseball in the history of the game, dancing with fate and establishing an unfathomable mark that has never been matched.

Major league baseball still doesn't know what to call it, but the players still around who saw Haddix tie Milwaukee Braves hitters in knots, watch the little southpaw destroy their timing and set down batter after batter, 36 of them in a row, for 12 innings, know what they saw. "I know I never saw anything else like it," Danny Kravitz said.[15]

Neither has anyone else.

"He pitched the greatest game ever pitched and he lost it," said Pirate Hank Foiles. "It was almost impossible. Almost, but not quite. That's the game."[16]

For one bright shining moment, Harvey Haddix mastered baseball the way no other pitcher ever has. He touched a level of perfection deemed impossible, ascending to a heavenly state in his game. He played with the fire of the gods, and then fell back to earth with singed fingertips. Forever after he was regarded as the pitcher who coped so nobly with crushing defeat, the embodiment of man's inability to maintain perfection.

Box Score:
Milwaukee 1, Pittsburgh 0

Game Played on Tuesday, May 26, 1959 (N) at County Stadium

Pit N	0	0	0	0	0	0	0	0	0	0	0	0	0–0	12 1
Mil N	0	0	0	0	0	0	0	0	0	0	0	1	1–1	1 0

Batting

Pittsburgh Pirates	AB	R	H	RBI	BB	SO	PO	A
Schofield ss	6	0	3	0	0	0	2	4
Virdon cf	6	0	1	0	0	0	8	0
Burgess c	5	0	0	0	0	0	8	0
Nelson 1b	5	0	2	0	0	0	14	0
Skinner lf	5	0	1	0	0	0	4	0
Mazeroski 2b	5	0	1	0	0	1	1	1
Hoak 3b	5	0	2	0	0	1	0	6
Mejias rf	3	0	1	0	0	0	1	0
Stuart ph	1	0	0	0	0	0	0	0
Christopher rf	1	0	0	0	0	0	0	0
Haddix p	5	0	1	0	0	0	0	2
Totals	**47**	**0**	**12**	**0**	**0**	**2**	**38**	**13**

Fielding—E: Hoak (5).
Batting—Team LOB: 8.

Milwaukee Braves	AB	R	H	RBI	BB	SO	PO	A
O'Brien 2b	3	0	0	0	0	1	2	5
Rice ph	1	0	0	0	0	0	0	0
Mantilla 2b	1	1	0	0	0	0	1	2
Mathews 3b	4	0	0	0	0	1	2	3
Aaron rf	4	0	0	0	1	0	1	0
Adcock 1b	5	0	1	1	0	2	17	3
Covington lf	4	0	0	0	0	0	4	0
Crandall c	4	0	0	0	0	0	2	1
Pafko cf	4	0	0	0	0	1	6	0
Logan ss	4	0	0	0	0	0	3	5
Burdette p	4	0	0	0	0	3	1	4
Totals	**38**	**1**	**1**	**1**	**1**	**8**	**39**	**23**

Fielding—DP: 3. Adcock-Logan-Adcock, Mathews-O'Brien-Adcock, Adcock-Logan.
Batting—2B: Adcock (3, off Haddix); SH: Mathews (1, off Haddix); IBB: Aaron (2, by Haddix); Team LOB: 1.

Pitching

Pittsburgh Pirates	IP	H	R	ER	BB	SO	HR
Haddix L (4–3)	12.2	1	1	0	1	8	0

IBB: Haddix (5, Aaron).

Milwaukee Braves	IP	H	R	ER	BB	SO	HR
Burdette W (8–2)	13	12	0	0	0	2	0

Umpires: HP—Vinnie Smith, 1B—Frank Dascoli, 2B—Frank Secory, 3B—Hal Dixon
Time of Game: 2:54
Attendance: 19,194

Starting Lineups

Pittsburgh Pirates	Milwaukee Braves
1. Schofield ss	O'Brien 2b
2. Virdon cf	Mathews 3b
3. Burgess c	Aaron rf
4. Nelson 1b	Adcock 1b
5. Skinner lf	Covington lf
6. Mazeroski 2b	Crandall c
7. Hoak 3b	Pafko cf
8. Mejias rf	Logan ss
9. Haddix p	Burdette p

Play by Play

PIRATES 1ST: Schofield popped to third; Virdon grounded out (catcher to first); Burgess flied out to left; 0 R, 0 H, 0 E, 0 LOB. Pirates 0, Braves 0.

BRAVES 1ST: O'Brien grounded out (shortstop to first); Mathews lined to first; Aaron flied out to center; 0 R, 0 H, 0 E, 0 LOB. Pirates 0, Braves 0.

PIRATES 2ND: Nelson singled to center; Skinner grounded into a double play (first to shortstop to first) [Nelson out at second]; Mazeroski struck out; 0 R, 1 H, 0 E, 0 LOB. Pirates 0, Braves 0.

BRAVES 2ND: Adcock struck out; Covington grounded out (second to first); Crandall grounded out (third to first); 0 R, 0 H, 0 E, 0 LOB. Pirates 0, Braves 0.

PIRATES 3RD: Hoak singled to second; Mejias forced Hoak (third to second); Haddix singled to pitcher [Mejias out at third (shortstop to third)];

Box Score

Schofield singled to right [Haddix to third]; Virdon flied out to left; 0 R, 3 H, 0 E, 2 LOB. Pirates 0, Braves 0.

BRAVES 3RD: Pafko flied out to right; Logan lined to shortstop; Burdette was called out on strikes; 0 R, 0 H, 0 E, 0 LOB. Pirates 0, Braves 0.

PIRATES 4TH: Burgess lined to center; Nelson grounded out (second to first); Skinner singled to center; Mazeroski flied out to center; 0 R, 1 H, 0 E, 1 LOB. Pirates 0, Braves 0.

BRAVES 4TH: O'Brien was called out on strikes; Mathews flied out to center; Aaron flied out to center; 0 R, 0 H, 0 E, 0 LOB. Pirates 0, Braves 0.

PIRATES 5TH: Hoak grounded out (shortstop to first); Mejias singled to right; Haddix grounded into a double play (third to second to first) [Mejias out at second]; 0 R, 1 H, 0 E, 0 LOB. Pirates 0, Braves 0.

BRAVES 5TH: Adcock grounded out (third to first); Covington flied out to left; Crandall flied out to left; 0 R, 0 H, 0 E, 0 LOB. Pirates 0, Braves 0.

PIRATES 6TH: Schofield grounded out (second to first); Virdon grounded out (first to pitcher); Burgess flied out to left; 0 R, 0 H, 0 E, 0 LOB. Pirates 0, Braves 0.

BRAVES 6TH: Pafko popped to first; Logan grounded out (shortstop to first); Burdette struck out; 0 R, 0 H, 0 E, 0 LOB. Pirates 0, Braves 0.

PIRATES 7TH: Nelson grounded out (pitcher to first); Skinner flied out to right; Mazeroski flied out to center; 0 R, 0 H, 0 E, 0 LOB. Pirates 0, Braves 0.

BRAVES 7TH: O'Brien grounded out (third to first); Mathews struck out; Aaron grounded out (third to first); 0 R, 0 H, 0 E, 0 LOB. Pirates 0, Braves 0.

PIRATES 8TH: Hoak was called out on strikes; Mejias grounded out (third to first); Haddix grounded out (shortstop to first); 0 R, 0 H, 0 E, 0 LOB. Pirates 0, Braves 0.

BRAVES 8TH: Adcock struck out; Covington flied out to left; Crandall grounded out (third to first); 0 R, 0 H, 0 E, 0 LOB. Pirates 0, Braves 0.

PIRATES 9TH: Schofield grounded out (second to first); Virdon singled to center; Burgess flied out to center; Nelson singled to right [Virdon to third]; Skinner grounded out (pitcher to first); 0 R, 2 H, 0 E, 2 LOB. Pirates 0, Braves 0.

Box Score

BRAVES 9TH: Pafko struck out; Logan flied out to left; Burdette struck out; 0 R, 0 H, 0 E, 0 LOB. Pirates 0, Braves 0.

PIRATES 10TH: Mazeroski grounded out (second to first); Hoak singled to left; Stuart batted for Mejias; Stuart flied out to center; Haddix grounded out (pitcher to first); 0 R, 1 H, 0 E, 1 LOB. Pirates 0, Braves 0.

BRAVES 10TH: Christopher replaced Stuart (playing RF); Rice batted for O'Brien; Rice flied out to center; Debut game for Joe Christopher; Mathews flied out to center; Aaron grounded out (shortstop to first); 0 R, 0 H, 0 E, 0 LOB. Pirates 0, Braves 0.

PIRATES 11TH: Mantilla replaced Rice (playing 2B); Schofield singled to left; Virdon forced Schofield (second to shortstop); Burgess grounded into a double play (first to shortstop) [Virdon out at second]; 0 R, 1 H, 0 E, 0 LOB. Pirates 0, Braves 0.

BRAVES 11TH: Adcock grounded out (shortstop to first); Covington lined to center; Crandall flied out to center; 0 R, 0 H, 0 E, 0 LOB. Pirates 0, Braves 0.

PIRATES 12TH: Nelson flied out to left; Skinner lined to first; Mazeroski singled to center; Hoak forced Mazeroski (shortstop to second); 0 R, 1 H, 0 E, 1 LOB. Pirates 0, Braves 0.

BRAVES 12TH: Pafko grounded out (pitcher to first); Logan flied out to center; Burdette grounded out (third to first); 0 R, 0 H, 0 E, 0 LOB. Pirates 0, Braves 0.

PIRATES 13TH: Christopher grounded out (pitcher to first); Haddix flied out to center; Schofield singled to left; Virdon grounded out (second to first); 0 R, 1 H, 0 E, 1 LOB. Pirates 0, Braves 0.

BRAVES 13TH: Mantilla reached on an error by Hoak; Mathews out on a sacrifice bunt (pitcher to second) [Mantilla to second]; Aaron was walked intentionally; Adcock doubled to center [Mantilla scored (unearned), Aaron to third, Adcock out at second (shortstop unassisted)]; 1 R (0 ER), 1 H, 1 E, 1 LOB. Pirates 0, Braves 1.

Chapter Notes

Chapter 1

1. Walter Langford interview with Harvey Haddix for Baseball Hall of Fame Library, July 3, 1987.
2. Bob Skinner, personal interview, May 22, 2008.
3. Langford interview.
4. Skinner interview.
5. Langford interview.
6. Ibid.
7. Dick Groat, personal interview, May 21, 2008.
8. Langford interview.
9. Groat interview.
10. Langford interview.
11. Ibid.
12. Bob Friend, personal interview, May 21, 2008.
13. Langford interview.
14. Ibid.
15. Ibid.
16. Ibid.
17. Bob Wolf, "High School Shortstop with 2-2 Record in Majors Tagged as Future Pitching Great," *Milwaukee Journal*, April 20, 1953.
18. Langford interview.
19. Wolf, "High School Shortstop."
20. Langford interview.
21. Ibid.
22. Ibid.

Chapter 2

1. Ralph Kiner and Joe Gergen, *Kiner's Korner: At Bat and on the Air—My 40 Years in Baseball* (New York: Arbor House, 1987), pp. 23-24.
2. John McCollister, *The Good, the Bad and the Ugly: Pittsburgh Pirates* (Chicago: Triumph Books, 2008), p. 38.
3. Joe Garagiola and Martin Quigley, *Baseball Is a Funny Game* (New York and Philadelphia: J.B. Lippincott, 1960), pp. 43-44.
4. Kiner and Gergen, *Kiner's Korner*, p. 12.
5. *Pittsburgh Pirates Team Media Guide*, 2007, p. 228.
6. Dennis DeValeria and Jeanne Burke DeValeria, *Honus Wagner: A Biography* (New York: Henry Holt, 1995), p. 3.
7. Ibid., pp. 167-168.
8. Ibid., p. 159.
9. Ibid., pp. 238-240.
10. Ibid., p. 240.
11. Clifton Blue Parker, *Big Poison and Little Poison: Paul and Lloyd Waner, Baseball Brothers* (Jefferson, N.C.: McFarland, 2003), p. 163.
12. Ibid.
13. Ibid., p. 3.
14. Ibid., p. 4.
15. Ibid., p. 70.
16. Kiner and Gergen, *Kiner's Korner*, p. 97.
17. Ibid.
18. Jim O'Brien, *We Had 'Em All the Way* (Pittsburgh: Geyer Printing, 1998), p. 214.

Chapter 3

1. Dick Groat, personal interview, May 21, 2008.
2. Dick Schofield, personal interview, May 21, 2008.
3. BaseballLibrary.com, www.baseballlibrary.com.
4. Samuel A. Andrews, "Bad Henry," *Black Sports Magazine*, May-June 1972.
5. Wayne Minshew, "Hank's 3,000-Hit Dream Born in '54," *The Sporting News*, May 23, 1970.
6. Vern Law, personal interview, May 21, 2008.

7. Walter Langford interview for Baseball Hall of Fame Library, July 3, 1987.
8. Bill Virdon, personal interview, May 21, 2008.

Chapter 4

1. Dick Schofield, personal interview, May 21, 2008.
2. Ibid.
3. Bob Skinner, personal interview, May 22, 2008.
4. Leonard Koppett, "Haddix Can Handle a Buffalo, but How About Met Pitchers?" *The New York Times*, January 5, 1966.
5. Ibid.
6. Dan Hoyt, "Berserk Buffalo No Match for Kitten; Haddix Kills 900-Pounder with .22," Unnamed newspaper, Baseball Hall of Fame Library Archives, December 12, 1964.
7. Skinner, personal interview.
8. "Harvey Won't Go Hungry in Philly," *Pittsburgh Press*, May 28, 1959.
9. Dick Groat, personal interview, May 21, 2008.
10. Ibid.
11. Ibid.
12. Schofield interview.
13. Lester J. Biederman, "Schofield Proving That He Has the Talent to Play with Anyone," *Pittsburgh Press*, September 13, 1960.
14. Schofield interview.
15. Tom Jones, "Dick Schofield Played in Three Different Decades," *Sports Collectors Digest*, June 23, 2000.

Chapter 5

1. Dick Groat, personal interview, May 21, 2008.
2. Bob Skinner, personal interview, May 22, 2008.
3. Walter Langford, interview for Baseball Hall of Fame Library, July 3, 1987.
4. Earl Lawson, "Adcock Won Statewide Acclaim When He Played Basketball with Louisiana State University of Louisiana Five," *Cincinnati Star and Post*, May 12, 1952.
5. Tom Swope, "Hitting Eye Discovered by Adcock in 12 Games," *Cincinnati Post*, March 27, 1952.
6. Bob Wolf, "Borrowed Weapon Smashes Dodgers into Submission," *Milwaukee Journal*, August 1, 1954.
7. Ibid.
8. Bob Friend, personal interview, May 21, 2008.
9. Les Biederman, "Pirates Tried Hard to Win for Haddix; Loss Hard to Take," *Pittsburgh Press*, May 27, 1959.
10. Ibid.
11. Mel Roach, personal interview, July 12, 2008.

Chapter 6

1. The Baseball Page.com, www.thebaseballpage.com.
2. Rich Westcott, *Sports Collector's Digest*, September 4, 1998.
3. Wikipedia, the Free Encyclopedia, www.en.wikipedia.org/wiki/.
4. Gene Schoor, *Lew Burdette of the Braves* (New York: G.P Putnam's Sons, 1960), pp. 16–17.
5. Ibid., p. 86.
6. Ibid., p. 101.
7. The Baseball Page.com, www.thebaseballpage.com.
8. Schoor, *Lew Burdette*, p. 101.
9. Ibid., p. 103.
10. Ibid., p. 104.
11. Bob Friend, personal interview, May 21, 2008.
12. Roy McHugh, "Lew Makes a Pitch for the Spitter," *Pittsburgh Press*, April 29, 1969.
13. Ibid.
14. Ibid.
15. Ibid.
16. "Burdette Sees Life 'Outside.'" CNS (news service, no byline), June 11, 1972.
17. Ibid.
18. Bob Skinner, personal interview, May 22, 2008.

Chapter 7

1. Dick Groat, personal interview, May 21, 2008.
2. Vernon Law, personal interview, May 21, 2008.
3. Andy Pafko, personal interview, May 21, 2008.
4. Milton Gross, "Pafko Pays Off," *Sport Magazine*, September 1952.
5. Pafko interview.
6. Andy Pafko (as told to Dave Condon), "I'm Lucky to be a Brave," *Sport Magazine*, June 1954.
7. Ibid.
8. Pafko interview.
9. Jack Barry, "Crosetti Letter Gave Logan Confidence He Needed to Master Shortstop Job," *Boston Globe*, August 17, 1952.
10. Larry Whiteside, "Old Favorite Johnny Logan on Brewer TV Team," *The Sporting News*, February 17, 1973.
11. Walter Langford, interview, Baseball Hall of Fame Library, July 3, 1987.
12. Dick Schofield, personal interview, May 21, 2008.
13. Hank Foiles, personal interview, May 23, 2008.
14. Ibid.
15. Elroy Face, personal interview, June 10, 2008.

Chapter 8

1. Bob Skinner, personal interview, May 22, 2008.
2. Jim O'Brien, "Maz and the '60 Bucs." (Pittsburgh: Geyer Printing, 1993), p. 416.
3. Wikipedia, the Free Encyclopedia, History of Pittsburgh, http://en.wikipedia.org/wiki/Pittsburgh.
4. BaseballLibrary.com, www.baseballlibrary.com.
5. John McCollister, *The Good, the Bad and the Ugly: Pittsburgh Pirates* (Chicago: Triumph, 2008), p. 99.
6. Wikipedia, Pittsburgh.
7. Harold Livesay, *Andrew Carnegie and the Rise of Big Business: Ode to Steelmaking* (Boston: Little Brown, 1975), p. 189.
8. PBS.org., American Experience.
9. Ibid.
10. William Kennedy, Sr., personal interview, May 27, 2008.
11. John Wideman, "My Town Pittsburgh Essay." PBS.org, April 18, 2008.
12. Hank Foiles, personal interview, May 23, 2008.
13. Kennedy interview.
14. Dick Schofield, personal interview, May 21, 2008.

Chapter 9

1. Bob Friend, personal interview, May 21, 2008.
2. Vernon Law, personal interview, May 21, 2008.
3. Walter Langford interview for Baseball Hall of Fame Library, July 3, 1987.
4. Mel Roach, personal interview, July 12, 2008.
5. Ibid.
6. Roland Hemond, personal interview, May 24, 2008.
7. Ibid.
8. Danny Kravitz, personal interview, May 26, 2008.
9. Roy Face, personal interview, June 10, 2008.

Chapter 10

1. Wikipedia, the Free Encyclopedia, www.en.wikipedia.org/wiki/.
2. John McCollister, *The Good, the Bad and the Ugly: Pittsburgh Pirates* (Chicago: Triumph, 2008), p. 44.
3. Ralph Kiner with Joe Gergen, *Kiner's Korner* (New York: Arbor House, 1987), p. 22.
4. McCollister, *The Good, the Bad and the Ugly*, p. 47.
5. Ibid., p. 49.
6. Joe Garagiola with Martin Quigley, *Baseball Is a Funny Game* (New York: J.B. Lippincott, 1960), p. 61.
7. Ibid., p. 101.

8. David Maraniss, *Clemente: The Passion and Grace of Baseball's Last Hero* (New York: Simon and Schuster, 2006), p. 73.
9. Ibid., pp. 61–62.
10. Ibid., pp. 62–63.

Chapter 11

1. "Hoak 'Tough Guy' in Pirate Drive," *Chicago Daily News*, no byline, August 27, 1960.
2. Ibid.
3. Bill Roeder, unreadable newspaper credit, Baseball Hall of Fame Library archives, July 12, 1957.
4. Ibid.
5. Dick Schaap, "Don Hoak: Whipcracker of the Pirates," *Sport Magazine*, January, 1961.
6. Arthur Daley, "Hoax by Hoak," *New York Times*, April 25, 1957.
7. Milton Gross, "Hoak Played with 8-Stitch Secret Injury," *Pittsburgh Press*, October 4, 1960.
8. Ibid.
9. Ibid.
10. Ibid.
11. Schaap, "Don Hoak: Whipcracker."
12. Ibid.
13. Roy Face, personal interview, June 10, 2008.
14. Jim O'Brien, *We Had 'Em All the Way* (Pittsburgh: Geyer Printing, 1998), p. 330.
15. Del Crandall, personal interview, June 10, 2008.

Chapter 12

1. Jim O'Brien, *We Had 'Em All the Way* (Pittsburgh: Geyer Printing, 1998), p. 9.
2. John McCollister, *The Good, the Bad and the Ugly: Pittsburgh Pirates* (Chicago: Triumph Books, 2008), p. 115.
3. O'Brien, *We Had 'Em*, p. 19.
4. McCollister, *The Good, the Bad and the Ugly*, p. 115.
5. Ibid.
6. Ibid.
7. O'Brien, *We Had 'Em*, p. 32.
8. McCollister, *The Good, the Bad and the Ugly*, p. 112.
9. Ibid.
10. William Kennedy, Sr., personal interview, May 27, 2008.
11. O'Brien, *We Had 'Em*, p. 88.
12. David Maraniss, *Clemente: The Passion and Grace of Baseball's Last Hero* (New York: Simon and Schuster, 2006), p. 87.
13. Maraniss, *Clemente*, p. 88.
14. O'Brien, *We Had 'Em*, p. 284.
15. Ibid., p. 303.
16. Ibid. p. 290.
17. Ibid. p. 45.
18. Ibid. p. 361.

Chapter 13

1. Dick Schofield, personal interview, May 21, 2008.
2. Jim O'Brien, *Maz and the '60s Bucs* (Pittsburgh: Geyer Printing, 1993), p. 396.
3. Ibid.
4. Ibid., p. 392.
5. Ibid., p. 393.
6. Ibid., p. 392.
7. Ibid., pp. 424–425.
8. Ibid., p. 393.
9. Ibid.
10. Andy Pafko, personal interview, May 21, 2008.
11. Andy Pafko, "I'm Lucky to Be a Brave," *Sport Magazine*, June, 1954.
12. Ibid.
13. Ibid.
14. Roy Face, personal interview, June 10, 2008.
15. Sandra Cozzi and James G. Robinson, BaseballLibrary.com, www.baseballlibrary.com, 2002.
16. Steve Stout, "The Greatest Game Ever Pitched," *The National Pastime: A Review of Baseball History*, Society for American Baseball Research, 1994.
17. Cozzi and Robinson.
18. Stout, "The Greatest Game Ever Pitched."

Chapter 14

1. Davis Maraniss, *Clemente: The Passion and Grace of Baseball's Last Hero* (New York: Simon and Schuster, 2006), p. 52.
2. Ibid., p. 53.
3. Bruce Markusen, *The Team That Changed Baseball* (Yardley, Pa.: Westholme, 2006), p. 82.
4. Ibid., p. 82.
5. Ibid., p. 109.
6. Ibid., p. 110.
7. Richard Goldstein, "Howie Haak, Baseball Pioneer in Latin America, Dies at 87," *The New York Times*, March 1, 1999.
8. Ibid.
9. Ibid.
10. America Online Baseball, http://members.aol.com/vibaseball/christopher.html.
11. BaseballLibrary.com, www.baseballlibrary.com, 2006.
12. Don Hoak and Myron Cope, "The Day I Batted Against Castro," *Sport Magazine*, June 1964.
13. Ibid.
14. Ibid.
15. Ibid.
16. Ibid.
17. Ibid.
18. James Campion, "Castro, Baseball and the Great Divide," *Aquarian Weekly*, April 26, 2000.
19. J. David Truby, "Castro's Curveball," *Harper's*, May 1989.
20. Frank Deford, "Liege Lord of Latin Hopes," *Sports Illustrated*, December 24, 1973.
21. Ibid.
22. Robert Cassidy, "Tommy Lasorda Recalls His Days in Cuba," Newsday, April 7, 2008.
23. Ibid.
24. Ibid.
25. Ibid.

Chapter 15

1. Wikipedia, the Free Enclyclopedia, www.en.wikipedia.org/wiki/.
2. Jim O'Brien, *Maz and the '60 Bucs* (Pittsburgh: Geyer Printing, 1993), p. 417.
3. Les Biederman, "Rookie Leads Three Rivals in Scramble," *Pittsburgh Press*, March 30, 1954.
4. "Pirates Call Skinner 'Best Natural Hitter' They've Seen in Years," Associated Press (no byline), April 23, 1954.
5. Ibid.
6. Wikipedia, the Free Encyclopedia, www.en.wikipedia.org/wiki/.
7. Bob Skinner, personal interview, May 22, 2008.
8. Ibid.
9. Ibid.
10. O'Brien, *Maz and the '60 Bucs*, p. 460.
11. Ibid., p. 464.
12. Skinner, personal interview.
13. O'Brien, *Maz and the '60 Bucs*, p. 465.
14. "Ball for Cooperstown: Hank's 3,000th," Associated Press (no byline), May 10, 1970.
15. O'Brien, *Maz and the '60 Bucs*, p. 466.

Chapter 16

1. Jim O'Brien, *We Had 'Em All the Way* (Pittsburgh: Geyer Printing, 1998), p. 213.
2. Jim O'Brien, *Maz and the '60 Bucs* (Pittsburgh: Geyer Printing, 1993), p. 177.
3. Bob Addie, "Murtaugh Left Everybody a Twinkle," *The Washington Post*, December 4, 1976.
4. Ibid.
5. Ibid.
6. Bill Virdon, personal interview, May 21, 2008.
7. O'Brien, *Maz and the '60 Bucs*, p. 177.
8. Ibid., p. 179.
9. Ibid., p. 178.
10. Ibid., p. 179.
11. Ibid., p. 177.
12. Walter Langford, Baseball Hall of Fame Library Archives, July 3, 1987.
13. Danny Kravitz, personal interview, May 26, 2008.
14. John McCollister, *The Good, the Bad and the Ugly: Pittsburgh Pirates* (Chicago: Triumph Books, 2008), p. 3.

15. O'Brien, *We Had 'Em*, p. 96.
16. "Danny Murtaugh, 59," Associated Press, no byline, December 3, 1976.
17. Richard Sandomir, "When Marichal and Spahn Dueled for a Game and a Half," *The New York Times*, July 2, 2008.

Chapter 17

1. Roland Hemond, personal interview, May 24, 2008.
2. Walter Langford, interview for Baseball Hall of Fame Library Archives, July 3, 1987.
3. Ibid.
4. Ibid.
5. Ibid.
6. Vernon Law, personal interview, May 21, 2008.
7. Ibid.
8. Eddie Mathews and Bob Buege, *Eddie Mathews and the National Pastime* (Milwaukee: Douglas American Sports Publications, 1994), p. 139.
9. Ibid., p. 183.
10. Bob Skinner, personal interview, May 22, 2008.
11. Del Crandall, personal interview, June 10, 2008.
12. Ibid.
13. Langford interview.
14. Roy Face, personal interview, June 10, 2008.

Chapter 18

1. Bob Friend, personal interview, May 21, 2008.
2. Ibid.
3. Dick Groat, *Bucs Silent About No-Hitter, Pittsburgh Press*, May 27, 1959.
4. Vernon Law, personal interview, May 21, 2008.
5. Dick Groat, personal interview, May 21, 2008.
6. Bill Virdon, personal interview, May 21, 2008.
7. Walter Langford, Baseball Hall of Fame Library Archives interview, July 3, 1987.

8. Jim O'Brien, *Maz and the '60 Bucs* (Pittsburgh: Dreyer Printing, 1993), p. 464.
9. Friend interview.
10. Wikipedia, the Free Encyclopedia, www.en.wikipedia.org/wiki/.
11. Ibid.
12. Ibid.
13. Ibid.

Chapter 19

1. Les Biederman, "Mazeroski Already at Work to Avoid Another Poor Year," *Pittsburgh Press*, November 29, 1959.
2. Ibid.
3. Jimmy Breslin, "Dick Stuart: Pittsburgh's Problem and Baseball's Dilemma," *True Magazine*, September 1959.
4. Ibid.
5. Ibid.
6. Stan Hochman, "The Man Who Hit 66 HRs," *Philadelphia Daily News*, March 14, 1962.
7. Jack Mann, "They Pay Stuart to Hit; What's the Glove for?" *Newsday* (exact date missing), 1959.
8. Ibid.
9. Les Biederman, "Buccos Revise Book on Stuart After Kid Flips Over New Leaf," *Pittsburgh Press*, November 6, 1959.
10. Breslin, "Dick Stuart."
11. Ibid.
12. Ibid.
13. Mel Roach, personal interview, July 12, 2008.
14. Chuck Greenwood, "Joe Christopher's MLB Debut Came in Haddix's Masterpiece," *Sports Collectors Digest*, July 14, 2000.
15. Dick Schofield, personal interview, May 21, 2008.
16. Bill Virdon, personal interview, May 21, 2008.
17. Hank Foiles, personal interview, May 23, 2008.

Chapter 20

1. Paul Green, "Felix Mantilla," *Sports Collectors Digest*, July 19, 1985.

2. Ibid.
3. Ibid.
4. Bob Friend, personal interview, May 21, 2008.
5. Danny Kravitz, personal interview, May 26, 2008.
6. Bill Virdon, personal interview, May 21, 2008.
7. Del Crandall, personal interview, June 10, 2008.
8. *Milwaukee Journal* (no byline), February 1, 1955.
9. "Joe Adcock, Former Ballplayer, 71," www.mlb.mlb.com., May 3, 1999.
10. R.G. Lynch, "Adcock Finally Cashing in on His Power," *Milwaukee Journal*, July 20, 1956.
11. Wikipedia, the Free Encyclopedia, www.en.wikipedia.org/wiki/.
12. Ibid.
13. Ibid.
14. Ibid.
15. Ibid.
16. Walter Langford, interview for Baseball Hall of Fame Library Archives, July 3, 1987.
17. Jim O'Brien, *Maz and the '60 Bucs* (Pittsburgh: Geyer Printing, 1993), p. 457.
18. Ibid., p. 465.

Chapter 21

1. Bob Prince, KDKA radio recording, May 26, 1959.
2. Dick Schaap, "Don Hoak: Whipcracker of the Pirates," *Sport Magazine*, January 1961.
3. Ibid.
4. Andy Pafko, personal interview, May 21, 2008.
5. Lou Chapman, "...And, in This Corner: Battling Johnny Logan!" *Baseball Digest*, February 1992.
6. Bob McCoy, "Keeping Score," *Milwaukee Sentinel*, July 5, 1980.
7. Prince, KDKA.
8. Amy Rabideau Silvers, "State Loses Sports Voice of Golden Era," *Milwaukee Journal-Sentinel*, December 13, 2003.
9. Ibid.
10. Earl Gillespie, WTMJ radio recording, May 26, 1959.
11. Walter Langford, interview for Baseball Hall of Fame Library Archives, July 3, 1987.

Chapter 22

1. Roland Hemond, personal interview, May 24, 2008.
2. Earl Gillespie, WTMJ radio recording, May 26, 1959.
3. Walter Langford interview for Baseball Hall of Fame Library Archives, July 3, 1987.
4. Bob Prince, KDKA radio recording, May 26, 1959.
5. Hal Bock, "A Look at Perfect and Not-so-perfect Games," Associated Press, May 26, 2002.
6. Vernon Law, personal interview, May 21, 2008.
7. Gillespie, WTMJ.
8. Ibid.
9. Prince, KDKA.
10. Bob Friend, personal interview, May 21, 2008.
11. Langford interview.
12. Del Crandall, personal interview, June 10, 2008.
13. Mel Roach, personal interview, July 12, 2008.
14. Hemond, personal interview.
15. Danny Kravitz, personal interview, May 26, 2008.
16. Bob Skinner, personal interview, May 22, 2008.
17. Jim O'Brien, *Maz and the '60 Bucs* (Pittsburgh: Geyer Printing, 1993), p. 466.
18. Les Biederman, "Pirate Lefty Hurls 12 Perfect Innings Before Bowing, 2-0," *Pittsburgh Press*, May 27, 1959.
19. Les Biederman, "Haddix's Perfect Game for Naught as Milwaukee Wins It in 13th Inning," *Pittsburgh Press*, May 27, 1959.
20. Ibid.
21. Ibid.
22. Skinner interview.
23. Dick Schofield, personal interview, May 21, 2008.

24. Baseball Almanac Fast Facts, http://www.baseball-almanac.com.
25. Ibid.
26. O'Brien, *Maz and the '60 Bucs*, p. 468.
27. Ibid.
28. Ibid.
29. Friend interview.

Chapter 23

1. Bill Kennedy, personal interview, May 27, 2008.
2. Ibid.
3. Ibid.
4. Ibid.
5. Sandy Grady, "Man About Sports—Haddix a Born Victim," *Philadelphia Bulletin*, May 27, 1959.
6. Ibid.
7. Les Biederman, "Haddix's Perfect Game for Naught as Milwaukee Wins It in 13th Inning," *Pittsburgh Press*, May 27, 1959.
8. Pat Livingston, "Mrs. Haddix Tuned in After 9th," Pittsburgh Press, May 27, 1959.
9. Ibid.
10. Ibid.
11. Ibid.
12. Pete Coutros, "Adcock Recalls Crushing Kitten," *New York Post*, July 28, 1989.
13. Ed Phetteplace, "Down the Baseball Trail" (no date), Baseball Hall of Fame Library Archives.
14. "Joe Adcock Dies at 71," CNN SI.com Web site, http://sportsillustrated.cnn.com, no byline, May 3, 1999.
15. Cleon Walfoort, "Adcock Ruled Out, Gets Two Base Hit," *Milwaukee Journal*, May 27, 1959.
16. Ibid.
17. "Harvey Haddix Makes History by Retiring 36 Straight Men," *Milwaukee Journal*, byline missing, May 27, 1959.
18. Ibid.
19. Del Crandall, personal interview, June 10, 2008.
20. Coutros, "Adcock Recalls Crushing Kitten."

21. "'Inspiring' Mayor Wires Haddix," *Pittsburgh Press*, no byline, May 28, 1959.
22. "First in History—No Pitcher Had Ever Retired 36 in Order," *Milwaukee Journal*, no byline, May 27, 1959.
23. Ibid.
24. "Haddix Recalls Perfect 12," Associated Press, May 27, 1979.
25. Dick Groat, personal interview, May 21, 2008.
26. Gene P. Carney, *Notes from the Shadows of Cooperstown*, September 22, 2001.
27. Steve Stout, "The Greatest Game Ever Pitched," *The National Pastime*, 1994.
28. Vernon Law, personal interview, September 21, 2008.
29. Ibid.
30. Ibid.
31. Ibid.
32. Ibid.
33. Ibid.

Chapter 24

1. Roy Face, personal interview, June 10, 2008.
2. Jim O'Brien, *Maz and the '60 Bucs* (Pittsburgh: Geyer Printing, 1993), p. 466.
3. Ibid.
4. Sandra Cozzi and James G. Robinson, "The Greatest Game Ever Lost," BaseballLibrary.com, www.baseballlibrary.com, February 6, 2008.
5. Ibid.
6. Joe Williams, "Fate Against Haddix," *New York World-Telegram*, May 29, 1959.
7. Ibid.
8. Les Biederman, "Harvey Wasn't Aware He Had Perfect Game," *The Sporting News*, June 3, 1959.
9. Ibid.
10. Dick Groat, personal interview, May 21, 2008.
11. David Maraniss, *Clemente: The Passion and Grace of Baseball's Last Hero* (New York: Simon and Schuster, 2006), p. 94.
12. Face, personal interview.
13. Ibid.
14. Mel Roach, personal interview, July 12, 2008.

15. Ibid.
16. Ibid.
17. Gene Schoor, *Lew Burdette of the Braves* (New York: G.P. Putnam's Sons, 1960), p. 166.
18. Ibid.
19. Biederman, "Harvey Wasn't Aware."

Chapter 25

1. Les Biederman, "Haddix Thinks Back: 'Impact of Greatest Game Slow Coming,'" *Pittsburgh Press*, May 27, 1960.
2. Dick Groat, personal interview, May 21, 2008.
3. Biederman, "Haddix Thinks Back."
4. David Maraniss, *Clemente: The Passion and Grace of Baseball's Last Hero* (New York: Simon and Schuster, 2006), p. 99.
5. Milton Gross, "Friend Recounts 'Painful' Season, Looks to Future," *Pittsburgh Press*, September 13, 1959.
6. Ibid.
7. Les Biederman, "Pirate Players Rate Bill Virdon with Best in National League," *Pittsburgh Press*, March 29, 1962.
8. Ibid.
9. Bill Virdon, personal interview, May 21, 2008.
10. Walter Langford interview for Baseball Hall of Fame Library Archives, July 3, 1987.
11. Ibid.
12. Ibid.
13. Ibid.
14. Bill Kennedy, personal interview, May 27, 2008.
15. Jim O'Brien, *Maz and the '60 Bucs* (Pittsburgh: Geyer Printing), p. 28.
16. Ibid., p. 82.
17. "Sidelines: That Rings a Bell; 12 Perfect Innings and 32 Years to Remember," *New York Times*, no byline, May 27, 1991.

Chapter 26

1. Tim Wiles, "Who's on Verse," *The New York Times*, March 31, 1996.
2. Weldon Myers, personal notes, Baseball Hall of Fame Archives, 1961.
3. Ibid.
4. Ibid.
5. Jack Slayton, "A Poetical Tribute to Haddix," *Lakeland Ledger*, May 4, 1961.
6. Weldon Myers, "Twelve Perfect Innings—a Pretty Good Game" (Lakeland, Fla.: The Commercial Press, 1961), Foreword.
7. Ibid., pp. 1–2.
8. Ibid., p. 3.
9. Ibid., pp. 6–8.
10. Myers, Baseball Hall of Fame Archives.
11. Myers, "Twelve Perfect Innings," p. 20.
12. Ibid., p. 27.
13. Ibid., pp. 54–56.
14. Ibid., p. 76.
15. Ibid., p. 81.
16. Slayton, "A Poetical Tribute to Haddix."
17. Ibid.

Chapter 27

1. Walter Langford, interview for Baseball Hall of Fame, July 3, 1987.
2. Ibid.
3. Les Biederman, "An Era Passes with Haddix," *Pittsburgh Press*, December 17, 1963.
4. Langford interview.
5. Ibid.
6. Si Burick, "Haddix Finds Happiness Chopping Corn, Fishing," *Dayton Daily News*, September 9, 1965.
7. "Haddox Retires," United Press International (no byline), September 9, 1965.
8. Burick, "Haddix Finds Happiness."
9. Leonard Koppett, "Haddix Can Handle a Buffalo, but How About Met Pitchers?" *The New York Times*, January 5, 1966.
10. Langford interview.
11. Barney Kremenko, "Haddix Enjoys Polishing Gems," *New York Journal-American*, January 15, 1966.
12. Earl Lawson, "No Coddling of Reds' Twirlers with Tutor Haddix in Command," *The Sporting News*, November 23, 1968.

13. "Sore-Arm Plague Stirs [Majors]," *The Sporting News,* 1966 (byline cut off, date cut off).
14. Langford interview.
15. Larry Claflin, "Haddix on Hot Seat as Red Sox Pitching Coach," *The Sporting News,* October 31, 1970.
16. Langford interview.
17. Ibid.
18. Ibid.
19. Ibid.
20. Sid Bordman, "Haddix has Perfected His Tale of Baseball Epic," *Kansas City Star,* May 1, 1984.
21. "It's Been 25 Years Since He Hurled Best Game Ever, and Lost," Associated Press (no byline), Baseball Hall of Fame Library Archives, May 1984.
22. Ibid.

Chapter 28

1. Baseball Reference.com., www.baseball-reference.com/.
2. Nonohitters.com, www.nonohitters.com/.
3. Hal Bock, "A Look at Perfect Games and Not-so-Perfect Games," Associated Press, May 26, 2002.
4. "Haddix Dies; Pitched Longest Perfect Game." Associated Press, January 9, 1994.
5. Bob Friend, personal interview, May 21, 2008.
6. Roy Face, personal interview, June 10, 2008.
7. Mike Celizic, "Rule on No-hitters Is Dumb," NBCsports.com, June 29, 2008.
8. Ibid.
9. "Haddix Dies," Associated Press.
10. Vernon Law, personal interview, May 21, 2008.
11. Bill Virdon, personal interview, May 21, 2008.
12. Danny Kravitz, personal interview, May 26, 2008.
13. Dick Groat, personal interview, May 21, 2008.
14. Virdon interview.
15. Kravitz interview.
16. Hank Foiles, personal interview, May 23, 2008.

Bibliography

Books

DeValeria, Dennis and Jeanne. *Honus Wagner: A Biography*. New York: Henry Holt, 1995.

Garagiola, Joe, and Martin Quigley. *Baseball Is a Funny Game*. Philadelphia: J.P. Lippincott, 1960.

Kiner, Ralph, and Joe Gergen. *Kiner's Korner: At Bat and on the Air — My 40 Years in Baseball*. New York: Arbor House, 1987.

Livesay, Harold. *Andrew Carnegie and the Rise of Big Business (Ode to Steelmaking)*. Boston: Little Brown, 1975.

Maraniss, David. *Clemente: The Passion and Grace of Baseball's Last Hero*. New York: Simon and Schuster, 2006.

Markusen, Bruce. *The Team That Changed Baseball: Roberto Clemente and the 1971 Pittsburgh Pirates*. Yardley, PA: Westholme, 2006.

Mathews, Eddie, and Bob Buege. *Eddie Mathews and the National Pastime*. Milwaukee: Douglas American Sports Publications, 1994.

McCollister, John. *The Good, the Bad and the Ugly: Pittsburgh Pirates*. Chicago: Triumph Books, 2008.

Myers, Dr. Weldon. *Twelve Perfect Innings — a Pretty Good Game*. Lakeland, Fla: The Commercial Press, 1961.

O'Brien, Jim. *Maz and the '60 Bucs*. Pittsburgh: Geyer Printing, 1993.

_____. *We Had 'Em All the Way*. Pittsburgh: Geyer Printing, 1998.

Parker, Clifton Blue. *Big Poison and Little Poison: Paul and Lloyd Waner, Baseball Brothers*. Jefferson, N.C.: McFarland, 2003.

Schoor, Gene. *Lew Burdette of the Braves*. New York: G.P. Putnam's Sons, 1960.

Newspapers

Boston Globe
Chicago Daily News
Cincinnati Post
Cincinnati Star & Post
Dayton Daily News
Kansas City Star
Lakeland Ledger
Milwaukee Journal
Milwaukee Journal-Sentinel
Milwaukee Sentinel
New York Post
New York Times
New York World-Telegram
Newsday
Philadelphia Daily News
Pittsburgh Press
Washington Post

Personal Interviews

Del Crandall
Elroy Face
Hank Foiles
Bob Friend
Dick Groat
Roland Hemond
Bill Kennedy, Sr.
Danny Kravitz
Vernon Law
Andy Pafko
Mel Roach
Dick Schofield
Bob Skinner
Bill Virdon

Publications

Aquarian Weekly
Baseball Digest
Baseball Encyclopedia 2005
Black Sports Magazine

Bibliography

Harpers Magazine
The National Pastime, the Society for American Baseball Research
Notes from the Shadows of Cooperstown
Pittsburgh Pirates Team Media Guide, 2007
Sport Magazine
The Sporting News
Sports Collectors' Digest
Sports Illustrated
True Magazine

Web Sites

America Online Baseball Pages
Baseball Almanac Fast Facts
BaseballLibrary.com
Baseballreference.com
CNN SI.com
Major League Baseball.com
NBCsports.com
PBS.org
Thebaseballpage.com
Wikipedia, the Free Encyclopedia

Baseball Hall of Fame Library

(The Baseball Hall of Fame Library contains many newspaper clippings on which the name of the publication or writer has been eliminated, or where the date has been omitted. Some archival nature of this type was used.)

Walter Langford recorded interview with Harvey Haddix.

News Services

Associated Press
CNS
United Press International

Radio

KDKA recording of Bob Prince
WTMJ recording of Earl Gillespie

Index

Aaron, Hank 1, 21, 22, 24, 35, 45, 55, 57, 77, 78, 79, 92, 94, 105, 118, 119, 120, 122, 137, 140, 148, 149, 159, 160, 174
Aber, Al 101
Abreus, Cuba 44, 82
Adcock, Joe 1, 11, 35, 36, 45, 57, 69, 76, 77, 79, 91, 104, 105, 108, 122, 123, 128, 135, 138, 140, 144, 147, 148, 149, 150, 156, 159, 178, 183
Alaska 46
Alaska Baseball League 86
Ali, Muhammad 143
Allegheny River 50
Alley, Gene 84
Allison, Bob 89
Almendares 88
American Association 14, 20
American League 120, 121, 124
American Tobacco Company 15
Ames, Red 124
Anderson, IN 31
Arlin, Howard 72, 73
Arredondo, Jose 186
Ashburn, Richie 77, 106
Athens Summer Olympics 89
Atlanta Braves 24, 92, 133, 160

Babushka power 73
Baltimore Orioles 31, 165, 179, 187
Banks, Ernie 78
Baseball Digest 78
Baseball Encyclopedia 8, 76
Baseball Hall of Fame 14, 16, 17, 21, 41, 56, 60, 77, 84, 94, 111, 112, 114, 117, 170, 171, 182, 183, 186
Batista, Fulgencio 88, 89
Bauer, Hank 179
Belen College 86
Bell, Cool Papa 84
Bell, Gus 66
Berardino, John 12, 13
Berra, Yogi 12, 129, 165, 168, 181
Bickford, Vern 131
Biederman, Lester 68, 164, 179
Black, Joe 124
Blenig, Rudy 57
Bookbinders 30
Boston Braves 12, 24, 40, 96, 105, 125, 133

Boston Pilgrims 15, 162
Boston Red Sox 15, 31, 112, 121, 152, 182
Boyceville, WI 46
Boyer, Clete 165
Bragan, Bobby 98
Brazle, Al 11
Brecheen, Harry 7, 8
Bridgewater College 172
Brigham Young University 22
Brooklyn Dodgers 12, 18, 35, 41, 45, 46, 59, 60, 63, 64, 65, 66, 69, 82, 83, 84, 90, 104, 113, 125, 152
Brooklyn Superbas 124
Brown, Joe E. 69
Brown, Joe L. 69, 83, 86, 92, 99, 100, 157
Bruton, Bill 121
Buffalo, NY 111
Buhl, Bob 80, 81
Burdette, Lew 2, 8, 11, 19, 20, 33, 38, 40, 41, 42, 43, 44, 54, 68, 76, 78, 80, 91, 92, 94, 102, 103, 104, 106, 108, 110, 115, 117, 122, 127, 129, 132, 135, 143, 156, 159, 160, 163, 176
Burgess, Smokey 7, 19, 54, 65, 76, 77, 78, 99, 108, 122, 157, 158, 186

California Angels 92
Campanella, Roy 41, 66
Canadian Baseball Hall of Fame 90
Caray, Harry 132, 133, 153
Carnegie, Andrew 51, 52
Carney, Gene 152
"Casey at the Bat" 171, 172
Cash, Dave 83, 84
Castro, Fidel 85, 86, 87, 88, 89
Catawba High School 8
Celizic, Mike 186
Chaffee, Nancy 13
Champion Lakes Golf Club 30
Chartiers, PA 14
Cher 97
Chester, PA 96
Chicago Bears 97
Chicago Cubs 18, 45, 46, 50, 62, 90, 124
Chicago White Sox 34, 57, 69, 90, 92, 101, 112, 116
Christopher, Joe 82, 85, 86, 118, 135, 140
Cienfuegos 87

Index

Cimoli, Gino 67
Cincinnati Red Stockings 124
Cincinnati Reds 1, 5, 7, 11, 18, 21, 35, 43, 53, 54, 65, 66, 124, 125, 150, 181, 187
Clemente, Roberto 19, 44, 63, 64, 71, 73, 74, 78, 82, 83, 85, 98, 102, 110, 114, 118, 158, 163, 164, 186
Cleveland, O. 111, 112
Cleveland Indians 90, 182
Clines, Gene 83
Coast Guard 57
Cobb, Ty 15
College Basketball Hall of Fame 31
Columbia, SC 120
Columbus, OH 9, 118
Commercial Press of Lakeland 171
Community Hospital of Springfield, OH 186
Converse College 172
Cope, Myron 77, 86, 97
County Stadium 1, 5, 20, 24, 33, 56, 92, 94, 98, 102, 103, 104, 105, 106, 119, 127, 132, 134, 140, 145
Covington, Wes 36, 69, 78, 79, 104, 123
Crandall, Del 19, 36, 69, 79, 103, 105, 106, 118, 122, 123, 140, 150
Crosby, Bing 18
Crosetti, Frankie 47
Cuba 83, 84, 85, 87, 89
Cuban League 88
Cy Young Award 22, 164

Dascoli, Frank 149
Davalillo, Vic 83
Davis, Tommy 160
Dean, Daffy 60
Dean, Dizzy 60
Deford, Frank 88
Del Greco, Bobby 61
Detroit Tigers 13, 41, 101, 112, 162
Dihigo, Martin 84
DiMaggio, Joe 40, 78
Ditmar, Art 165, 167
Doby, Larry 84
Dominican Republic 86, 88
Donahue, Pat 8, 9
Douglas, Whammy 7
Dreyfuss, Barney 14, 50, 51
Drysdale, Don 131
Duke University 30, 61
Durocher, Leo 45, 46

Ebbets Field 35
Ed Sullivan Show 183
Elias Sports Bureau 101
Ellis, Dock 83
Evansville (minors) 120

Face, Elroy 48, 58, 61, 64, 69, 80, 106, 155, 158, 159, 164, 165, 167, 168, 185
Feller, Bob 35, 78
Fenway Park 152
Fidrych, Mark 41
Foiles, Hank 29, 48, 53, 54, 76, 119, 187
Fontaine, Bob 115
Forbes Field 13, 16, 50, 51, 53, 63, 70, 72, 129, 164, 165, 167, 169
Ford, Whitey 165, 166, 168
Fort Myers, FL 163
Fowler, Art 89
Freeman, Herschel 124
Frick, Ford 66, 67, 153
Friend, Bob 8, 36, 42, 53, 54, 61, 62, 64, 67, 68, 74, 107, 111, 121, 129, 138, 145, 153, 157, 161, 164, 165, 168, 185

Galbreath, John 60
Gallagher, Thomas J. 150
Galvin, Pud 111
Gandhi, Mahatma 61
Garagiola, Joe 12, 62
Gardner, Horace 120
Gashouse Gang 60
General Hospital 13
Giles, Warren 43, 66, 67, 149, 150, 153, 157
Gillespie, Earl 133, 136, 138
Gilliam, Junior 66, 160
Golf Digest 78
Gonder, Jesse 71
Grady, Sandy 147
Green, Fred 80
Green Bay Blue Jays 133
Green Bay Packers 133
Green Weenie 73
Greenberg, Hank 13
Greengrass, Jim 131
Gretzky, Wayne 15
Grimes, Burleigh 42, 43
Grimm, Charlie 131
Groat, Dick 6, 16, 19, 29, 30, 31, 32, 33, 44, 61, 64, 74, 76, 92, 98, 99, 107, 108, 110, 114, 121, 129, 135, 151, 157, 158, 163, 164, 187
Gustine, Frankie 53

Haak, Howie 82, 83, 85, 86, 87, 88
Haddix, Ann 28
Haddix, Harvey (son) 28
Haddix, Marcia 28, 125, 126, 148, 154, 156, 182, 187
Haddix, Teri 28
Halley's Comet 1
Haney, Fred 12, 36, 56, 63, 91, 104, 118, 120, 135, 137, 159, 160

206

Index

Harlem Globetrotters 20
Harmon, Merle 133
Harrah, OK 17
Harshman, Jack 101
Havana Hilton 89
Havana Sugar Kings 90
Hazo, Sam 75
Hebner, Richie 83
Hemond, Roland 57, 102, 136, 140
Hernandez, Jackie 83
Hernon, Jack 164
Herzog, Whitey 181
Hirdt, Steve 101
Hoak, Don 6, 7, 19, 36, 42, 43, 53, 65, 67, 68, 69, 86, 87, 94, 102, 106, 115, 129, 130, 131, 136, 137, 143, 156, 157, 158, 163, 164, 177, 186
Houston Astros 34, 92, 122, 141
Howard, Elston 165
Hubbard, Cal 67
Hubbell, Carl 39
Huntington Avenue Grounds 15

Iliad 171
Illinois state government 32
International League 90
International League Hall of Fame 90
Iron City beer 49, 52
Isabella, Puerto Rico 120
Iwo Jima 65

Janowicz, Vic 62
Javier, Julian 163
Jaws 107
Johnson, Walter 112, 151
Jordan, Michael 97
Joss, Addie 112
Josten's 32

Kansas City Athletics 180
Kansas City Monarchs 62
KDKA 72, 73, 126, 127, 137, 148
Kennedy, William, Jr. 146, 147, 169
Kennedy, William, Sr. 52, 53, 73, 128, 146, 147, 169, 170
Kiner, Ralph 12, 13, 18, 61, 62, 96
King, Nellie 71
Kline, Ron 61
Klippstein, Johnny 124
Kluszewski, Ted 33, 34, 57
Koosman, Jerry 181
Korea 46
Koufax, Sandy 137
Kravitz, Danny 54, 58, 76, 100, 121, 140, 187
Kubek, Tony 165

La Jolla, CA 91
Lakeland, FL 171
Landis, Kenesaw Mountain 60
Larsen, Don 112, 113, 152
Lasorda, Tommy 88, 89
Latrobe, PA 49
Law, Vernon 22, 45, 55, 61, 62, 64, 71, 103, 138, 153, 157, 158, 163, 167, 168, 186
Leigh, Janet 13
Leonard, Buck 84
Lincoln, NE (minors) 116
Logan, Johnny 34, 47, 66, 79, 110, 121, 122, 130, 131, 132, 133, 176
Los Angeles 70
Los Angeles Angels 186
Los Angeles Dodgers 88, 159, 160
Louisiana State University 35

Mack, Connie 8, 9
Magee, William A. 51
Major League Baseball: no-hitter definition 184, 185, 186; officials 3
Managua, Nicaragua 186
Mantilla, Felix 120, 121, 122, 130, 135, 136, 137, 138, 142, 143, 144, 149, 176
Mantle, Mickey 22, 40, 53, 78, 94, 165, 166, 167
Maraniss, David 63
Marianao, Cuba 87, 88
Marichal, Juan 39, 101
Marines 65
Maris, Roger 165, 167
Marquette University 133
Massachusetts 83
Mathews, Eddie 1, 19, 21, 35, 44, 45, 55, 57, 68, 78, 79, 93, 94, 103, 104, 105, 108, 118, 119, 122, 137, 148, 159, 160
Mathewson, Christy 151
Mauch, Gene 92
Mauldin, Bill 97
Mayfield, KY (minors) 91
Mays, Willie 21, 53, 77, 78, 101, 165
Mazeroski, Bill 19, 29, 31, 34, 36, 54, 94, 114, 115, 128, 129, 130, 137, 163, 169, 170, 186
McGraw, John 14
McGraw, Tug 181
McIntyre, Harry 124
Medway, OH 8
Mejias, Roman 19, 44, 47, 68, 82, 85, 102, 103, 115, 118
Milwaukee, WI 1, 5, 12, 56, 75, 79, 90, 144
Milwaukee Braves 1, 2, 5, 6, 8, 11, 19, 20, 21, 24, 33, 35, 36, 37, 38, 40, 45, 46, 47, 54, 55, 56, 57, 58, 66, 69, 80, 81, 92, 93, 94, 98, 101, 102, 104, 105, 108, 110, 111, 117, 118, 121, 122, 123, 124, 125, 128, 129,

Index

130, 131, 132, 133, 134, 135, 136, 137, 140, 142, 143, 145, 148, 149, 151, 153, 155, 156, 157, 158, 159, 160, 162, 165, 176, 180, 181, 183, 184, 185, 187
Milwaukee Brewers (minors) 20
Milwaukee Brewers 132
Minoso, Minnie 85
Missouri 60
Mizell, Vinegar Bend 163, 166
Mobile, AL 22
Monongahela River 14, 50
Montgomery, AL 120
Montreal Royals 63, 82
Morgan, J.P. 52
Morgan, Ray 152
Murtaugh, Danny 1, 6, 19, 21, 32, 34, 54, 58, 80, 83, 84, 96, 97, 98, 99, 100, 101, 106, 114, 115, 118, 125, 135, 137, 142, 157, 158, 159, 163, 167, 168, 186
Murtaugh, Kate 97
Musial, Stan 47, 53, 77, 78, 182
Myers, Dr. Weldon 171, 172, 173, 174, 175, 176, 177, 178

National Baseball Congress 86
National League 1, 6, 10, 11, 12, 13, 14, 15, 19, 21, 32, 33, 41, 42, 43, 53, 57, 60, 68, 76, 84, 92, 96, 104, 105, 111, 114, 115, 118, 124, 142, 149, 157, 158, 162, 163, 165, 181
Neal, Charlie 66
Negro Leagues 62, 84
Nelson, Rocky 19, 21, 33, 34, 54, 69, 90, 91, 94, 98, 110, 115, 123, 128, 131, 136, 137, 156, 163, 174, 186
New Orleans Pelicans (minors) 96, 100
New York Giants 14, 18, 36, 46, 86, 91, 124
New York Mets 12, 86, 180, 181, 182
New York Yankees 19, 24, 38, 40, 47, 56, 67, 104, 112, 122, 152, 163, 165, 166, 167, 168, 187
Nitro, WV 38
Nixon, Richard 137
Norfolk, VA 42
Northwestern University 31

O'Brien, Eddie 20
O'Brien, Jim 70, 72
O'Brien, Johnny 20, 21, 54, 55, 76, 94, 108, 118, 120, 174
Ohio River 50
Ohio State 62
Ohio Wesleyan 59
Okinawa 65
Oklahoma University 70
Oliver, Al 83, 84
O'Malley, Walter 59

O'Neill, Steve 43
Otero, Reggie 90
Owens, Brick 152

Pafko, Andy 45, 46, 47, 54, 78, 79, 94, 105, 110, 117, 128, 131, 176
Pafko, Ellen 79
Pagan, Jose 83
Paige, Satchel 84, 86
Pan American Games 89
Panama 83
Peary, Danny 80
Pendleton, Jim 7
Perez, Tony 85
Perini, Lou 132
Petit, Paul 61
Philadelphia 30
Philadelphia Athletics 9, 112
Philadelphia Phillies 11, 43, 72, 77, 83, 84, 92, 96, 98, 106, 124, 159, 187
Pineland, Texas 62
Pinson, Vada 150
Pirate City 83
Pittsburgh, PA 49, 50, 125, 127
Pittsburgh Alleghenies 14
Pittsburgh Pirates 1, 2, 5, 6, 7, 11, 12, 13, 14, 16, 17, 18, 19, 20, 22, 24, 26, 29, 30, 33, 36, 39, 41, 42, 43, 44, 48, 49, 50, 51, 53, 54, 55, 56, 58, 59, 60, 61, 62, 63, 64, 65, 67, 69, 70, 71, 72, 73, 74, 75, 80, 82, 83, 84, 86, 88, 90, 91, 92, 94, 96, 97, 98, 99, 100, 102, 103, 104, 106, 107, 108, 110, 111, 114, 115, 116, 117, 118, 119, 121, 122, 124, 125, 128, 132, 133, 134, 135, 138, 140, 141, 142, 143, 145, 146, 150, 153, 155, 156, 157, 158, 161, 162, 163, 164, 165, 166, 167, 168, 179, 181, 182, 183, 185, 187; Hall of Fame 183
Pittsburgh Press 164
Pittsburgh Steelers 97
Podres, Johnny 36
Polo Grounds 18, 35
Portsmith, OH 59, 90
Post, Wally 66
Powers, John 7
Prince, Betty 74
Prince, Bob 70, 71, 72, 73, 74, 75, 91, 94, 95, 102, 114, 127, 128, 132, 137, 138, 146, 154, 159, 170
Prio, Carlos 88
Providence, RI 111
Puerto Plata, Puerto Rico 88
Puerto Rico 10, 63, 82, 83, 84, 86, 186

Reese, Pee Wee 41
Rice, Del 118, 119, 120, 121
Richardson, Bobby 165

Index

Richmond, Lee 111
Rickey, Branch 9, 18, 20, 59, 60, 61, 62, 64, 82, 83, 85, 88, 91, 97, 157, 158
Rickey, Branch, Jr. 115, 116
Rizzuto, Phil 133
Roach, Mel 37, 56, 118, 140, 159, 160
Roberts, Christine 62, 63
Roberts, Curt 62, 63
Roberts, Robin 39
Robertson, Bob 84
Robertson, Charlie 112
Robinson, Frank 182
Robinson, Jackie 41, 60, 62, 63, 82, 84
Robinson, Rachel 62
Rock, Sergeant 97
Rolling Rock beer 49
Rooney, Art 97
Rowswell, Rosey 70, 71, 72
Ruth, Babe 13, 15, 21, 94, 115, 116, 117, 152
Ryan, Nolan 181

Sain, Johnny 40
St. Louis Browns 59
St. Louis Cardinals 7, 8, 9, 10, 11, 27, 31, 32, 33, 59, 60, 67, 69, 90, 92, 118, 153, 182, 183, 187
Sanchez, Raul 66
Sandburg, Carl 97
San Diego Padres (minors) 92
San Francisco Giants 101, 159
Sanguillen, Manny 83, 85
Santurce, Puerto Rico 63
Schoendienst, Red 21, 56, 121
Schofield, Dick 19, 20, 21, 27, 31, 32, 44, 47, 48, 53, 71, 76, 99, 102, 108, 119, 121, 122, 123, 135, 143, 163, 174
Schofield, Dick, Jr. 31
Schroeder Hotel 5, 143
Seattle University 20
Seaver, Tom 181
Sheboygan, WI 31
Shore, Ernie 152
Sisler, George 59, 116
Skinner, Bob 5, 6, 16, 19, 29, 30, 34, 43, 49, 50, 54, 62, 64, 69, 78, 91, 92, 93, 94, 105, 110, 128, 141, 142, 143, 158, 163, 164
Skinner, Joel 34, 92
Skowron, Bill 165, 168
Smith, Hal 158, 163, 164
Smith, Mayo 21
Snead, J.C. 74
Snead, Sam 74
Snider, Duke 41
South Atlantic League 22, 35, 120
South Vienna, OH 8, 9
Spahn, Warren 40, 55, 101, 152, 159, 160

Spartanburg, SC 172
Sport magazine 46
The Sporting News 182
Sports Illustrated 88
Springfield, OH 125, 148, 186
Stargell, Willie 83, 100
Steinbrenner, George 122
Stengel, Casey 12, 112, 165, 167, 168
Stennett, Rennie 83
Stuart, Dick 34, 90, 98, 115, 116, 117, 118, 119, 129, 158, 163, 169
Sukeforth, Clyde 82

Taxin, John 30
Taylor, Elizabeth 13
Tebbetts, Birdie 43, 77
Temple, Johnny 131
Terry, Ralph 167, 169
Texas League 35
Texas telegram 154
Thomas, Frank (1950s) 69
Thomas, Frank (1990s) 69
Thomson, Bobby 46
Three Rivers Stadium 50, 83, 183
Tiltonsville, OH 114
Titanic 117
Toney, Fred 124
Topps baseball cards 20
Toronto (minors) 90
Traynor, Pie 13, 16, 17, 68
Truman, Harry 98
Turley, Bob 165, 168
Twelve Perfect Innings: A Pretty Good Game 171, 172, 173, 174, 175, 176, 177, 178

Uecker, Bob 47
University of Havana 86
University of Michigan 59
University of Pittsburgh 16, 31, 50, 70
University of Virginia 172
University of Wisconsin 133

Vancouver (minors) 180
Vander Meer, Johnny 125, 160
Van Gogh, Vincent 119
Vaughan, Hippo 124
Venezuela 83, 86
Vernon, Mickey 97
Vincent, Fay 184
Virdon, Bill 19, 24, 26, 30, 44, 55, 67, 76, 99, 108, 119, 121, 122, 123, 132, 135, 157, 163, 165, 167, 170, 187
Virgin Islands 82, 86, 118

Wagner, Honus 13, 14, 15, 16, 51, 163
Waner, Lloyd 13, 16, 17, 18, 163

Index

Waner, Paul 13, 16, 17, 18, 122
Ward, John Montgomery 111
Washington Post 97
Washington Senators 97, 152, 162
Weaver, Jered 186
Werth, Jayson 31
Westinghouse 72
Westrum, Wes 180, 181
White, Charlie 35, 36
Wichita, KS 86
Wideman, John 52
Wiles, Tim 171, 172
Williams, Ted 31, 53
Wilson, Hack 13
Wiltse, Hooks 124

Wisconsin 5, 40, 45, 46, 56, 57, 79, 105, 133
Wisconsin Sports Hall of Fame 133
Wisconsin State League 133
Witt, George 80
Woods, Jim 127
Worcester, MA 111
World Series 1, 7, 13, 15, 16, 19, 31, 32, 38, 45, 56, 60, 64, 67, 90, 91, 92, 104, 112, 128, 142, 152, 159, 162, 163, 165, 167, 169, 170, 179, 180, 182, 187
World War II 65, 78, 133

Yankee Stadium 165, 167
Young, Cy 15, 112, 151

www.ingramcontent.com/pod-product-compliance
Ingram Content Group UK Ltd.
Pitfield, Milton Keynes, MK11 3LW, UK
UKHW041959140426
5217IPUK00015B/885